The Metropolitan
Experiment in Alaska

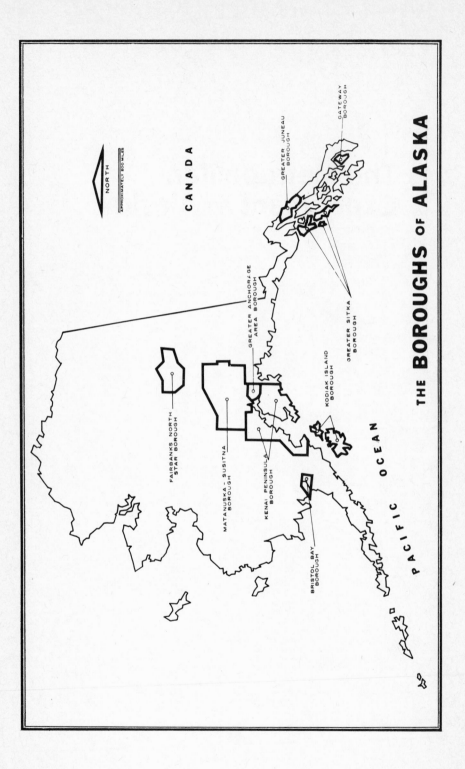

THE **BOROUGHS** OF **ALASKA**

NORTH
APPROXIMATELY 200 MILES

CANADA

PACIFIC OCEAN

GREATER JUNEAU BOROUGH

GATEWAY BOROUGH

GREATER SITKA BOROUGH

KODIAK ISLAND BOROUGH

GREATER ANCHORAGE AREA BOROUGH

FAIRBANKS NORTH STAR BOROUGH

MATANUSKA- SUSITNA BOROUGH

KENAI PENINSULA BOROUGH

BRISTOL BAY BOROUGH

TABLE 1

ORGANIZED BOROUGHS, STATE OF ALASKA

Classification	1960 Census Population or Estimate	Estimated Sq. Miles	Incorporation Date
First-Class Borough			
Greater Juneau Borough	9,745	3,100	Sept. 24, 1963
Second-Class Boroughs			
Bristol Bay Borough	1,015	1,200	Oct. 2, 1962
Gateway Borough	8,874	1,250	Sept. 6, 1963
Greater Anchorage Area Borough	66,600[a] (Est.)	1,500	Jan. 1, 1964
Greater Sitka Borough	6,150 (Est.)	2,900	Sept. 24, 1963
Kenai Peninsula Borough	9,053	15,000	Jan. 1, 1964
Kodiak Island Borough	4,450[b] (Est.)	4,500	Sept. 24, 1963
Matanuska-Susitna Borough	5,188	23,000	Jan. 1, 1964
Fairbanks North Star Borough	25,000[c] (Est.)	7,500	Jan. 1, 1964

[a]Excluding residents of Elmendorf AFB (base proper) and Fort Richardson (base proper).

[b]Excluding residents of Kodiak Naval Station (base proper).

[c]Excluding residents of Eielson AFB (base proper) and Fort Wainwright (base proper).

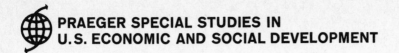

PRAEGER SPECIAL STUDIES IN
U.S. ECONOMIC AND SOCIAL DEVELOPMENT

The Metropolitan Experiment in Alaska

A STUDY OF BOROUGH GOVERNMENT

Edited by
Ronald C. Cease
and
Jerome R. Saroff

FREDERICK A. PRAEGER, Publishers
New York · Washington · London

The purpose of the Praeger Special Studies is to make specialized research monographs in U.S. and international economics and politics
available to the academic, business, and government communities. For
further information, write to the Special Projects Division, Frederick
A. Praeger, Publishers, 111 Fourth Avenue, New York, N.Y. 10003.

FREDERICK A. PRAEGER, PUBLISHERS
111 Fourth Avenue, New York, N.Y. 10003, U.S.A.
77-79 Charlotte Street, London W.I, England

Published in the United States of America in 1968
by Frederick A. Praeger, Inc., Publishers

Library of Congress Catalog Card Number: 67-29432

Printed in the United States of America

To

Senator Harold Z. Hansen

PREFACE

Boroughs are a form of areawide local government unique to Alaska.

The four years since the formation of boroughs have been a period of conflict, consolidation, and growth. It is rare to be present at the birth of a new form of government, and Alaskans are fortunate to be witnesses and participants in just such an event. Though Alaska is different from the other forty-nine states, it is nonetheless instructive to examine the borough experiment in Alaska. For the borough may serve the function of areawide or metropolitan government.

Two events are likely to take place within the next twenty-five years throughout the country: A number of constitutional conventions will be called to rewrite obsolete constitutions; and some form of more efficient and effective governmental organization or means of local intergovernmental cooperation for metropolitan areas will be created. On both counts the Alaskan experience anticipates that of other parts of the country. Thus, it is instructive to observe and analyze the first few years of operation of the Alaskan experiment, the borough.

In selecting contributors to this volume, we sought those individuals who are or have been key participants in the development of Alaskan local government. We requested our contributors to give particular emphasis to areas of difficulty, confusion, and conflict in order to indicate clearly some of the problems and pitfalls of metropolitan government in Alaska. Thus, if there is an emphasis on conflict, it is because we want to point up the problem areas.

In order to give a rounded, yet vigorous, picture of the growth and evolution of the borough, we decided to bring together a number of chapters based on an "adversary" approach, combined with several others which serve as points of reference. With deliberation we informed our contributors that each should concentrate on presenting his own view of events. The tension which is apparent among a number of the accounts verifies the usefulness of the adversary approach. The clash of different opinions, different evaluations, and different conclusions provides the material from which the reader can draw his own conclusions.

One major area of ambiguity runs through many of the chapters. It is whether the borough is "metropolitan" or "regional" government. Actually, the borough is a regional form of government. The main question is whether it is a metropolitan region or some other sort of region. The most populous boroughs in Alaska constitute metropolitan regions, focusing as they do on a central city and its surrounding trade area. However, in some of the more sparsely populated or geographically larger boroughs, this description does not apply. We do not see a need to impose one definition or another, but note that, depending on the circumstances, the borough can be used as a flexible and adaptable tool of government. Nevertheless, the majority of boroughs do include central cities and their trading areas. Hence the emphasis on the borough as a form of metropolitan government.

After only four years of actual borough operation, most of the major actors are still on the scene. The interests and emotions of the participants are still warm and still clearly remembered. It is thus appropriate to catch quickly the early stages of the growth of metropolitan government in Alaska.

This effort to evaluate the borough will be of use to two different groups. People in other parts of the country interested in metropolitan government can observe and, perhaps, learn from the

Alaskan experience. Residents of Alaska will have
a historical record of what the first few years of
borough government were like, from the participants
themselves. Thus, the twin goals of instruction
and history will be served.

Research and compilation for this study were
completed in early 1967, and this volume indicates
the borough situation as of that date. The passage of an act (c. 137, SLA 1967) authorizing a
first-class borough and all cities within the borough to unite to form a single unit of home rule
local government, and the election of a Charter
Commission in Juneau (which is now at work), have
not changed our analyses or conclusions.

There are many to whom we wish to acknowledge
indebtedness. Particular appreciation, of course,
goes to our contributors, busy men all, who somehow
managed to find enough time in their schedules
to compose chapters for this study. We thank them
for their efforts and for their unfailing courtesy
and good humor.

A number of persons who have made contributions to the development of Alaskan local government reviewed the manuscript. For their host of
suggestions we thank John C. Doyle, long-time
director of the Alaska Legislative Council; Gregory
Machyowsky, counsel, Legislative Council; Douglas
Bailey, Assistant Attorney General, State of
Alaska; James Nordale, deputy director of the
Alaska Local Affairs Agency; Roger W. Pegues,
director of the Local Affairs Agency, 1960-62; and
Gary Thurlow, executive assistant to former Governor William A. Egan of Alaska, 1961-64.

Robert W. Pavitt, Alaska State Federal Assistance Coordinator, was of major assistance in crit-
icizing and editing the manuscript. Adrianne
Brockman provided the layout and drafted the borough map.

Our secretary, Carol A. K. Anderson, performed
cheerfully and efficiently throughout the procedure
of drafting and redrafting.

Finally, we thank our wives, Jane and Natalie. It is no mere gesture to state that without their patience the manuscript could not have been completed.

Ronald C. Cease

Jerome R. Saroff

CONTENTS

Chapter   Page

ABBREVIATIONS

ACLA	Alaska Compiled Laws Annotated
ALG	Alaska Local Government, the publication of the Local Affairs Agency
AS	Alaska Statutes, plus title number and chapter and section where appropriate
PAS	Public Administration Service
PUD	Public Utility District
SLA	Session Laws of Alaska

The Metropolitan
Experiment in Alaska

CHAPTER **1** THE BOROUGH:
HISTORY, POWERS,
AND ORGANIZATION

By Ronald C. Cease
and
Jerome R. Saroff

Alaska became the forty-ninth state on January 3, 1959, when the formalities of admission to the Union were completed with the Formal Proclamation of Statehood.[1] On that date, the Constitution of the State of Alaska, adopted by the delegates to the State Constitutional Convention on February 5, 1956, and ratified by the citizens of the Territory on April 24, 1956, went into operation. This document is the most modern of state constitutions. Among its many model provisions, it provides for a simplified and potentially integrated system of local government.

At the time of statehood, Alaska had a minimum system of local government. The Territory contained nearly forty cities, eight independent school districts, one incorporated school district and six public utility districts, but no counties or area-wide political subdivisions.[2] Outside the cities and special districts there was no local government whatsoever.

The Organic Act, passed by Congress in 1912, created a Territorial legislature and permitted it to enact legislation relating to local government. Congress, however, prohibited the creation of counties without specific Congressional approval. Apropos of this prohibition, a joint publication of

1

the Alaska Legislative Council and the Local Affairs Agency comments:

> Many commercial interests in Alaska
> fought against the Organic Act gener-
> ally and the creation of counties
> specifically. Counties have tradi-
> tionally been financed by a property
> tax. Most of the property outside
> incorporated cities in Alaska was
> owned by mineral and fishing inter-
> ests. Delegate Wickersham[3] apparent-
> ly believed that these interests
> would succeed in defeating the entire
> Organic Act if the restriction on the
> creation of counties were not includ-
> ed in the Act.
>   This was another of those times
> when the self-interest of a special
> group ultimately served . . . the ad-
> vantage of the general public, saving
> Alaska from the archaic county system
> of local government.[4]

Otherwise, the Alaska Territorial Government
dealt with political subdivisions in much the same
manner as most states deal with their local units
of government. However, the traditional state-
local legal relationship did not apply, since

> local governments in Alaska derive
> their powers both from the Territo-
> rial Legislature and from acts of the
> National Congress. In this sense lo-
> cal governments must look to a dual
> sovereignty to determine the source
> and extent of their powers. Also,
> the full extent of the powers of the
> territorial legislature in dealing
> with its local subdivisions has never
> been fully determined.[5]

The Federal Government empowered the Alaska Territorial legislature to provide for local governments

in those instances where Congress had not acted.
The Territory's cities and special districts operated under both Federal and Territorial legislation.[6]

CITIES

Alaska Territorial law authorized the incorporation of three classes of cities and a village
form of local government. Except for the adoption
of home-rule charters, there has been little change
in the system since statehood.

Territorial statutes provided almost no control over the incorporation of cities, except to
set minimum population and area standards for the
various classes. Unfortunately, many communities
which met the standards and should have incorporated did not and were not required to do so. On the
other hand,

> communities completely unable to fi-
> nance and administer necessary local
> government functions can be and have
> been incorporated. An area on the
> outskirts of an existing city could
> possibly be incorporated. . . . The
> municipal code does not prevent the
> fragmentation of a community by the
> unwise, but legal, incorporation of
> a satellite city, say a subdevelop-
> ment near Anchorage or Juneau. The
> courts, while presumably able to pre-
> vent the incorporation of a city,
> have apparently done so only twice.[7]

State law on the incorporation of cities is nearly
identical to Territorial legislation.[8]

SPECIAL DISTRICTS

School Districts

The first public school districts in Alaska were city school districts.[9] The city school district was (and is) under the general supervision of a local elected school board, but was dependent upon action of the city council for the local share of the school budget.

In addition to the city school district, which is not a local unit of government, the Territorial legislature created two special school districts: the incorporated school district and the independent school district.

The establishment of incorporated school districts with taxing powers was authorized in 1917 for areas outside cities. At the time of statehood, Alaska had only one incorporated school district.[10]

"In order to extend city school districts into the suburban areas which sourrounded many of Alaska's cities and in which many students live,"[11] the legislature in 1934 provided for the incorporation of independent school districts, encompassing both a city or cities and the surrounding contiguous area. Like the incorporated school district, the independent school district had power to levy a property tax and, contingent on voter approval, a sales tax. However, the district's taxing authority was generally limited to the area of the district outside cities. The cities provided financial support as determined by their councils. Alaska had eight independent school districts at the time of statehood.

The Public Utility District

Legislation to permit the incorporation of public utility districts (PUDs), Alaska's other form of special district,[12] was enacted by the

Territorial legislature in 1935, under special Congressional authorization. The PUD, unlike the incorporated and independent school districts, was a
multipurpose unit of local government, quasimunici-
pal in nature. Although PUDs had a wide range of
permissible powers and functions, few were created
and only one or two of these provided extensive
services.

THE ALASKA STATE CONSTITUTION
AND LOCAL GOVERNMENT

When the State Constitutional Convention met
at the University of Alaska during the winter of
1955-56, the delegates recognized the need to improve Alaska's system of local government.[13] The
need for a unit of government to provide local
services on an areawide basis was particularly apparent.

One of several working committees established
by the convention was the Committee on Local Government. Its task was to propose a system of local
government capable of meeting the future needs of
Alaska's people. The committee studied the local
government patterns within the other states, as
well as in Canada and Europe. The secretary of the
committee noted:

> The basic results of most studies were
> that there wasn't much we could learn;
> the main lesson lay in what not to do.
> And so local government, as contained
> in the Constitution, sort of turns
> its back on the past and steps into
> the future. It assumes a form that
> should be workable through decades,
> or even centuries, if necessary, to
> come.[14]

The committee, in essence, followed the recommendation of the influential Public Administration Service (PAS), consultant to the convention, which had

warned that "the approach to local government that
considers only traditional structures, forms and
powers would seem to offer little hope of solving
many of the problems that characterize this entire
field of government."[15]

Recognizing the great diversity of Alaska's
communities, the convention delegates considered it
essential that the State's local government system
be flexible. Consequently, they felt that the
State Constitution should provide for only the basic local government framework. The chairman of
the Committee on Local Government stated:

> We believe that we should just draw
> the outline of this local government
> structure; we should leave a great
> deal of it and will need a great deal
> of help from the state in setting up
> the exact boundaries and the exact
> laws and rules under which they [lo-
> cal governments] shall operate.[16]

While this approach did permit great flexibility,
it also opened the way to later conflict as to
constitutional intent.

Two Units of Local Government

The philosophy of the Constitution's local
government article, Article X, is contained in the
first sentence: "The purpose of this article is to
provide for maximum local self-government with a
minimum of local government units, and to prevent
duplication of tax levying jurisdictions." Only
two units of local government are authorized: the
borough and the city. "The State may delegate taxing powers to organized boroughs and cities only."
(Art. X, sec. 2) Special districts established
under the Territory are recognized only as transitional units. The Constitution provides that:

> Special service districts existing at
> the time a borough is organized shall

> be integrated with the government of
> the borough as provided by law. (Art.
> X, sec. 15)
>   Cities, school districts, health
> districts, public utility districts,
> and other local subdivisions of gov-
> ernment existing on the effective
> date of this constitution shall con-
> tinue to exercise their powers and
> functions under existing law, pending
> enactment of legislation to carry out
> the provisions of this constitution.
> New local subdivisions of government
> shall be created only in accordance
> with this constitution. (Art. XV,
> sec. 3)

In a significant disagreement, a number of
convention delegates argued for the continuation of
the school district as a separate unit of local
government, and an amendment was proposed to that
end. A second amendment was proposed adding "public utility districts, public improvement districts,
health districts"[17] as units of local government.

However, the majority of the delegates accepted the thesis of simplified local government. The
amendment to grant local government powers to
school districts was defeated: forty-three nays,
nine yeas, and three absent. The second amendment
was withdrawn.

The intent of Article X is to create an integrated local government system. At the convention
interest was shown in the establishment of a single
unit of local government. The Committee on Local
Government considered the following organizational
arrangements for Alaska's cities:

> Abolition of cities and their recon-
> stitution as special urban tax dis-
> tricts within the larger unit.
>   Retention of existing cities but
> prohibition of future incorporations.

> Retention of cities over a spec-
> ified population and assessment level
> and abolition of those below such lev-
> el.
>   Retention of all cities and per-
> mission for future incorporation and
> separation of all cities from the sur-
> rounding unit.[18]

"The need for compromise in light of the political
and social reality in Alaska,"[19] however, prevented
the adoption of any of these proposals. "It was
the opinion of the Committee that while . . . [the
abolition of cities] had very definite advantages
of completely unified government, . . . it was too
drastic a step to take at one point . . . to abol-
ish these units altogether."[20] Thus, the provision
for two units of local government was a retreat
from an ideal considered too advanced to be politically acceptable. The committee hoped, however,
that the long-run relationship between the city and
borough would gradually lead to unified local government:

> Our local concept has been based not
> upon a separation of the two basic
> units of government, the borough and
> the city, but [upon] as close an in-
> tegration of functions between the
> two as possible. It was felt, for
> instance, that we should not . . .
> follow the pattern you find in most
> stateside counties where you have
> exact [sic] same functions being car-
> ried on separately at these two lev-
> els of government with their own
> hierarchy of officials and separate
> capital investments. It was our
> thought that <u>wherever functions over-
> lap, they should be integrated</u>.[21]
> [Emphasis added.]

Article X contains a number of provisions for the
purpose of facilitating interaction between the

borough and the city: Among these are grants of
authority for cooperative agreements for the transfer of functions from the city to the borough, and
the requirement that the city's representatives on
the borough governing body must be from the city
council.

Cities

The local government article of the Constitution did not alter the legal status of Alaska's
existing cities. Discussion at the convention indicated that "cities will, of course, remain . . .
much as they are today or with possibly slight
changes."[22] First-class cities may, however, according to the Constitution, adopt home-rule charters and "the legislature may extend home rule to
other . . . cities." (Art. X, secs. 9 and 10)
Cities "may be merged, consolidated, classified,
reclassified, or dissolved in the manner provided
by law." (Art. X, sec. 7)

Boroughs

The "borough," by definition, means a place
organized for local government purposes. It is not,
as is true of counties, simply a unit for State administrative purposes. "The whole treatment of
borough government in Article X is in terms of municipal functions and powers, with emphasis on home
rule for organized boroughs and on the interchange-
ability of functions and powers between boroughs
and cities."[23]

There was much debate at the convention over
the name of this unit of government.[24] Alaska Local Government reports that:

> The Constitutional Convention chose
> not to use the word "county" to avoid
> having the courts apply judicial de-
> cisions relating to counties in other
> states to local government in Alaska.
> It chose a new word to show its intent

prohibited by law or charter." (Art. X, sec. 11)
[Emphasis added.] This means that the legislative
body of a home-rule city or borough has, if not
prohibited, any power that is constitutionally
available to the State legislature. A member of
the Committee on Local Government stated:

> The old approach to county government
> was that they existed and had their
> authorities only in those specifical-
> ly delegated to them and specifically
> spelled out to them by the legisla-
> ture or by the Constitution. The
> other approach . . . had been called
> the Texas Plan.[26]
> . . . under that plan they allocate
> such powers to the intermediate form
> of government and the cities as are not
> specifically reserved or eventually
> withdrawn by the state itself.[27] [sic]

The constitutional provisions on home rule are
thus brief and simple. There is no enumeration of
local government functions. As to the problem of
interpreting home-rule powers, the Minutes of the
Committee on Local Government provide the following
guidelines:

> Specifically reviewed were provisions
> authorizing the adopting of home rule
> charters. It was generally agreed
> that procedure should be left to the
> legislature and to the local govern-
> ment body. The grant of powers is to
> be based upon "legislative powers"
> rather than a specific enumeration.
> . . . Nor was it felt desirable that
> the grant be on the basis of powers
> covering "local affairs" or "local
> government". . . . The grant of
> "legislative" power would be subject
> to restrictions contained in the con-
> stitution, to powers specifically
> withheld by the legislature and to

powers withheld by the people in the
adoption of their local charters.[28]

It was clearly and consciously recognized that
Alaska would "be pioneering in interpreting the
home rule provisions and it would be extremely fal-
lacious to rely on the experiences of other states
with their entirely different and inapplicable constitutional language."[29] In a farsighted move to
assist the courts, the Constitution directs that "a
liberal construction shall be given to the powers
of local government units." (Art. X, sec. 1)

Home rule, however, "should not mean the
State's withdrawal from all obligations within the
local area."[30] As one member of the committee
stated:

> In Alaska it is particularly impor-
> tant that we provide a local govern-
> ment system that will have the maximum
> amount of flexibility, with a maximum
> amount of home rule, and at the same
> time with the maximum amount of state
> interest and participation in local
> affairs.[31]

The State has the power to establish and classify boroughs and cities, to prescribe powers of
noncharter governments, to withhold authority from
home-rule boroughs and cities, and to exercise advisory, review, and control functions. Moreover,
the State's interest in local government is recognized by the constitutional provisions for the creation of a boundary commission and a local government agency. The commission is given major authority in the establishment and alteration of local
government boundaries:

> A local boundary commission or board
> shall be established by law in the
> executive branch of the state govern-
> ment. The commission or board may
> consider any proposed local government

> boundary change. It may present pro-
> posed changes to the legislature dur-
> ing the first ten days of any regular
> session. The change shall become ef-
> fective forty-five days after presen-
> tation or at the end of the session,
> whichever is earlier, <u>unless disap-
> proved by a resolution concurred in
> by a majority of the members of each
> house</u>. The commission or board, sub-
> ject to law, may establish procedures
> whereby boundaries may be adjusted by
> local action. (Art. X, sec. 12) [Em-
> phasis added.]

It was recognized that it was not only desirable but essential for local governments to have
access to expert assistance and advice. Thus:

> An agency shall be established by law
> in the executive branch of the state
> government to advise and assist local
> governments. It shall review their
> activities, collect and publish local
> government information, and perform
> other duties prescribed by law. (Art. X,
> sec. 14)

FROM STATEHOOD TO THE
MANDATORY BOROUGH ACT

The first Alaska State legislature convened in
late January, 1959, less than a month after the
Formal Declaration of Statehood was signed.[32] Its
immediate and pressing concern was the organization
of the new State's administrative machinery. There
appeared to be no imminent need to implement the
local government provisions of the Constitution.
The Constitutional Convention, in fact, recognized
that the legislative implementation of Article X
could not be accomplished overnight when it provided, in Section 3 of Article XV, that the State's
special districts "shall continue to exercise their

powers and functions under existing law pending
enactment of legislation to carry out the provisions of this constitution." Says the Public Administration Service:

> Thus the Constitution protects the
> State against a break or crisis in
> the continuing functioning of local
> institutions and gives the Governor,
> the Legislature, and the people of
> Alaska reasonable time to adjust the
> laws and practices of local govern-
> ment to the requirements of the Con-
> stitution after statehood itself has
> become a fact.[33]

Public Administration Service Proposals and Early State Action

The PAS proposed that during the first year of
statehood the legislature and the Governor limit
themselves to "a few simple things" in the local
government field. It recommended that they (1) enact home-rule legislation, (2) establish a department of local affairs, (3) create the local boundary commission, and (4) make provision for the study
of local government problems before establishing
long-range policies.

Although the legislature took no action on the
fourth PAS proposal, it did implement the other
three recommendations.[34] Chapter 196, SLA, 1959,
provided for the adoption of home-rule charters by
first-class cities. The Organization Act of 1959
created the Local Affairs Agency in the Office of
the Governor,[35] and also established the Local
Boundary Commission in the Local Affairs Agency.[36]
The Local Affairs Agency was to become extremely
important as the principal adviser to the legislature on local government problems and as a resource
and source of support for the borough governments.

Members of the Boundary Commission were appointed by the Governor on November 1, 1959, and

held an organizational meeting soon thereafter.
Following the meeting, the Commission held a number
of hearings throughout the State, particularly on
the matter of establishing borough governments.
On February 2, 1960, it submitted a report of its
findings to the legislature.[37] The report contained a number of recommendations and suggestions
regarding borough government, including a request
for legislation to permit the creation of boroughs
by local action.

The Borough Act of 1961

Although the legislature took no action on the
commission's recommendations, it recognized the
need for additional information on borough government and directed the Legislative Council and the
Local Affairs Agency to prepare a report and specific proposals on borough government to be submitted at the next legislative session.[38]

After months of research, drafting, and review,
the two agencies in 1961 submitted the Final Report
on Borough Government and a suggested borough
bill.[39] The bill was introduced into the legislature at the request of the Governor and the Legislative Council and, with some amendments, became
the first State borough statute, commonly referred
to as the Borough Act of 1961.[40] The act provided
for the incorporation, classification, organization,
and functions of borough government. Despite subsequent amendments, it remains the basic borough
statute.

The act established a single unorganized borough: "All areas in the state which are not within
the boundaries of an organized borough constitute a
single unorganized borough." (sec. 1.01) On the
transition of special service districts it provided
that:

> Special service districts existing on
> the effective date of this Act[41] may
> continue to exercise their powers and

functions under existing law until
July 1, 1963, or until such time
within this period that they are integrated into city or organized borough government, annexed to or incorporated as cities, or established as
service areas in the unorganized borough. (sec. 1.03)[42]

Borough Incorporation

In considering the incorporation of organized
boroughs, the Local Affairs Agency and the Legislative Council indicated that:

Standards for incorporation of organized boroughs need not and probably
should not be rigid. Local governments are human institutions, and
rigid or precise standards are not
applicable to them. Each unit must
be judged by itself to determine what
is best for it.[43]

The legislature adopted this flexible approach.
No minimum population base, no set geographic size,
and no specific economic standards are required.
However, the Borough Act does set general guidelines. It stipulates that:

No area may be incorporated as an organized borough unless it conforms to
the following standards:
     1. the population of the area
proposed for incorporation shall be
interrelated and integrated as to its
social, cultural, and economic activities . . . and shall be large enough
and stable enough to warrant and support the operation of organized borough government;
     2. the boundaries of the pro-
posed organized borough shall conform
generally to the natural geography of

the area proposed for incorporation,
shall include all areas necessary and
proper for the full development of
integrated local government services . . . ;
    3. the economy of the proposed
organized borough shall encompass a
trading area with the human and financial resources capable of providing an adequate level of governmental
services . . . ;
    4. the transportation facilities
in the area proposed for incorporation
shall be of such a unified nature as to
facilitate the communication and exchange necessary for the development
of integrated local government and a
community of interests. (sec. 2.03)

The Local Affairs Agency and the Local Boundary
Commission were given the responsibility of determining whether proposed borough incorporations met
these standards.

    Under the act, no less than 25 per cent of the
voters within each first-class city and 25 per cent
of the voters outside each first-class city must
petition for borough incorporation. The petition
includes the class of the proposed borough, the
name and borough seat, the boundaries, the composition and apportionment of the assembly, and the request, if any, for additional powers. This is
filed with the Local Affairs Agency, which investi-
gates to determine whether the proposed incorporation meets the standards. The agency reports its
findings to the Local Boundary Commission, which is
required to hold at least one hearing in the area
proposed for incorporation. The commission may
then either accept the petition, reject it, or accept it with changes in the proposed boundaries,
composition, and apportionment of the assembly, or
additional areawide powers, if such changes will
make the petition conform to the standards.

Borough Classification

The Borough Act provides for two classes of
organized borough: first- and second-class. Classifications of local governments are usually based
on population and sometimes on geographical location. However, <u>the only difference between the two
classes of organized boroughs is one of powers</u>. No
population distinctions are made, and any area of
the State may petition for either class.

Both first- and second-class boroughs must
provide for three areawide functions: (1) education, (2) planning and zoning, and (3) property tax
assessment and collection. Additional areawide
powers may be added either by the voters or by
transfer from cities to the borough. Areawide powers are those exercised by boroughs <u>both inside and
outside of cities</u>. "<u>No city of any class, whether
home rule or not, within an organized borough may
exercise any areawide power . . . once that power
is being exercised by an organized borough</u>." (sec.
3.31) [Emphasis added.]

The distinction between first- and second-
class boroughs lies mainly in the powers <u>which may
be exercised in the area outside cities only</u>. In
the borough area outside cities a first-class borough may exercise any powers granted by statute to
first-class cities. On the other hand, in the same
area, a second-class borough may exercise only
those powers which are specifically approved by the
borough voters residing outside cities.

Borough Study Groups and 1962
Amendments to the Borough Act

The passage of the Borough Act of 1961 encouraged the organization of a number of borough study
groups throughout the State.[44]

In May, 1961, the Local Affairs Agency prepared a <u>Borough Incorporation Manual</u> to assist persons interested in creating an organized borough.

Reliance was placed upon local study groups to
stimulate public interest in borough government.
The manual encouraged the establishment of study
groups broadly representative of their communities:

> The borough study group should be com-
> posed of members representing each
> section and interest in the largest
> possible area under consideration for
> incorporation. The number joining
> the group should be large enough to
> provide such representation. An un-
> wieldy size is not an important con-
> sideration. The group can be broken
> down into working committees later.[45]

As a result of suggestions received from these
study groups, from persons interested in borough
government, and from opinions expressed at public
meetings held in various parts of the State, the
Local Affairs Agency in 1962 proposed a number of
amendments to the Borough Act. These suggestions
were incorporated as Chapter 110, SLA, 1962.

Chapter 110 contained two major changes to the
Borough Act. One reduced the number of required
borough petition signatures in the Anchorage and
Fairbanks areas from 25 to 15 per cent. The other
altered the sections of the act relating to assembly apportionment, gave a majority of seats on the
borough assembly to the areas outside first-class
cities, and provided for a weighted vote on enumerated areawide matters and functions.

THE MANDATORY BOROUGH ACT

When the first session of the third State legislature convened in Juneau on January 29, 1963, it
was apparent that the integration of the State's
special service districts into constitutional forms
of local government and the problems of organized
borough government would demand much of the legislators' time. Although the original Borough Act

had become law almost two years earlier, only a single organized borough, the small Bristol Bay Borough in western Alaska, had been incorporated. And although the Local Affairs Agency had received two other borough incorporation petitions, it was obvious that "local initiative" wasn't working and that boroughs were not being formed voluntarily.

Public Confusion and Opposition

Borough study groups were active throughout the State. The staff of the Local Affairs Agency had been assisting these groups in explaining to the public the concept of and need for organized borough government. Borough petitions had been prepared and were being circulated in the Anchorage and Fairbanks areas.

Opposition or apathy to the incorporation of borough governments, however, was widespread. Basic informational questions were continually being asked: "What is a borough? Why don't we have counties? Why didn't the Constitution or the legislature stipulate borough boundaries? Why do we need a borough anyway?"

Local residents who did not live within incorporated local governments and, consequently, did not pay local taxes were in many instances opposed to the formation of boroughs.[46] School officials and school organizations, such as the PTA, continually agitated to create fiscal autonomy for school districts. For example, the superintendent of the Fairbanks Independent School District stated:

> The borough was established by the constitutional convention. The borough and the status of the school district in relation to the borough was not a concept fostered or advocated by representatives of the public schools in this state, but was an idea sponsored by the PAS . . . and backed by the League of Alaskan Cities.

> Public education leaders in the
> state protested the position relegated
> to the public school district by the
> constitution.[47]

A Foundation for Alaska's Public Schools,[48] a
report on Alaska's school system financed by the
Ford Foundation, was severely critical of the Borough Act and recommended that all references in the
act to education be repealed as contrary to the intent of the Constitutional Convention. For their
part, supporters of borough government felt that
the foundation study's use of Constitutional Convention minutes was an unscholarly selection of
votes and comments, which altered the convention's
actual position that education and local school organizations be part of the general purpose government.[49]

Borough Bills

The 1963 legislature was thus faced with two
salient problems on the issue of organized borough
government: (1) Much of the public was either confused or hostile, or both; and (2) under the provisions of the Borough Act of 1961, special districts
could operate under existing law only until July 1,
1963. If new legislation were not forthcoming by
that time, it was assumed that the functions and
property of districts not located within borough or
city government would escheat to the State. To
most members of the thinking public and the legislature this was intolerable. The legislature thus
had only two practical options: (1) to extend the
life of the special districts or (2) to require the
incorporation of organized boroughs.

Three borough bills were introduced during the
session: Senate Bill No. 17, which extended the
life of special districts to July, 1970, and two
bills requiring the incorporation of organized bor-
oughs--House Bill No. 62 and House Bill No. 90.
The Senate unanimously passed Senate Bill No. 17,
after amending it to extend the 1963 cut-off date

for special districts for a single year, and then took no further action on borough legislation until it received House Bill No. 90 from the House.

House Bill No. 62

House Bill No. 62 was introduced by the Rules Committee at the request of the Governor. Under the provisions of the bill, organized boroughs could still be incorporated by local option petition. However, in those areas meeting the standards for borough incorporation and not incorporated by local option, the State Board of Education could provide for the establishment of second class boroughs for school purposes.

House Bill No. 62 had the active support of the State Department of Education, the State Board of Education, and several members of the legislature. Although State and local school officials preferred the continuation of the State's independent school districts, it was becoming apparent to many of them that the failure to implement the Constitution's provisions on local government was causing great uncertainty in the entire State school system.

Strong borough supporters, however, were lukewarm toward the bill. They refused to accept the thesis that a second-class borough should be simply a glorified school district. Moreover, they were critical of the provision of House Bill No. 62, which gave the initiative for establishing organized boroughs to the State Board of Education. Borough supporters, concerned with the need for local government and local government functions other than public education, advocated the passage of House Bill No. 90. They were prepared to accept House Bill No. 62 if House Bill No. 90 foundered. Although the Governor had introduced House Bill No. 62, he had no strong feelings about it.

The Mandatory Borough Act
(House Bill No. 90)

Greater support developed for the passage of House Bill No. 90 than for House Bill No. 62. Nearly unanimous support was given to the bill by the leaders of the various local borough study groups. The Governor at first appeared indifferent to the bill. However, he actively supported it when it reached the Senate.[50]

House Bill No. 90, commonly referred to as the Mandatory Borough Act, was originally introduced by Representative John L. Rader, House Democratic Minority Leader from Anchorage. Following lengthy argument, several public hearings, a number of amendments, and intense parliamentary maneuvering, the bill passed the House and Senate as Committee Substitute for House Bill No. 90 and was signed into law by the Governor.[51]

Borough powers and organization set up under the 1961 Borough Act remained the foundation upon which the 1963 Mandatory Borough Act rested.

The Borough Act of 1961 provided for the incorporation of organized boroughs exclusively by local option. This procedure did not change under the Mandatory Borough Act. Boroughs could still be incorporated by local option. However, if boroughs were not incorporated by local option prior to October 1, 1963, in eight designated election districts,[52] the areas were to be mandatorily incorporated as first- or second-class organized boroughs on January 1, 1964.

In the areas designated for incorporation borough officers were to be selected and borough class and the form of borough executive (chairman or manager) were to be determined at an election to be held between October 1 and December 15, 1963. Borough seats and borough names were to be later chosen by the assemblies of the new boroughs.

Under the terms of the Mandatory Borough Act,
special districts located within the designated
election districts could continue to exercise their
powers and functions under AS 07.10.130-140.[53]
These sections permitted the governing body of the
borough, the assembly, to determine when to assume
the activities being performed by the special districts within the boundaries of the borough. However, special districts could be integrated no
later than two years after the incorporation of the
organized borough and, during this transitional period, the exercise of certain powers by the special
districts had to meet with the approval of the borough assembly.

"Start-up" incentives were given to organized
boroughs under the Mandatory Borough Act. They
were land grants and money.

In language similar to that in the Alaska
Statehood Act, the Mandatory Borough Act granted to
organized boroughs the right to select 10 per cent
of the vacant, unappropriated, unreserved State
lands located within their boundaries no later than
five years after such lands were made available.
Further, each organized borough was entitled to $10
for every voter within the borough who voted in the
last general election. No borough, however, was to
receive less than $25,000. It was intended that
the grants of money would be used for the "purpose
of defraying the cost of transition to borough government and in order to provide for development and
interim governmental operations."[54]

The sponsors of the act were aware that the
mandatory incorporation feature would be highly unpopular with many segments of the general public.[55]
It was hoped, however, that the money and land
grant provisions would reduce this opposition.

A number of factors combined to create the
legislative climate necessary for the passage of
the Mandatory Borough Act:

1. A need for additional services on the

local level, particularly in those areas
adjacent to cities.

2. A desire on the part of numerous local res-
    idents and groups for increased local con-
    trol of essentially local functions.
    Coupled with this was an interest of the
    State administration in creating local gov-
    ernments, so that the local areas could
    perform and pay for local services.

3. A growing need to equalize local tax bur-
    dens.

4. The necessity to integrate the special ser-
    vice districts into constitutional forms
    of local government.

In indicating why he supported the passage of
the Mandatory Borough Act, Governor Egan later commented:

> . . . we who favor borough formation
> are urging that people accept more re-
> sponsibility for government decision
> on the local level so that those deci-
> sions are not left to the state gov-
> ernment. We are not imposing decisions
> on Alaskans. We are providing them
> with greater opportunity to make their
> own decisions.
>
> In the past few years I have re-
> ceived phone calls, letters and peti-
> tions demanding that this or that
> teacher be fired, that a drainage
> ditch along a privately owned subdi-
> vision street be filled, that grammar
> school students be transferred to a
> local junior high school building,
> and junior high school students to
> the grammar school building, that
> streets be built, private properties
> be zoned to eliminate snake exhibits
> and junkyards, and so on. Who is in

the best position to decide whether
a school needs a fence, which house
will have a sewer, which streets
should be paved, who should get side-
walks and street lights, where junk-
yards can be set up? The traditional
and, I believe, the correct answer is
that these decisions should be made
by the people affected--they will
make the best, the fairest, and the
most economical decisions.
. . . In one sense we are strip-
ping off a layer of government. Decisions formerly made by state officials in Juneau will no longer be
made there. Substitution of local
government for state government does
not add a layer [of government].[56]

THE DETERMINATION OF BOROUGH BOUNDARIES
AND THE ESTABLISHMENT OF
ORGANIZED BOROUGHS

On January 1, 1964, Alaska had nine organized
boroughs. Five of these were incorporated under
the local option provisions of the Borough Act of
1961; four pursuant to the Mandatory Borough Act.

The Governor signed the Mandatory Borough Act
on April 12, 1963. Before this date the Local Affairs Agency had received petitions[57] for four proposed boroughs. Between May 1 and July 12, petitions were submitted for five more.

The Local Affairs Agency investigated and prepared formal reports on seven of the nine petitions.
The Local Boundary Commission, upon receipt of the
findings and recommendations of the agency, held
fourteen hearings on the seven petitions. It rejected one petition of the seven as not meeting the
standards of the Borough Act and accepted six,
though not before enlarging the proposed boundaries
on four petitions. Six local option borough incorporation elections were scheduled by the Secretary

of State for the month of September, 1963, and four
were approved by the voters.[58]

The Local Boundary Commission
and Borough Boundaries

As indicated, the Alaska Constitution provides
that "each borough shall embrace an area and population with common interests to the maximum degree
possible." (Art. X, sec. 3) The Borough Act of
1961 implemented this by requiring that "the population of the area proposed for incorporation shall
be interrelated and integrated as to its social,
cultural, and economic activities."[59] In reviewing
a borough petition, the Local Affairs Agency determines whether the proposed borough is a "natural
community" and exhibits a "community of interests":

> When it is stated that organized bor-
> oughs are local governments for natural
> communities, it does not mean that they
> are local governments for the limited
> community of the city, of the suburb,
> or of a group of farms or homesteads.
> It means that they are local govern-
> ments for an entire natural community
> made up of a combination of cities,
> suburbs, and groups of farms or home-
> steads. The concept of natural commu-
> nity upon which borough government is
> based is that of a community of per-
> sons with common interests in schools,
> economic development, health and wel-
> fare, flood control, resources and
> markets, job opportunities, shopping,
> entertainments, roads, land use, and
> so forth. Admittedly, a group of
> persons in a limited community share
> a common interest in all these things,
> but their common interest is also
> shared by others for miles around,
> and all these persons and groups are
> a part of the same natural community.[60]

Thus, when the agency questions whether a proposed borough "embrace[s] an area and population
with common interests to the maximum degree possible" [emphasis added], it advises the Local Boundary Commission to accept the petition, but to "consider closely the suggested borough boundaries
[proposed by the petitioners]"[61] and to enlarge
boundaries if necessary to meet the standards of
the Borough Act.

As a rule, the Local Boundary Commission has
followed a concept of large boroughs. The First
Report to the Second Session of the First Alaska
State Legislature states:

> . . . the Commission's present think-
> ing [is] that organized boroughs,
> particularly in Alaska, were to be
> large in size--otherwise they would
> be duplicating the service area's
> jurisdiction. No opinion is expressed
> at this time as to just how large the
> borough should be, for there are other
> considerations to be weighed: for
> example, the population density would
> be an important factor, but, it is
> felt, in view of existing conditions
> in Alaska, the general rule should
> be large boroughs, and the exception
> should be small boroughs.
>   It should be remembered that
> when "counties" or intermediate forms
> of government were originally formed
> in other states, one of the major
> factors in determining size was travel
> time. Generally, the areas were con-
> fined to ones in which the county
> seat could be reached by horse and
> buggy within twenty-four hours from
> any point in the county. Using this
> measure in Alaska, and the common
> mode of travel, be it air, road, or
> even boat, a borough in Alaska can
> encompass sizeable areas.[62]

Although the report further states that "in any
event, the Commission is not wedded to this position, and is prepared to vary its concept if it can
be shown that its approach is erroneous,"[63] its decisions on borough petitions (subsequent to the
acceptance of the Bristol Bay Borough petition) indicate that it has not essentially deviated from the
large borough concept.[64] This concept was in fact
strengthened by the Mandatory Borough Act, which
provided for boroughs the size of election districts.*

Local Option Borough Elections

The borough incorporation elections were bitterly contested in the Anchorage, Fairbanks, and
Juneau areas. Little opposition developed in the
Ketchikan and Sitka areas and, although opposition
was evident in Kodiak, the major public reaction
there was indifference.

The Gateway (Ketchikan) and Greater Sitka Boroughs were incorporated by large margins. Incorporations were achieved by narrow margins in the
Juneau and Kodiak areas. However, the proposed
Captain Cook (Anchorage) Borough was defeated by
more than 3 to 1, while the proposed North Star
(Fairbanks) Borough was defeated by nearly 3 to 2.

Opposition to the proposed Captain Cook Borough, though perhaps more organized, was typical
of the hostility toward boroughs which developed
elsewhere. Defeat of the first class proposal, anticipated weeks before the election, was attributed
to several types of opposition, sometimes in combination:

1. Opposition by the predominantly agricul-
    tural Matanuska-Susitna Valley communities
    to inclusion in the same borough with

---

*Editors' Note: Alaska's 586,400 square miles
are divided into nineteen election districts.

the more populous and more urban Anchorage area.

2.   Opposition to a first-class borough.

3.   Opposition to borough government per se.

A group, calling itself the Committee for Common Sense Government, advertised extensively in the Anchorage newspapers against the incorporation of the Captain Cook Borough. It indicated its opposition to both a large borough and a first-class borough. Some of its advertisements, however, reveal that its basic opposition was to any borough government. On September 10, 1963, it lamented that the Anchorage area already had:

> Too much government--we have seen too much of state government and city government ignoring the wishes of the people.
> Too much bureaucracy--we have seen the number of state employees mushroom to the point where there are now more than five thousand--one for every twelve taxpayers.
> Too many taxes--Federal Income, Social Security, State Income, State E.S.C., liquor, gasoline, cigarette, automobile, school . . . and numerous others.[65]

Although a number of Anchorage groups endorsed the Captain Cook Borough proposal, none actively campaigned for incorporation. Many members of the Borough Information Committee, an offshoot of the Anchorage Borough Steering Committee,* energetically supported the large borough proposal. However,

---

*Editors' Note: For a discussion of the Anchorage area Borough Steering Committee, see Chapter 9, written by Richard W. Fischer.

the committee, calling itself only "a citizens'
voter service committee interested in presenting
factual information,"[66] refused to publicly take a
stand on the issue of large borough vs. small borough.

Mandatory Borough Incorporation

On October 1, the director of the Local Affairs Agency notified the Secretary of State to
schedule elections for the selection of borough officers and the determination of borough classification and type of executive in those areas designated in the Mandatory Borough Act which had not voluntarily incorporated: The Anchorage, Matanuska-
Susitna Valley, Fairbanks, and the combined Seward-
Cook Inlet election districts. Elections were
scheduled and held in all four areas on December 3.
The voters chose second-class boroughs and the
chairman form of executive in all instances. On
January 1, 1964, the four areas became incorporated
units of local government.[67]

THE LEGAL AND POLITICAL STRUGGLE TO
REPEAL THE MANDATORY BOROUGH ACT

The Mandatory Borough Act was one of the most
controversial statutes ever passed by an Alaskan
legislature. It was bitterly criticized throughout
the State from its introduction by Representative
John L. Rader. Many critics maintained that they
were not opposed to borough government, but resented what they considered State eagerness to "stuff
boroughs down their throats."[68] Others indicated
their opposition to the borough per se. The latter
attitude was colorfully portrayed by a Fairbanks
resident:

> There is a kind of animal in tropical
> rivers called a crocodile that works
> at both ends. What it doesn't mash
> with its tail it gobbles up with its
> teeth.

> Destroy this monster before it
> destroys the community!
> Kill it now!
> I think it will be a long time
> before the scars of this monster will
> heal.[69]

The repeal or suspension of the Mandatory Borough Act was the subject of a referendum petition,
several court cases, a request for a special session of the legislature,[70] and two 1964 legislative
bills. All attempts to scuttle the act failed.

On September 10, 1963, the Secretary of State
certified a referendum petition which apparently
rendered the Mandatory Borough Act subject to the
consideration of the State's voters at the 1964
August primary. Although the Secretary accepted
the petition, he did so reluctantly as he was "unable to establish with reasonable certainty that
the petition does not bear the required . . . eligible signers."[71] For Alaska did not then and
still does not have voter preregistration.[72]

Several days earlier, on September 4, two residents of the Kenai Peninsula initiated proceedings
in the State Superior Court, Third Judicial District (Anchorage), alleging that the Mandatory Borough Act was unconstitutional. On September 13,
three days after the Secretary of State certified
the referendum petition, the plaintiffs filed an
amended complaint in which they held that the referendum petition suspended the operation of the
Mandatory Borough Act until the measure was considered by the voters at the 1964 statewide primary
election. Finally, on October 16, they applied for
a preliminary injunction to enjoin the director of
the Local Affairs Agency and the Secretary of State
from acting under the Mandatory Borough Act.

The court rendered a decision on November 14.[73]
The judge denied the request for injunction and
ruled "that the filing of the [referendum] petition
did not suspend further the effective date of"[74]

the Mandatory Borough Act. In December, the plaintiffs appealed the decision of the lower court to
the State Supreme Court and requested a judgment
prior to January 1, 1964, the date that boroughs
were to be incorporated under the Mandatory Borough
Act. However, the court did not render a decision
until January 15. It then sustained the order of
the Superior Court denying the petitioners a preliminary injunction.[75]

In another development, on September 14, 1963,
Senator Yule Kilcher from the Kenai Peninsula formally requested the speaker of the House in the
latter's capacity as chairman of the Legislative
Council "to take the necessary action to effect a
special session of the Alaska State Legislature in
October of 1963, with the express purpose of recon-
sidering the Mandatory Borough Act."[76] On September 20, the chairman called a meeting of the Legislative Council to determine a means of polling
State legislators as to their stand on calling a
special session. On a straight party vote,[77] the
council rejected the request to poll legislators.
Neither the House nor the Senate formally polled
legislators on this matter although legislators in
several areas were "polled" by the newspapers.

Opponents of the Mandatory Borough Act had
every hope that repeal of the Act would be the
first order of business of the 1964 legislative
session. However, although two bills relating to
the mandatory features of the 1963 Act were introduced,[78] the legislature took no action to repeal
or amend the act. Both bills were "political" and
neither was considered serious legislation by most
members. A majority of the lawmakers had no desire
to further agitate the borough conflict. They appeared anxious to settle the issue in order to direct their attention to major State economic problems.

Action to enjoin the Secretary of State from
placing the Mandatory Borough Act on the ballot
for referral to the people was initiated by two

residents of Spenard in the Anchorage area on October 31, 1963.[79] They alleged that the Mandatory Borough Act was local legislation and pointed out that the Constitution prohibits the use of the referendum on local or special legislation. (Art. II, sec. 19)

On April 28, 1964, upon the agreement of all parties, the Superior Court ordered the consolidation of <u>Walters and Mullen</u> v. <u>Cease, et al</u>.[80] and <u>Gill and Norene</u> v. <u>Cease, et al</u>. in view of the apparent similar or identical issues raised.

On June 19, the court determined that the Mandatory Borough Act was not subject to referendum, on the ground that the Constitution requires the establishment of boroughs.[81] The judge refused to consider whether the act was local or special legislation. Six days later he enjoined the Secretary of State from placing the question of the Mandatory Borough Act on the ballot. On July 2, Walters and Mullen filed with the Supreme Court a "Petition for a Writ of Review of the Injunction of the Superior Court." On August 7, four days prior to the statewide primary election, the Supreme Court ruled that "the lower Court's injunction was properly issued."[82]

BOROUGH FUNCTIONS AND POWERS

The organized borough in Alaska is a municipal corporation. It is a form of areawide government for a natural community, that is, government not limited to a city, nor to a suburb, nor to a rural area, but which includes all three. The organized borough has certain areawide functions that are denied to the cities within it, and has certain functions that may be exercised only in the area outside cities.

Although the Constitution leaves the determination of borough functions to the legislature,[83] the minutes of the Constitutional Convention

indicate delegate sentiment that "all functions that
can best be carried out on the unified basis [should]
be transferred to the borough."[84]

Areawide Borough Functions

The 1961 <u>Final Report on Borough Government</u>
suggested that "while an organized borough may have
very broad powers, its powers within a city may be
limited at first to those which are absolutely
necessary for areawide government."[85] The legislature at this time imposes upon an organized borough
only three governmental functions and these three
are areawide: to educate its children; to provide
a rational land use program; and to have property
assessed and property taxes collected by one agency.

Education

Each organized borough is a school district.
First- and second-class boroughs must establish,
maintain, and operate a system of public schools
in the manner provided by general law.[86] State
laws relating to teachers' salary and tenure, to
State financial support, to supervision by the
State Department of Education, and other State laws
relating to schools are applicable to borough
school operations.

Each borough school district has an elected
school board composed of five members[87] and borough
schools are under the supervision and control of
the school board. Responsibility for the preparation of the school budget belongs to the board,
but the adoption of the budget is contingent on
the approval of the borough assembly.[88] The assembly has the authority to determine <u>how much</u> money
is to be made available from local sources for
school purposes. The only instances where the assembly has the authority and duty to determine <u>how</u>
school money shall be spent are in regard to actual
construction and initial equipment of school buildings and subsequent capital improvements.

Planning, Platting, and Zoning

In the past, planning and zoning in Alaska were limited to cities, which had no control over land use patterns in areas beyond city limits. Platting had been exercised by city planning commissions and by platting boards operating in the area of independent school districts outside first-class cities. The Borough Act consolidated the platting responsibility and filled the planning vacuum which existed between city and State by providing for an areawide borough planning, platting, and zoning function.[89]

Planning commission members are appointed by the borough executive with the approval of the assembly. A city, however, may continue to support a planning commission in an advisory capacity. Appointment of borough planning commission members from a first-class city must be made from the city advisory commission, if there is one.

Even though planning and zoning is an areawide borough function, city councils may continue to perform as boards of adjustment within their boundaries. However, the borough assembly is the board of adjustment for the area outside cities and for cities which do not exercise this power. The Local Affairs Agency and borough executives have on several occasions proposed that the Borough Act be amended to delete any reference to the city council as a separate board of adjustment. This recommendation, however, has been opposed by many of Alaska's cities, and no legislative action has been taken.

Property Tax Assessment and Collection

The third areawide power of an organized borough is property tax assessment and collection.[90] In many areas of the State two or more units of local government had assessed and collected real and personal property taxes, with a glaring lack of uniformity. Delegates to the Constitutional

Convention recognized the need for areawide assessment and collection. A member of the Committee on
Local Government stated:

> I think you can have better government
> at less expense by correlating the tax-
> ing activities and channeling them
> through one body with one set of ap-
> praisers, one set of collectors, one
> set of condemners and tax sale ex-
> perts, and having that money go into
> one fund for distribution by a general
> body elected by all of the people no
> matter what level of government we
> operate at. [sic][91]

In discussing sources of local tax revenue,
the Final Report on Borough Government indicated
that the major weakness in the local property tax
was inadequate assessment.

> The property tax has one egregious
> weakness: assessment. Assessment
> is a major problem in most states.
> The primary reasons for this are
> lack of uniformity in assessment,
> inadequate assessment standards and
> a lack of trained or experienced
> assessors in local units. It ap-
> pears that the cure for this weak-
> ness is closer state supervision of
> property assessment and assessment
> on an areawide basis by an areawide
> agency.[92]

Areawide assessment can be achieved by "an
areawide agency," the organized borough. Within
an organized borough only the borough government
is authorized to assess and collect local property
taxes. The city, however, continues as a tax levying unit, and taxes levied by cities and collected
by the borough must be returned in full to the cities in which collected. A home-rule city may continue to grant its own exemptions or exclude

property from city and borough taxes. It must, however, appropriate to the borough sufficient funds
to equal revenues lost by the borough because of
exemptions or exclusions made by the city. An organized borough may adjust its property tax structure to that of any home-rule city within it.

Resource Development

The Borough Act does not delegate an areawide
function in resource development to the organized
borough. However, the provision of the Mandatory
Borough Act which authorizes the organized borough
to select and use at its discretion 10 per cent of
the vacant, unreserved, or unappropriated State
lands within its boundaries in effect gives the
borough an additional areawide function. Resource
development, unlike other areawide borough functions, however, is not exclusive to the borough.

Borough land selection will have an important
effect upon the development of the organized borough, particularly as lands are selected for recreational uses. It is now too early to gauge the
extent and direction of that effect.

Assumption of Borough Functions[93]

The powers exercised by cities and special
districts[94] continue to be exercised by them until
such time as the borough assumes the powers, but
no later than two years after the date of incorporation. Ordinances, rules, resolutions, regulations, procedures, and orders in effect prior to
the assumption of these powers by the organized
borough remain in effect until superseded by action of the borough.

Before assuming any function, the organized
borough must consult with the officials of the
city or special district concerned and arrange for
an orderly transfer. Written notice of assumption,
usually in the form of letter or resolution, is
made by the borough to the city or district.

Integration of School Districts
and State Schools[95]

The Borough Act stipulates that school districts[96] existing within an organized borough must
be integrated into the borough within two years
after it is incorporated.[97] This has occurred.

The organized borough succeeds to all the
rights, powers, debts, and duties of any school
district within it. In addition, the borough succeeds to the title and interest in real and personal property held by the district. The borough
assembly may levy and collect special charges,
taxes, or assessments including interest for the
purpose of amortizing bonded indebtedness previously incurred by the school district, for continuing
services in the area, or for future indebtedness
in the area.

After the incorporation of an organized borough, but before it assumes the functions of education, no school district within it can assume new
bonded indebtedness, make any contract, or transfer
any assets without the consent of the borough assembly.

Although, under the law, the organized borough
is permitted a maximum two-year transition period
in which to integrate city and independent school
districts, it is responsible immediately upon incorporation for the administration of State schools
within its area. However, the Attorney General has
ruled that "as a practical matter, the [State] Department of Education must continue its administration of such a school for a brief period until such
arrangements for an orderly transfer can be made by
the borough assembly and the Department of Education."[98] Approximately thirty-five State-operated
schools have been taken over by boroughs.

Additional Areawide Functions

The Borough Act provides general standards for the acquisition of supplemental areawide powers by organized boroughs:[99]

> In addition to the areawide powers re-
> quired by this title, those areawide
> powers which can be exercised more
> efficiently and economically on an
> areawide basis or through the use of
> service areas by the organized bor-
> ough shall be assigned to the pro-
> posed borough. In determining effi-
> ciency and economy, the present and
> anticipated benefit and cost of op-
> eration, responsiveness to people
> served, ability to operate over ex-
> tended distances, the feasibility
> of integration, and other factors
> shall be considered.[100]

Areawide powers, in addition to the three required by the Borough Act, may be added either by the voters or by transfer from a city to the borough.

In the former instance, which applies only to second-class boroughs, a vote on a proposed area-wide power may not be held unless the Boundary Commission determines that the proposal meets the standards for the assignment of areawide powers.[101] This procedure involves filing a petition with the Local Affairs Agency, which is handled in much the same manner as local option borough incorporation petitions. The agency conducts an investigation to determine "the feasibility and practicability of the borough's exercising the additional power or powers," and the Local Boundary Commission holds at least one hearing in the borough in order to elicit public comment on the proposal. Immediately after publication of its findings and those of the commission, the agency notifies the borough assembly to hold an election in the borough on the question of adding to the borough's powers. If more

a population basis, except that (1) if a first-
class city or the area outside first-class cities
had a population more than twice as large as the
remaining population of the borough, its delegation
could exceed the remaining members of the assembly
only by two, and (2) if a first-class city or the
area outside first-class cities had a population
not more than twice as large as the remaining population of the borough, its delegation could exceed
the remaining members of the assembly by only one.[104]

The control of both areawide and nonareawide
borough functions by city councils (representing
the majority of the borough's population) presented
borough supporters with a major problem. Noncity
residents and residents of cities other than first-
class cities were bitterly critical. Though they
had no legitimate complaint as to the exercise of
areawide functions, they did have a valid complaint
about city council dominance over nonareawide matters. This problem was quickly recognized: "The
problem, as I see it, is to give the representatives of the majority of the people a controlling
voice in the affairs which pertain directly to
them, that is, the functions performed in the area
outside cities only."[105]

The Weighted Vote

The suggested solution was embodied in amendments to the Borough Act in 1962.[106] These provided new standards for assembly composition and
apportionment and for a weighted vote. Under the
amendments, the assembly is apportioned to represent the total population of the borough without
giving an overwhelming advantage to either first-
class cities or to the borough area outside first-
class cities. The area outside first-class cities
in each borough has one more representative on the
borough assembly than the total number of assemblymen who represent first-class cities. If a majority of borough population lives outside a first-
class city or cities, weighted voting is not used.

However, in those boroughs where a majority of
the borough population resides in a first-class
city or cities, the assembly uses two systems of
voting--a weighted voting system when dealing with
areawide functions enumerated in AS 07.20.070(d),
and a nonweighted vote on all other matters.

AS 07.20.070(c) of the Borough Act as amended
(1962) provides that "no action of the assembly is
valid or binding unless adopted by a majority of
all the votes to which the assembly is entitled on
the question." [Emphasis added.] When the assembly deals with nonareawide functions or nonenumer-
ated areawide functions and activities, the number
of possible votes equals the number of assembly
members; i.e., each member has a single vote. On
the other hand, when the assembly votes on enumerated areawide borough functions, assembly action
requires a majority of the total possible number of
votes within the assembly. This number is greater
than the assembly membership, hence, the term
"weighted vote."

The weighted vote is determined as follows:[107]

If one first-class city has a majority of the
borough population, the votes of the assemblymen
representing that city are weighted by dividing
the number of all other assembly seats plus one by
the number of all assembly seats apportioned to
the first-class city with the majority of population. If, however, one first-class city does not
have a majority of the borough population, but two
or more first-class cities have a majority, the
votes of the assemblymen representing all the
first-class cities are weighted by dividing the
number of all assembly seats apportioned to the
area outside cities plus one by the number of all
assembly seats apportioned to the first-class
cities.

Many persons assume that the weighted vote
applies to all areawide borough functions. Although the enumeration under AS 07.20.070(d) does

cover substantially all areawide functions, it does not include all.[108] The functions enumerated are:

1. Education

2. Planning and zoning

3. Assessment and collection of taxes

4. Additional areawide powers acquired by transfer or by petition and vote

5. Levying areawide taxes for areawide functions

6. Incurring indebtedness on an areawide basis for areawide functions.

In practice, there is little uniformity in the use of the weighted vote. There is general misunderstanding of the law, which is not as clear as it should be and does not, of course, cover all contingencies. In some boroughs there has been and continues to be a continual wrangle over the weighted vote. It is maintained, on the one hand, that the device is abused by the city, and on the other, that it is used to deny equitable representation to the city. In those areas where there is no great hostility or divergent policy lines between the city and the rest of the borough it has not been a problem because it has not been used, or has not been used systematically.

Although the creation of the weighted vote was an attempt to provide a method of equitable voting on areawide and nonareawide functions, it is mechanically and psychologically a failure. Moreover, there is question whether it violates the "one man, one vote" doctrine of the United States Supreme Court. The City of Juneau has filed a suit against the Greater Juneau Borough on the entire issue.[109] A decision, however, had not been rendered at the time of this writing.

Reapportionment

The two features of local government most
likely to become obsolete are boundaries and the
apportionment of the governing body.

The Constitution is silent on the matter of
assembly reapportionment. It does, however, provide for the automatic reapportionment of the State
House of Representatives after each decennial census by a nonlegislative agent--the Governor. The
Constitutional Convention intended that the borough
assembly would be reapportioned in a similar manner
by a State agency.

The legislature provides for alternate methods
of borough assembly reapportionment through the
Borough Act.[110] The assembly may reapportion itself whenever the apportionment of seats no longer
meets the standards prescribed by the Act. In
addition, fifty qualified borough voters may petition the assembly or the Local Affairs Agency to
reapportion the assembly. Evidence that reapportionment is essential to meet the apportionment
standards must accompany the petition. The assembly or the agency is then required to investigate
the evidence and reapportion the assembly if it determines that the existing apportionment violates
the standards.

In its investigation and reapportionment the
assembly or agency uses the latest Bureau of the
Census figures or "any method necessary to determine most accurately the actual population."[111]

Reapportionment by the Local Affairs Agency
has priority over reapportionment by the assembly.
The new apportionment of assembly seats is effective at the beginning of the next regular election.
Thus, adequate safeguards for assembly reapportionment are provided.

Nomination, Selection, and
Election of Officers

Candidates for assemblyman from areas of the
borough outside first-class cities are nominated by
petition of fifty qualified voters who must be residents outside any first-class city.[112] They are
elected only by voters living outside of first-
class cities. The Borough Act provides that the
representatives of first-class cities on the assembly shall be appointed by and from the city councils, but is silent about the method of appointment. In practice a city council usually selects
the city's borough representatives by a simple majority vote of the council. However, many city residents find selection by the council unsatisfactory.
They desire an opportunity to vote directly for
council-assemblymen. Several proposals have been
made to provide for dual election by State law, but
at this writing none of these have been enacted.[113]

The Borough Act provides for both election at
large and by sections.[114] Except in the Anchorage
area, all assemblymen from outside first-class
cities were initially elected at large. However,
the assembly can subsequently establish sections
for the future election of assemblymen "in order
to provide representation to separate and distinct
areas within the borough."[115]

To date, only the Fairbanks North Star Borough
has established borough sections. The initial borough sections in the Greater Anchorage Area Borough
were established by the Local Affairs Agency.[116]

All borough elections are nonpartisan. However, many of the State's Democrats are unhappy
with this procedure because they feel that nonpartisan elections favor the selection of Republicans. Accordingly, a number of Democrats in the
legislature have made several unsuccessful attempts
to change the law to permit partisan borough elections. These moves have been highly criticized as
running counter to the Alaskan tradition of nonpartisan local elections.

The term of office for members of the assembly
is the same as that of councilmen in the largest
first-class city within the borough, or three years
if there is no first-class city within the borough.
A majority of the State's first-class cities have
council terms of two or three years.

The Borough Act permits the assembly to set
different election dates and different terms of
office for assemblymen, but no term of office may
exceed three years. Most assemblies have set assembly terms at three years. Since the State's cities
have staggered council terms, most boroughs have
adopted the same arrangement.

The assembly elects from its members a presiding officer and a deputy presiding officer. The
assembly also appoints a clerk who is responsible
for the administrative and clerical needs of the
assembly. In a majority of the boroughs the borough chairman officially or unofficially served as
assembly clerk at the early assembly sessions.

THE BOROUGH EXECUTIVE

The Alaska Constitution contains no reference
to the borough executive, and the minutes of the
Constitutional Convention shed little light on the
subject. However, what little delegate sentiment
there was reveals a preference for the strong unified executive. "Judging by the type of chief executive the Convention chose for the state,"
states the Final Report on Borough Government, "it
is safe to assume that the Convention would never
have gone on record as favoring a weak mayor plan
of government for an organized borough. Other than
that it is impossible to show a constitutional intent favoring any particular plan."[117]

The Borough Act provides for a strong chief
executive, with the citizens of each organized
borough given an option between an elected or appointed executive. If the executive is elected he

is known as the "borough chairman"; if appointed,
as the "borough manager." Whether elected or appointed, almost all executive power is vested in a
single executive.

The borough chairman is responsible for the
proper administration of all borough affairs placed
in his charge by the Borough Act. It is his duty
to appoint, suspend, and remove all borough officers
and employees, though he may delegate this power to
other borough officers in regard to their subordin-
ates. His removal of employees is subject to review of the borough assembly. School administrators and teachers, however, are under the State
Teachers' Tenure Act and are not under his jurisdiction.

The Borough Act specifies that the chairman
shall direct and supervise the functions of all
borough officers and employees, the care and custody of all borough buildings,[118] all real and
personal property of the borough, and the construction, maintenance, and operation of borough roads,
buildings, and other public works.

The chairman may introduce ordinances and
take part in the discussion of all matters coming
before the assembly, but he may not vote. However,
he may veto any ordinance, resolution, motion, or
order of the assembly, and his veto may be overridden only by "two-thirds of all the votes to
which the assembly is entitled on the question."[119]

The borough manager has all the powers and
duties of the borough chairman except that he may
not introduce ordinances and he has no veto power.
Unlike the borough chairman, the manager has no
fixed term. He is appointed by the assembly and
serves at its pleasure.

The first chairman of an organized borough
established by local option is selected at the
incorporation election. The first chairmen of
boroughs incorporated under the Mandatory Borough

Act were elected by the voters on December 3, 1963.
Significantly, the borough chairman is elected at
large by all areas of the borough, including first-
class cities. The candidate receiving the most
votes at the election is declared elected. Borough
voters may adopt the manager plan at the initial
borough election or may at a later date petition
for a vote on the question.

The term of office of the borough chairman is
the same as that of the mayor in the largest first-
class city in the borough, or three years if there
is no first-class city. The assembly may provide
for a longer or shorter term by ordinance. All
boroughs with the chairman form of executive, except the Greater Juneau Borough, have set the term
of the chairman at three years. The chairman of
the Greater Juneau Borough has a four-year term.

Although all of Alaska's first-class cities
with full-time executives, except the City of
Juneau,[120] operate on the manager plan, the voters
within eight of the State's nine organized boroughs
have chosen the elected executive form of borough
government. Only the Bristol Bay Borough in western
Alaska has a borough manager. In the June, 1963,
issue of Alaska Local Government, the director of
the Local Affairs Agency succinctly noted the advantages of an elected chairman:

> The borough chairman is the one bor-
> ough official elected at large.[121]
> His political base is the entire
> borough, the cities as well as the
> outlying areas. The chairman is the
> only borough institution that has
> political support and the power to
> mollify group animosities and to
> bring truly integrated and accepted
> areawide local government to an
> area. No other form of executive
> for local government has the ad-
> vantages of an elected areawide
> executive with real executive
> powers.[122]

The voters throughout the State overwhelmingly selected the chairman form of borough government. Only in the Fairbanks and Anchorage areas, the two largest urban areas in the State, did the manager system even receive over 40 per cent of the vote.

CHANGES IN BOROUGH AND CITY BOUNDARIES

Annexation to and exclusion from cities and organized boroughs are accomplished through recommendations of the State Local Boundary Commission and through local action pursuant to the Annexation Act of 1957[123] or home-rule charter provisions.

The Constitutional Convention intended that all alterations in the boundaries of cities and organized boroughs should be reviewed and regulated by a State agency. To this end, the Local Boundary Commission was set up in the executive branch of the State government under Section 12, Article X, of the State Constitution. The Commission may consider any proposed local government boundary change[124] and may present proposed changes to the legislature during the first ten days of any regular session. Commission proposals become law forty-five days after presentation to the legislature unless disapproved by a resolution concurred in by a majority of the members of each house. Section 12 also provides that "the commission or board, subject to law, may establish procedures whereby boundaries may be adjusted by local action."

Section 12 is the result of convention sentiment that "local political decisions do not usually create proper boundaries." The Minutes of the Committee on Local Government reveal that:

> There was some feeling that the citizens of a local unit should have some check upon the revision of their boundaries. . . . At the same time, however, it was recognized that an objective analysis of relative

> needs between adjacent units could
> only be made on a level higher than
> the local units.[125]

The Committee stated that the advantage of State
action:

> lies in placing the process at a level
> where area-wide or state-wide needs
> can be taken into account. By placing
> authority in this third-party, argu-
> ments for and against boundary change
> can be analyzed objectively.[126]

Although the Constitutional Convention intended that all local government boundary changes
should be reviewed and regulated by the Local Boundary Commission, this has not been the case in practice. The commission has not established "procedures whereby boundaries may be adjusted by local
action." Despite questions as to the constitutionality of the Annexation Act of 1957, cities have
continued to use it. Moreover, home-rule advocates
argue that since no law or charter specifically
prohibits a home-rule government from changing
boundaries, a home-rule city may alter boundaries
simply by ordinance. Thus far, however, no home-
rule city has attempted to annex solely by council
directive.

The Local Boundary Commission has to date made
two recommendations for changes in borough boundaries. One of these, made in 1964, reduced the Fairbanks North Star Borough to approximately one third
the size of the area incorporated as a borough under
the Mandatory Borough Act. The other (1966) altered the boundaries of the Matanuska-Susitna,
Greater Anchorage area, and Kenai Peninsula Boroughs. The changes in the boundaries of the three
boroughs essentially involved unpopulated areas.

The commission has made fifteen recommendations for changes in city boundaries. Five of
these concerned the City of Fairbanks and significantly altered its boundaries.

Although a number of commission recommendations have been controversial, none to the date of this writing has been rejected by the legislature.

Future Changes in Local
Government Boundaries

Until additional boroughs are created in Alaska, it will be a relatively easy matter to alter borough boundaries.

Changes in city boundaries, however, will not be so easy to accomplish, for the existence of organized boroughs appears to have had an adverse effect on the ability of cities within boroughs to annex. The PAS anticipated this:

> Once the borough has been established
> there will be a tendency to resist
> annexation to the city even when it
> may be by far the most economical
> and efficient way of extending par-
> ticular services already being con-
> ducted by the city as a going con-
> cern.[127]

Residents of the urban fringe in a number of cities are seeking municipal services from the borough and not the city. Although the Constitution precludes the use of service areas if a service can be provided through annexation to a city, the borough assembly (without the weighted vote) is the initial judge as to whether this limitation is applicable to the establishment of particular service areas. And borough residents from outside first-class cities and borough assemblymen representing the outlying areas, generally preferring the establishment of service areas, have opposed city annexations.

City officials, however, endorse annexation as a means of retaining control of areawide borough functions. The weighted vote applies only if a first-class city or cities has the majority of a

borough's population. In many parts of the State,
the population in the area adjacent to the city is
growing more rapidly than the population within the
city. Thus, if annexation is stalled, the population of the borough's outlying areas could surpass
the population of its first-class city and cause
the city to lose its use of the weighted vote on
areawide matters. In fact, when the Local Boundary
Commission conducted hearings in the City of Fairbanks in 1962 and 1963 to consider the annexation
of certain areas to the city, a member of the Fairbanks Borough Study Group requested that the annexation be denied or at least postponed until after a
borough were incorporated in the greater Fairbanks
area. She indicated her fear that adding population to the city would guarantee it the use of the
weighted vote.[128]

TAXATION

The general property tax and the general sales
tax are the major sources of local tax revenue in
Alaska. They are used exclusively by local governments. "Alaska local governments," states the
Legislative Council, "actually occupy a tax position that can be envied by many of their counterparts in the other states, as they have available
two important revenue sources that are not concur-
rently utilized by the State."[129]

Although the organized borough may levy the
same taxes as a first-class city, it may not tax
city residents for nonareawide borough functions.
The Borough Act provides that first- and second-
class boroughs "may levy areawide taxes for areawide functions and taxes limited to the area outside cities for functions limited to the area outside cities."[130]

> Tax and other revenue measures
> levied on an areawide basis may
> be expended on general adminis-
> tration costs and on areawide

functions only. Tax and other revenue
measures levied in the area outside
cities only may be expended on functions which render services to the
area outside cities only.[131]

Almost all local governments employ the general property tax. In Alaska, cities (except
fourth class)[132] and organized boroughs may assess,
levy, and collect a general tax on the assessed
valuation of all taxable real and personal property.

State law allows cities and organized boroughs
to impose up to a 3 per cent consumers' sales tax
on all retail sales, rentals, and services made
within the respective jurisdictions, subject to a
local referendum.

A particular problem in the sales tax area
arises from the fact that both the city and the
organized borough may levy a 3 per cent sales tax.
Thus, it is legally possible to have a 6 per cent
sales tax levied on goods and services sold within
a city--a 3 per cent areawide borough tax and a 3
per cent city tax. At first view this does not appear to present a real problem, since no sales tax
may be imposed without a local referendum. The
Borough Act, however, provides for the assumption
of an independent school district sales tax levy
by the organized borough in which a district is
located. As the old independent school district
could levy a 2 per cent sales tax in the area outside cities, the borough had the option to apply
the district levy either on an areawide basis for
areawide functions or on a nonareawide basis for
nonareawide functions, without a local referendum.

The problem of adjusting borough and city
sales taxes has caused serious strain between city
and borough governments. Boroughs have continued
the district sales taxes. Cities, however, have
been loath to abandon any part of their taxes, but,
on the other hand, have not been anxious to see a
major increase in the tax levied within the city

by the borough.   The problem has been particularly
severe in the Fairbanks area.   Prior to the assumption of the education function by the Fairbanks
North Star Borough, the City of Fairbanks levied a
3 per cent sales tax within the city and the Fairbanks Independent School District levied a 2 per
cent tax outside the city.   The borough voted to
continue the district tax on an areawide basis and,
consequently, the residents of the city pay a 5 per
cent tax.   All efforts so far to get the borough
and the city to compromise on the issue have failed.

General law (non-home rule) cities and boroughs may tax property up to thirty mills and con-
sumer sales up to 3 per cent.   Alaska has no legal
limitation, however, on the amount of debt that
cities and organized boroughs may incur.   "There
are no clear guidelines in this field,"[133] states
the planning and public services manual of the
Local Affairs Agency, although "investors in municipal bonds have used 10 per cent of a municipality's assessed valuation as a rule-of-thumb limit
on general obligation bonds."[134]

THE BOROUGH IN OPERATION

Except for the Bristol Bay Borough, organized
boroughs have been in operation for slightly more
than four years.   During this period they have
encountered a number of problems and have found
themselves in serious conflicts with school districts and cities.   However, in light of the difficulties in setting up a new unit of local government and in working out relationships with existing
units and systems, it is amazing that in most areas
the problems have not been greater or the conflicts
more severe.

Though each borough has ostensibly assumed the
mandatory powers required by the Borough Act, several have not completely or effectively done so in
law or in fact.   Differences in personality, in
philosophy, and in local political climate have

worked to corrode borough authority. In several instances where cooperative agreements were used to
ease the transfer of functions and delineate borough-
city or borough-school district relationships, the
agreements have been used as a means of returning a
function to the initial authority while retaining
the facade of borough control. (Any agreement or
contract which delegates borough legislative authority to a city or school system is probably ultra
vires. However, at the time of this writing none
of these arrangements has been tested in court.)

In spite of problems and conflicts encountered
in assuming the required functions, several boroughs
have acquired additional powers, on either an areawide or nonareawide basis. In all but a few instances, supplemental areawide powers were gained
through petition and a vote of the people; in only
one or two cases has a city voluntarily transferred
a power to a borough.

Early Problems

In the summer of 1964, less than a year after
the incorporation of the "mandatory" boroughs, the
Local Affairs Agency queried the nine boroughs,
"What have been your major organizational problems?"
The response is shown on Table 2. Although a number of the problems listed are no longer relevant
or major, they indicate the types of difficulties
that developed early.

Legislation and Proposed Legislation

Most of the difficulties experienced by the
boroughs have been essentially legal or political
in nature. However, labeling a problem "legal"
is often an answer or excuse for political conflict.

Legal problems have centered around vague, unclear, contradictory, or outdated sections in the
law. However, what appears vague or unclear to
some is not so to others. Borough powers are largely drawn by reference from the powers of cities, as

TABLE 2

MAJOR ORGANIZATIONAL PROBLEMS AS INDICATED
BY EACH ORGANIZED BOROUGH, 1964[a]

Borough	Problems
Bristol Bay	Budgetary conflict between borough assembly and school board
Gateway	Use of sales tax levied by independent school district and difference in fiscal years between city and district
Greater Juneau	How to handle dedication of sales tax for schools
Greater Anchorage Area	Lack of general public understanding regarding boroughs
Kenai Peninsula	Lack of funds to establish tax program[b]
Kodiak Peninsula	Lack of funds to carry over until next year's tax receipts are received[b]
Matanuska-Susitna	Lack of funds[b]
North Star	Conflict between city and borough over sales tax levied by independent school district

[a]Taken from ALG (June–July, 1964), pp. 8-9.

[b]The Kenai Peninsula, Matanuska-Susitna, and Kodiak Island Boroughs are large units of local government with small scattered populations. Although they received money grants of $10.00 per voter, these funds were quite insufficient to establish an initial property assessment program. The Matanuska-Susitna Borough reluctantly established such a program on largely a self-assessment basis. The other two units were able to find other revenues to meet the purpose.

indicated in the Municipal Code (AS 29). School
legislation is found in the Education Code (AS 14),
although provisions concerning borough-school district relationships are in part in borough legislation (AS 07). Attempts to "clarify" the law have
generally been efforts to achieve a political
breakthrough or victory by one side or another, by
changing the rules of the game. Each side, be it
the city, the borough, or the school district, has
sought to have the laws changed to increase its
power and to give it predominance.

Following a 1963 directive of the legislature, [135] the Local Affairs Agency drafted a substantive revision of the State's statutes on local
government. Although the directive apparently related only to a revision of the law on cities, the
agency made the decision to propose a consolidation
of the Municipal Code, the Borough Act, and those
portions of the Education Code dealing with school
districts. The suggested revision was introduced
into the 1965 legislature by the Senate Local Government Committee as Senate Bill No. 101.

Senate Bill No. 101, as introduced, sought to
enlarge the power of boroughs over the operation
of schools, and increase the authority of boroughs
in relation to cities by strengthening borough control over planning and zoning, and so on.

Senate Bill No. 101 was well received by the
boroughs but was bitterly attacked by the State's
largest cities and by the school districts, which
considered the measure too pro-borough. [136] Consequently, the agency became a lightning rod, drawing
the ire of city and school district officials, but
receiving support and appreciation from the boroughs.

The Senate Local Government Committee spent
the entire session reviewing the provisions of
Senate Bill No. 101. The committee was chaired by
Senator Harold Z. Hansen, who had been chairman of
the House Local Government Committee during the
1961-62 session. In reviewing the bill, the

committee, which had no staff of its own, used the services of the Local Affairs Agency. At the end of the session the committee introduced a Committee Substitute for Senate Bill No. 101. The concerted opposition of school officials forced the deletion from the bill of material initially taken from the Education Code.

The question of borough-school relationships was aggravated not only by Senate Bill No. 101 but also by several other Senate bills which, unlike Senate Bill No. 101, sought to give additional authority to the schools and thus downgrade borough authority. In an attempt to arrive at a solution acceptable to both sides, the chairman of the House Local Government Committee arranged a meeting attended by several officials of the State and of the Greater Juneau Borough, including the school superintendent. The group worked out a plan which it felt would be acceptable to both borough school and general government officials. The plan, for example, permitted the borough assembly to provide for a centralized treasury, but authorized the establishment of a centralized* accounting system only with the approval of the school board. The House Local Government Committee, with minor modifications, accepted the plan. It was written into a pro-school Senate bill and became House Committee Substitute for Senate Bill No. 146. The bill, known as the "Compromise Bill of 1965," passed the legislature and became law as Chapter 82, SLA, 1965.

During the summer and fall of 1965, the Legislative Council conducted hearings throughout the State on a number of items, including the revised

---

*
Editors' Note: "Centralized treasury" and "centralized accounting" are used throughout this book interchangeably with "central treasury" and "central accounting." "Centralized treasury" and "centralized accounting" is the language employed in the statutes.

Municipal Code (Committee Substitute for Senate Bill
No. 101). The hearings indicated that, although
school officials were not entirely pleased with the
revised code, their criticisms were not pronounced
since the most controversial items had already been
deleted. However, the city representatives were
most unhappy with Committee Substitute for Senate
Bill No. 101. At a council hearing held before the
Alaska Municipal League at its annual convention,
league officials stated that the bill was unacceptable. They indicated a hope that the league could
draft a substitute revised code to be considered by
the 1966 legislative session.[137]

The staff of the Legislative Council prepared
a summary of the testimony on Committee Substitute
for Senate Bill No. 101 given at the council's hearings. When the 1966 session of the legislature convened, this summary was presented to the Senate
Local Government Committee for review. For the remainder of the session the committee worked on Committee Substitute for Senate Bill No. 101, revising,
substituting, and editing. Near the end of the session it passed the revised Municipal Code, as the
Second Committee Substitute for Senate Bill No. 101.
The bill went to the Judiciary Committee where it
languished and died.[138]

To complicate the situation further, the 1965-
66 legislature had a revised Education Code (AS 14)
under study and review. It was generally recognized that the Education Code was badly out of
date. The revised code contained a number of provisions dealing with borough-school relationships.
The substance of these provisions and their inclusion within the code drew the fire of borough supporters. Consequently, in order not to delay and
possibly halt the passage of the Education Code,
its supporters removed the offending sections.
These were introduced as a separate bill, House
Bill No. 509. The Education Code, a necessary and
desirable measure, then passed easily.

As for House Bill No. 509, borough officials

found it unacceptable. Though not delighted with
the "Compromise Bill of 1965," they felt they had
accepted it in good faith and had done their best
to live with it. They did not feel that they could
compromise with school officials further. Nevertheless, after concerted effort by school officials
and their legislative supporters, the bill passed
the legislature.[139] The Governor allowed the bill
to become law without his signature. However, he
indicated that:

> I am not entirely satisfied with Sec-
> tion 2, which raises a question of
> whether total amount of the entire
> budget shall be subject to Assembly
> action, or only the funds to be made
> available from local sources. It has
> been the policy of the State of Alaska
> that all monies from whatever sources
> shall be openly disclosed and appro-
> priated for the expenditure of public
> funds. I would hope that this same
> policy would extend to the local
> political subdivisions.
>   I am therefore allowing House
> Bill 509, amended by the Senate, to
> become law without my signature
> (Chapter 129, SLA 1966), and with a
> request to the Commissioner of Edu-
> cation that he closely study the ef-
> fect of actions taken under this Act,
> and report to me. Should these re-
> views indicate appropriated monies,
> from all sources, have not been fully
> disclosed, it would be my intention
> to have remedial legislation intro-
> duced at the next session of the
> Alaska Legislature.[140]

Chapter 129 contains major provisions which
give further authority to school boards. It specifies that the borough has authority for only the
share of the school budget raised from local
sources. The boroughs had wanted control over the

total budget regardless of the source of funds.
Authority as to school building design is also
altered:

> Within 30 days after receipt of the
> budget the assembly shall determine
> the total amount of money to be made
> available from local sources for
> school purposes, and shall furnish
> the school board with a statement of
> the sum to be made available. [Empha-
> sis added.]
>   The school board is responsible
> for the design criteria of school
> buildings. Subject to the approval
> of the assembly, the school board
> shall select the appropriate profes-
> sional personnel to develop the de-
> signs. The school board shall sub-
> mit preliminary and subsequent de-
> signs for a school building to the
> assembly for approval or disapproval.
> If the design is disapproved, a re-
> vised design shall be prepared and
> presented to the assembly.[141]

Evaluation

The borough is creating a place for itself on
the Alaskan political landscape because it is providing services and benefits to the public that
heretofore did not exist or did not exist on an
areawide basis. Gradually the boroughs appear to
be creating a "constituency" which supports and de-
fends them, though not uncritically. The borough
is now an accepted fact and not even the most
adamant borough opponent believes it possible to
eliminate it.

Although the borough is here to stay and is
recognized as an integral part of the State's governmental structure, relationships among boroughs,
cities, and school districts do not follow a fixed
pattern. The borough has generally lost ground to

the school districts, and there is a possibility
that, in this area, its powers may be further
eroded. Where the city is concerned, however, the
borough has increasingly gained authority. In discussing the acquisition of additional areawide powers by borough governments, John L. Rader has remarked: "Each time a city gives up something, it
dies a little."[142]

NOTES TO CHAPTER 1

1. A short introduction to Alaska's geography,
population, and economy will be found in Appendix A.
For a discussion of the Alaska statehood movement,
see George W. Rogers, The Future of Alaska: Economic Consequences of Statehood (Baltimore: The
Johns Hopkins Press, 1962), passim.

2. The independent school district was an
areawide form of local government, but it was limited to the single purpose of education.

3. James Wickersham was for many years the
Territory's voteless delegate to the U.S. House of
Representatives.

4. Alaska, Alaska State Legislature, Legislative Council, and Office of the Governor, Local Affairs Agency, Final Report on Borough Government
(Juneau, January, 1961), p. 17. Hereafter cited as
Final Report.

5. Alaska, Alaska State Legislature, Legislative Council, Local Government in Alaska: Problems
and Alternatives, Publication No. 21-6 (Juneau,
1954), p. 2.

6. The Constitution provides that "all laws
in force in the Territory of Alaska on the effective date of this Constitution and consistent
therewith shall continue in force until they

expire by their own limitation, are amended, or repealed." (Art. XV, sec. 1.)

7. Final Report, pp. 28-29.

8. A petition, court hearing, court order,
and local election are required to incorporate
cities.

9. The Territory had more city school districts than other types of school districts. This
is also true of the State.

10. The term "incorporated school district"
is misleading. The incorporated school district
and the independent school district were both incorporated districts under law. The incorporated
school district was designed for only those areas
outside of towns, where the people desired to tax
themselves for school costs and manage their own
schools.

11. Final Report, p. 24.

12. Legislation authorizing the establishment
of health districts was enacted in 1955, Session
Laws of Alaska, 1955, chap. 163. (Hereafter cited
as SLA.) However, none were incorporated under
the Territory and none can now be formed under the
State Constitution.

13. It should be noted that, unlike most
constitution-makers, the delegates to Alaska's Constitutional Convention operated under ideal conditions. No one knew whether the document to be
drafted would ever become operative. ("This constitution shall take effect immediately upon the
admission of Alaska into the Union as a state."
Art. XV, sec. 25.) Thus, the delegates were not
under the pressures felt by most legislative bodies
and, consequently, had greater opportunity to develop a model document.

14.   Victor Fischer, speech before the Anchorage Chamber of Commerce, Anchorage, Alaska, n.d., p. 1.

15.   Public Administration Service, _Constitutional Studies_, prepared on behalf of the Alaska Statehood Committee for the Alaska Constitutional Convention (3 vols.; Chicago, November, 1955), III, 54.   Under the auspices of the Statehood Committee, PAS prepared a number of background studies for the Convention.

16.   Alaska, Alaska Legislative Council, Minutes of the Daily Proceedings, _Minutes of the Alaska Constitutional Convention_ (Juneau: State of Alaska, March, 1965), p. 2611.   Hereafter cited as _Minutes_.

17.   _Ibid._, p. 2699.

18.   Alaska Constitutional Convention, _Minutes of the Committee on Local Government_, 1955-56, No. 19.

19.   _Final Report_, p. 41.

20.   _Minutes_, p. 2654.

21.   _Ibid._, p. 2625.

22.   _Ibid._, p. 2612.

23.   Public Administration Service, _Local Government under the Alaska Constitution_ (Chicago, January 9, 1959), p. 53.   In addition to its background studies for the convention, PAS prepared a number of studies dealing with the problems of transition to statehood.

24.   A number of names besides "borough" and "county" were suggested: from "section," "township," "province," and "division" to such Alaskanized names as "denali," "tundraburg," "nunat," and "munipuk."   The name "borough" was finally chosen by majority vote.

25. Alaska, Office of the Governor, Local Affairs Agency, Alaska Local Government (May, 1962), p. 1. Alaska Local Government was a monthly publication of the Local Affairs Agency. Hereafter cited as ALG.

26. A copy of John P. Keith's City and County Rule in Texas (Austin: Institute of Public Affairs, University of Texas, 1951) was used extensively by the Committee on Local Government.

27. Minutes, p. 2613. The Final Report defines the Texas Plan in general terms as follows: "The Texas Plan parallels that relationship which exists between the federal government and the states in the following respect. The states are free to act on matters of concern to the federal government until such time as the federal government decides to act for the benefit of the nation as a whole. The same prerogative is permitted to the local government. They may act in any matter unless prohibited by general state law, or denied them by charter." (p. 36)

28. Minutes of the Committee on Local Government, No. 24.

29. Victor Fischer, speech before the Anchorage Chamber of Commerce, n.d., p. 4.

30. Minutes of the Committee on Local Government, No. 18.

31. Minutes, p. 2617.

32. The regular session of the Alaska State legislature meets each year on the fourth Monday in January. (Art. II, sec. 8.)

33. Local Government under the Alaska Constitution, p. 4.

34. The first State legislature also redesignated the incorporated village a city of the

fourth class (SLA, 1959, chap. 79) to meet the constitutional requirement that "all local government
powers shall be vested in boroughs and cities."

35. Ibid., chap. 64: "The Local Affairs
Agency shall administer a state program to provide
assistance to local communities, including assistance in fiscal problems, incorporation and organization problems, legal matters, engineering, purchasing, planning, and the recruitment of technical
and specialized personnel." The legislature apparently did not feel that the establishment of a separate department of local affairs was warranted.

36. The commission consists of five members
appointed by the governor for overlapping five-year
terms: one each from the old major senatorial election districts, and one from the State at large who
serves as chairman. The commission meets only
periodically. Its members are unsalaried, but do
receive per diem and travel expenses.
     Under the law, the Local Affairs Agency
provides staff services to the commission. The
director of the agency, or his representative, at-
tends commission hearings and meetings and partici-
pates in commission decisions, but has no formal
vote.

37. Alaska, Office of the Governor, Local
Boundary Commission, First Report to the Second
Session of the First Alaska State Legislature
(Juneau, February 2, 1960).

38. Senate Concurrent Resolution No. 23.

39. Preliminary Report on Borough Government
(Juneau: State of Alaska, December, 1960) was sub-
mitted to the legislators and the general public in
December, 1960.

40. SLA, 1961, chap. 146.

41. The act did not become effective until
October 1, 1961.

42. This section was amended by the Mandatory Borough Act in 1963.

43. Final Report, p. 47.

44. Several groups and organizations informally began the study of borough government prior to 1961.

45. Alaska, Office of the Governor, Local Affairs Agency, Borough Incorporation Manual (2d rev. ed.; Juneau, May, 1962), p. 3.

46. Many public schools within the State were located outside school districts and were totally financed and operated by the State through the State Department of Education. The biggest of these schools have been within organized boroughs since January 1, 1964.

47. Charles Lafferty, Superintendent, Fairbanks Independent School District, Memorandum, Subject: House Bill No. 488 (1962 amendments to the Borough Act), March 30, 1962, p. 1.

48. Erick L. Lindman, et al. (Los Angeles, Calif.: Ford Foundation, September, 1961). Hereafter cited as A Foundation for Alaska's Public Schools.

49. For further discussion of the foundation report, see Chapter 6, written by Donald M. Dafoe.

50. The political composition of the third Alaska State legislature was: House of Representatives--twenty Democrats, twenty Republicans (in control); Senate--fifteen Democrats, five Republicans. The Governor was William A. Egan, a Democrat.

51. The bill became Chapter 52, SLA, 1963.

52. These areas contained the major clusters of population and each had one or more special districts.

53.   Alaska law was codified in 1962.   All
legislation is categorized in approximately fifty
titles.   Alaska Statutes, Title 07, deals with boroughs.   Alaska Statutes is cited as AS, plus title
number, and chapter and section where appropriate.

54.   SLA, 1963, chap. 52.   The money and land
grant provisions of Chapter 52 are general provisions applicable to all organized boroughs, including any incorporated after January 1, 1964.

55.   A delegate to the Constitutional Convention made the comment: "If we . . . force it
[local government] upon the people, I think you
are going to have it taken with resentment and
probably a lack of good local government."   [sic]
(Minutes, p. 2651)

56.   Keynote Address, Thirteenth Annual Con-
vention of the Alaska Municipal League (Seward,
Alaska: October 23-26, 1963), as reported in ALG
(October, 1963), p. 5.

57.   Exclusive of the Bristol Bay Borough petition.   The Bristol Bay Borough was incorporated on
October 2, 1962.

58.   The "gun behind the door" feature of the
Mandatory Borough Act obviously influenced the
elections, but to what extent is difficult to state
with precision.

59.   AS 07.10.030(1).

60.   ALG (March, 1962), pp. 2-3.

61.   See Alaska, Office of the Governor, Local
Affairs Agency, Incorporation of the Captain Cook
Borough: Report to the Local Boundary Commission
on a Proposal to Incorporate an Organized Borough
in the Anchorage Area (Juneau, May, 1963), p. 17.

62.   Part 1, p. 9.

63.   <u>Ibid</u>., p. 10.

64.   The large borough concept ran counter to
the small borough approach advocated by many of the
State's local borough study groups.

65.   "Too Much!," <u>Anchorage Daily News</u>, p. 3.

66.   See "The ABC's of Boroughs," <u>Anchorage
Times</u>, September 14, 1963.

67.   The assemblies of the four boroughs subsequently adopted the following borough names:
          Matanuska-Susitna (Palmer-Wasilla-
             Talkeetna Election District No. 7)
          Greater Anchorage Agea (Anchorage Elec-
             tion District No. 8)
          Kenai Peninsula (combined Seward and
             Kenai-Cook Inlet Election Districts
             Nos. 9 and 10)
          North Star (Fairbanks Election District
             No. 19, as designated prior to reappor-
             tionment in 1961), later changed to
             Fairbanks North Star.

68.   "You Can't Hurry A Borough," <u>Anchorage
Times</u>, February 28, 1963, p. 4.

69.   As quoted in "July 15 Set for Takeover of
Schools," <u>Fairbanks Daily News-Miner</u>, June 12, 1964,
p. 7.

70.   The referendum petition, the court cases
testing the State's constitutional and statutory
referendum provisions, and the request for a
special session of the legislature were all "firsts"
for the new State.

71.   Quoted in "Reluctant Secretary Certifies
Borough Petition," <u>Daily Alaska Empire</u>, Juneau,
September 10, 1963, p. 1.

72.   A number of home-rule cities have adopted
preregistration although their authority to do so
has been questioned in light of the constitutional

provision which implies that only the legislature
may act in this area. "The legislature may provide
a system of permanent registration of voters. . . ."
(Art. V, sec. 4)

73. Walters and Mullen v. Cease, et al.,
Anchorage, Alaska, Superior Court, No. 63-1411,
November 14, 1963.

74. Ibid., p. 3.

75. Walters and Mullen v. Cease, et al., 388
P.2d 263 (1964).

76. As quoted in "Legislature Asked To Convene," Anchorage Times, September 14, 1963, p. 1.

77. Five Democrats and three Republicans.
The Legislative Council contains ten members. For
the 1963-64 legislative term, the council had six
Democrats and four Republicans. At the September
20 session of the council, two members, a Democrat
and a Republican, were absent.

78. House Bill No. 345 proposed the repeal
of the entire Mandatory Borough Act. The House
Local Government Committee sponsored a substitute
for the bill, which proposed not the repeal of the
entire act, but the dissolution of the four boroughs
incorporated under it.

79. Gill and Norene v. Cease, et al., Alaska,
Superior Court, "Complaint," Anchorage, October 31,
1963. Prior to the Superior Court decision in
Walters and Mullen v. Cease, et al., Gill and
Norene had moved to intervene as plaintiffs in the
case in order to request the Court to declare the
Mandatory Borough Act a special act. This motion
was opposed by Walters and Mullen. The application
for intervention was denied.

80. The earlier Superior and Supreme Court
decisions in Walters and Mullen v. Cease, et al.
had not considered the constitutionality of the
Mandatory Borough Act.

81. This decision and the November 14 Superior Court decision (see p. 33 above) were rendered by different judges.

82. Walters and Mullen v. Cease, et al., 394 P.2d 670 (1964). Unlike the Superior Court, the Supreme Court rendered its decision on the ground that the Mandatory Borough Act was local legislation.

83. Art. X, sec. 3: "The Legislature shall classify boroughs and prescribe their powers and functions."

84. Minutes, p. 2654.

85. Final Report, p. 55.

86. The Borough Act initially provided that borough school districts would be operated "in the manner provided by law for city school districts, except as provided otherwise by this title." School officials were unhappy with the "except as provided otherwise" phrase, since they felt it was open-ended and gave too much authority or potential authority to the officials of the general borough government. On the other hand, borough officials generally felt that it was unfortunate that the operation of borough school districts was tied to city school law, which was badly in need of revision. However, no basic changes were made in the school section of the Borough Act (AS 07.15.330) until 1965; a revised Education Code was not adopted until 1966. See this chapter, pp. 57 ff.

87. Districts with an average daily membership exceeding 5,000 pupils have an elected school board of seven members. The Anchorage and Fairbanks borough school districts have seven-member boards.

88. However, if within thirty days of the receipt of the school budget, the assembly has not indicated to the board the amount of money it will make available, "the amount requested in the budget

is automatically approved." (AS 07.15.330, as
amended in 1966.)

89. AS 07.15.340. A controversy has developed over whether the planning and zoning power
includes the responsibility for building codes.
The Attorney General, the Local Affairs Agency, the
State Director of Planning and Research, and a number of borough officials maintain that it does.
City officials vehemently deny it. For discussion
on this question, see Chapter 7, by Claude Millsap,
Jr.; Chapter 8, by Joseph R. Henri; and Chapter 10,
by Karl Walter.

90. AS 07.15.320. The law does not give the
borough the areawide responsibility for the administration of local sales taxes.

91. Minutes, p. 2703.

92. Final Report, p. 71. Closer State supervision over local assessments has been initiated
through the use of a Property Appraisal Manual for
Alaska Assessors (Alaska, Office of the Governor,
Local Affairs Agency [Juneau, 1963]).

93. See AS 07.10.130 and AS 07.10.140.

94. As well as platting boards. All special
districts have to date been integrated into borough
or city government.

95. A State school is defined as one operated
by the Department of Education and entirely financed
by nonlocal funds.

96. City, incorporated, and independent school
districts.

97. AS 07.10.130. The same provision also applies to PUDs. The integration of PUDs has been
achieved through the best and most practical means
at hand. Three of the State's six PUDs have been
integrated into cities. The other three have been
integrated into boroughs.

98.   1963 Opinions of the Attorney General,
No. 23.

99.   Boroughs may also be reclassified, but
this has so far not occurred. A first-class borough may adopt or repeal a home-rule charter in the
same manner as a first-class city (AS 29.40.010-090).
Second-class boroughs may be reclassified as first-
class boroughs in essentially the same manner as
second-class boroughs acquire additional functions
by petition after incorporation, except that only
residents outside cities are eligible to vote on
the question.

100.   AS 07.10.050.

101.   Although the law does not specifically
indicate, the commission probably has sufficient
authority to deny a petition for an additional
power on the basis that the proposal violates the
standards. However, it has not to date denied any
of the numerous requests for additional powers
(both areawide and nonareawide) which it has considered.   In the transfer of powers from cities to
boroughs, the question of standards is a matter to
be decided by the city council and the borough
assembly.

102.   AS 07.15.710.

103.   Borough legislation gives direct city
representation on the assembly only to first-class
cities.

104.   Borough Act of 1961, prior to 1962 amendment, sec. 2.04.

105.   Roger W. Pegues, Director of the Local
Affairs Agency, in a letter to Ronald C. Cease,
Assistant Professor of Political Science, University of Alaska, College, Alaska, September 29, 1961,
p. 1.

106.   SLA, 1962, chap. 110.

107.   Condensed from AS 07.20.070(d), as amended.

108.   The drafters of the 1962 amendments to the Borough Act felt that it was impossible to make a categorical distinction between areawide and non-areawide borough matters.   "I want to emphasize," states Roger W. Pegues, former director of the Local Affairs Agency, "that we purposely made a decision to limit the weighted vote to those specified functions."   Letter from Roger W. Pegues, Seattle, Washington, to Ronald C. Cease, Portland, Oregon, November 15, 1966.   Hereafter cited as Letter from Pegues to Cease.

109.   City of Juneau v. Greater Juneau Borough, Civil Action No. 65-317, Superior Court, First Judicial District, Alaska.   For discussion of the weighted vote controversy in the Juneau area, see Chapter 7, by Claude Millsap, Jr.; Chapter 8, by Joseph R. Henri; and Chapter 10, by Karl Walter.

110.   AS 07.20.030.

111.   AS 07.10.180.

112.   Candidates for borough chairman and for the school board are nominated by petition of fifty qualified voters residing anywhere within the borough.

113.   The City of Fairbanks initially provided by ordinance for direct election of assemblymen by designating certain council positions as dual council-assembly seats, but subsequently repealed the ordinance.

114.   Section boundaries must be established in such a way as to provide, insofar as possible, clarity of boundaries, compactness of area, equal voter representation among different sections, and homogeneity of interest within sections.   No section may have a number of voters which is less than one half that of any other section, as determined from the records of the last general election. (AS 07.30.100[a])

A candidate representing a specific section runs against another candidate from the same section. The outcome, however, is determined by at-large voting outside cities. In 1965 the legislature altered the provisions on sections to permit the establishment of a "ward" system in any borough with over 40,000 people (now applicable only to the Greater Anchorage Area Borough). Under this legislation, each section may elect its own assemblyman.

115. AS 07.30.100(a).

116. In October, 1965, the voters of the Greater Anchorage Area Borough adopted the "ward" system of sections.

117. Final Report, p. 3.

118. However, AS 07.15.330 provides that "the borough school board shall provide custodial services and routine maintenance for school buildings and shall appoint, compensate, and otherwise control personnel for these purposes."

119. AS 07.25.080.

120. The City of Juneau has a full-time mayor.

121. Members of the borough school board are also elected at large, although the assembly may provide for the election of board members by zones. Unlike the borough executive and members of the assembly, however, board members represent only one borough function.

122. ALG, p. 4.

123. AS 29.70.

124. Proposed boundary changes may be initiated by (1) a municipality, (2) an individual, (3) a group, (4) the director of the Local Affairs Agency, (5) the Boundary Commission, and (6) the legislature. See Alaska, Administrative Code

(Juneau, Alaska: Secretary of State, 1962), Title
6, Division 2, p. 501.

125. No. 18, December 4, 1955.

126. "Commentary on Proposed Article on Local
Government," December 19, 1955, p. 6. Quoted in
Fairview Public Utility District No. 1 v. City of
Anchorage, 368 P.2d 540 (1962).

127. Local Government Under the Alaska Constitution, p. 70.

128. Mrs. James Dalton, letter to the Local
Boundary Commission, Fairbanks, November 29, 1962.
The letter was read before the commission at its
first hearing on the petition to annex the Island
Homes area to the City of Fairbanks. Mrs. Dalton
was subsequently elected to the borough assembly,
where she still serves.

129. Alaska, Alaska State Legislature, Legislative Council, Revenue and Taxation in Alaska
(Juneau, January, 1962), Part II, p. 92.

130. AS 07.15.010(7)(A)(B).

131. AS 07.15.040.

132. There are few distinctions between
first-, second-, and third-class cities. They
share many of the same powers and duties and have
similar forms of municipal government. The powers,
duties, structure, and operation of the fourth-
class city, however, are quite different from the
others. The chief differences are that it may not
levy a property tax or special assessments; it has
no responsibility for the operation and maintenance
of local schools; and it has a weak mayor-council
form of government.

133. Alaska, Office of the Governor, Local
Affairs Agency, Borough Manual, Vol. III: Planning, Zoning and Public Services (Juneau, 1963),
p. 57.

134. *Ibid*.

135. House Concurrent Resolution No. 14.

136. City and school district officials frequently complain that the Local Affairs Agency is
too vehement a supporter of borough government.

137. The league did not draft a substitute
revision although it did prepare a section-by-
section analysis of the bill.

138. Though both the schools and cities fought
the proposed revision of the Municipal Code and
their combined opposition defeated it, their opposition did not center on the same items. Each group,
in its own way, according to its perceived interests,
objected to particular sections of the Municipal
Code. It is significant that neither cities nor
schools joined hands to present a common front
against this legislation.

139. The Senate version of the bill, Committee Substitute for House Bill No. 509, was accepted
in the House by only a narrow margin.

140. Letter from the Hon. William A. Egan,
Governor of Alaska, to the Hon. Hugh J. Wade, Secretary of State, Juneau, Alaska, May 2, 1966.

141. *SLA*, 1966, c. 129 (*AS* 07.15.330 as
amended).

142. Comment to the authors.

CHAPTER **2** LEGISLATIVE
HISTORY

by John L. Rader

In striving to form viable units of local
self-government, the people of Alaska have used
the courts, the executive branch of their Territorial Government, and the local subdivisions themselves. It was only after a series of repeated
failures that in 1963 the State legislature finally exercised the authority which had previously
been delegated to others. A brief look at these
attempts and failures may shed some light on the
historical events that preceded the passage of
Alaska's Mandatory Borough Act.

THE EXPERIMENT WITH JUDICIAL
SUPERVISION AND LOCAL
INITIATIVE

From the early days of Territorial Government,
great reliance was placed on judicial creation and
supervision of units of local government. The law
provided that upon the petition of a certain number of residents, the judge could order an election
for incorporation "if he be satisfied that it is
for the best interest and welfare of the community. . . ."[1] In the case of annexation it was provided that if "no private rights will be injured
by granting the petition and if it is just and
reasonable that the annexation take place, the
court shall [order an election]."[2]

The usual rules of law were inadequate.
Courts, depending upon the individual judge, handled these political questions in such a manner
that neither the citizens, the lawyers, nor the
judges knew from one proceeding to the next what
the guidelines for decision would be, or even what
evidence might be considered relevant.[3] In the
early days this rather arbitrary system apparently
worked as a matter of necessity. In the various
mining and fishing communities the people organized
locally to help themselves, or else they did without. There was no other option. The Territorial
and Federal Governments were unable to supply police or fire protection, schools or roads. However, subsequent to World War II, this gradually
changed.

My personal contact with these problems began
in 1954 when I became the attorney for the City of
Anchorage. It was at that time that United States
District Judge, George Folta, aptly described the
situation in a case entitled "Annexation to the
City of Anchorage (the Rogers Park Area)."[4] The
case illustrates the broad problems not only of
annexation proceedings, but also of incorporation.
The very opponents of annexation became the prime
movers to incorporate as independent cities certain portions of the urban area. Those opposed to
annexation could, by circulating a petition for incorporation, gather unto themselves the financial
and political support of people who recognized the
need for local government but distrusted the government of the City of Anchorage; or felt that they
would lose their identity and be swallowed up in
the larger community.[5]

In the case cited it was a question whether
a particular neighborhood should incorporate or
annex. The Judge found that:

> . . . the area sought to be incor-
> porated is a part of and undistin-
> guishable from a large urban area
> which also embraces the City of An-
> chorage, and that experience teaches

that an area of that kind is best
served and administered by one
municipality.

The petitioner city has
long ago outgrown its boundaries
to such an extent that the population of the adjacent area ex-
ceeds that of the city. Just
outside of the corporate limits,
numerous dives and like places
have been operated with virtual
impunity because of the lack of
law enforcement in areas outside
of incorporated towns. These
create a major police problem
for the city. From the initiation of the first annexation proceeding about a year ago, the city
has encountered the most determined and unprecedented opposition.

Every impediment and dila-
tory tactic has been employed by
the opponents of annexation, except the homesteaders, to obstruct
and harass the city in every move
in connection with its efforts to
extend its boundaries in the traditional manner to include the
adjacent areas. Such opposition
does not appear to be in the public interest or in good faith.
Much of it stems from the operators of illicit and disreputable
places who resist annexation in
order to avoid police regulation.
Their number is augmented by members of the armed forces who are
here only for the period of their
enlistment, assignment or tour of
duty and who have no stake in the
community or Territory and who,
in the meantime, are desirous of
avoiding all taxation.

The distinguished Judge ordered the annexation elections to be held and denied the petition for an incorporation election.[6] One cannot argue with his findings of facts as to the unpoliced districts which had grown up in the environs,[7] but one must argue with the implication that these represented the only substantial opposition to annexation. For example, in the very case cited, the Judge eliminated two large homesteads from the annexation area. The opposition of the "homesteaders" was most substantial and successful. Although there were very few actual "homesteaders," they were the largest land owners, and usually had few improvements on their land. The holding of large undeveloped tracts within a generally developed area made it most difficult to provide proper utilities, roads, and municipal services.

Everyone, in Alaska particularly, admires a "sturdy homesteader" or "pioneer." However, the Judge's sentimental attachment to the homesteader almost destroyed the feasibility of local government. He had only a vague notion of the politics of local government and understood the mechanics even less, but he had a capacity for growth.

By April, 1955, Judge Folta had become more informed as to the makeup of the community and the existence of opposition to government by others than the operators of liquor establishments with police problems. He said,

> The areas sought to be annexed are a part of one compact, urban community comprising the metropolitan area of Anchorage, and, except for the invisible corporate boundaries, are a part of the city's social and economic existence. The real boundaries extend away beyond the corporate boundaries. Moreover, not only do the streets of the city extend through these areas, but they

bear the names originally given
them by the city and the areas
themselves are indistinguishable
from that part of the city adjacent thereto. The opposition in
part is traceable to the failure
of the city during the boom to extend its facilities and services
into the areas as they developed.
This delay resulted in the extension of privately owned utilities
and the organization of public
utility districts. The situation
is such that the annexation law
appears to be inadequate, and gerrymandering, or the appearance
thereof, would appear to be ex-
cusable in attempting to cope with
it; otherwise it may well develop
that several municipalities will
be carved out of this one community, each with a government of its
own, resulting in a multiplication
of facilities and services, increased tax burdens, and inevitable judicial conflict and
chaos. . . :[8]

The owners of large tracts, be they homesteaders, speculators, investors, or otherwise,
uniformily opposed annexation. In the Anchorage
area these tracts were not agricultural in nature,
nor did they have any mineral, timber, or other
natural resource value. They occupied space
adjacent to a growing community and the owners,
by and large, wanted to hold the property with as
little taxes as possible while awaiting development.[9]

Of interest in the quotation from Judge
Folta is a reference to gerrymandering. The
boundaries of the various annexation areas and
therefore the ultimate city boundaries followed
highly erratic lines. As discussed in the

earlier case cited, the Judge excluded two homesteads. The distinguished Judge attributed this
gerrymandering not to his own decisions but rather
to what he termed "inadequate law."

The situation as it existed in Anchorage was
closely paralleled by that in Fairbanks[10] as well
as in several of the communities in southeastern
Alaska.

The experiment with judicial supervision of
local initiative was to terminate in 1957.[11] The
judicial system of the Territory consisted of the
United States Federal District Courts, with appeals directly to the Ninth Circuit Court of Appeals in San Francisco. These United States
District Courts were beginning to break down, due
to serious overloading of both judicial and non-
judicial functions. In 1957 annexation was determined to be one of the latter, and the courts
refused further supervision.[12]

THE EXPERIMENT OF LOCAL INITIATIVE
WITH NO SUPERVISION

The Territorial legislature responded to the
1957 decision of the court by providing a method
of annexation whereby interested persons could
petition the city council. The council would
order a public hearing after which, assuming that
it found the annexation to be desirable, it would
order an election. Persons opposing annexation
were reluctant to appear before a city council
which they viewed as their primary antagonist. As
a practical matter, the result was that there was
no forum in which the pros and cons of annexation
could be explored, publicly aired, and made available to the people. Although there were some annexations after the judicial experiment and before
statehood, these were very badly misunderstood and,
furthermore, did not meet the need for local government in the urban and suburban areas. The
situations as described by the courts became worse.

A LEGISLATIVE FAILURE AND AN EXECUTIVE
FAILURE TO SOLVE THE PROBLEM OF
TAX INEQUITY

The citizens of Alaska who had incorporated
themselves into cities or school districts (public
utility districts were not very important in this
respect) found themselves penalized by the tax
structure. Under Territorial law, those who lived
in a city or school district were required in all
instances to provide a substantial portion of the
cost of education. Local government generally
relied on property or sales tax, or both. There
was a tendency to withdraw Territorial police protection from cities. The Federal Government, at
that time, was largely responsible for roads and
highways through the Bureau of Public Roads. It
was the general policy of the Federal Government,
or at least it so appeared, to substantially withdraw from those areas which became cities, forcing
the local residents to assume road construction
and maintenance, both of which had heretofore been
provided free of charge.

The Territorial Legislature of 1949, which
was controlled by the Democratic Party and operated
under the influence of a strong Democratic governor, Ernest Gruening (now United States Senator),
made an initial attempt to provide some relief
from these inequities by enacting a Territory-wide
general property tax. The proceeds were refunded
to the local entity if collected in an incorporated
city, school district, or public utility district.
If the area was not incorporated, the proceeds
went into the treasury of the Territory. The
merits of a property tax are not germane to this
chapter. What is pertinent is that the measure was
an attempt to equalize the tax burden by requiring
those in the unincorporated areas to contribute
something to the cost of the services received.
This reform, however, was short-lived.

The matter of a Territorial tax became a

partisan political issue. The election of a Republican President of the United States and the
appointment of a Republican governor for the Territory of Alaska resulted in the repeal of the
property tax act by the 1953 Republican-controlled
Territorial Legislature. There were substantial
mining and fishing interests which were greatly
opposed to the tax; as were the homesteaders,
trappers, Indians, and Eskimos. This combination
firmly re-established the tax inequity favoring
those who were getting free services from the Territory by refusing and failing to incorporate. It
appeared that to equalize taxes in Alaska one
would need--and perhaps must create--a vested interest to protect the tax reform and combat the
interests which benefited financially from the
inequity.

In a further attempt at reform, the 1951
Territorial Legislature provided for the mandatory
creation of school districts. The act authorized
the Territorial Board of Education to discontinue
the operation and maintenance of any school run by
the Territory, "when in the judgment of the Board,
the school enrollment is large enough and the community financially able, to partially support its
own schools as an organized school district under
the laws for school district organization."13
The Board of Education was appointed by the Territorial governor and confirmed by the Territorial
legislature. Since the single largest expense of
local government in Alaska is education, this
far-reaching act could have been very important in
solving some of the tax inequities as well as setting a general pattern for local government

The 1951 legislature, however, had merely
authorized the reform. After years of inaction,
the 1957 legislature gave the board stronger direction,14 but the reform was still merely per-
missive. During the period between 1957 and the
coming of statehood in 1959, the Board of Education indulged in some vague talk about incorpo-
rating several communities in areas which had

schools of several hundred students. However,
such a hue and cry was raised by the communities
concerned that the Board of Education lost its will
to perform. That the legislation provided for a
piecemeal approach was a debilitating factor. When
a community was singled out for incorporation, that
community would point to many other communities
similarly situated which were continuing to escape
taxation and incorporation. The Board of Education could not incorporate them all at once and,
as a practical matter, was unable to incorporate
them one at a time. The board capitulated, and
the Territorial governor did not see fit to address himself in a meaningful way to the problems
and delinquencies of his Board of Education.

THE TRANSITION FROM TERRITORIAL
GOVERNMENT TO STATE GOVERNMENT
1959-62

In 1959 the first State legislature implemented the State Constitution relative to the
judiciary and the executive. Following the constitutional directive, it established the Local
Boundary Commission and the Local Affairs Agency.[15] Understandably the legislature was greatly
preoccupied with the problems of governmental
structure at the State level during this initial
session. Additionally, the first State governor
was ill and incapacitated through all except the
closing days of the session. Little was said
about local government at that time except for
one bill on public utility districts (Senate Bill
No. 89), which was vetoed.[16]

Shortly before the close of the 1959 session
of the legislature, I became Attorney General.
Truly the problems of transition in the executive
department of the State Government commanded the
full attention of the Governor and his cabinet
during the next several years. Because of my
interest in local government and boroughs, on
several occasions I discussed with the Governor

practical problems of local government as well as
constitutional and legal problems. The Local
Affairs Agency was staffed and located within the
Governor's office, but no general solutions to the
State's problems of local government were transmitted by the executive branch to the 1960 legislature.

The Local Affairs Agency and the Boundary
Commission did, however, exercise their powers to
consolidate and define city boundaries. The
commission presented to the legislature its recommendation that an area completely surrounded by
the City of Anchorage be annexed to the city.
Because this recommendation was not disapproved
by both houses of the legislature, it became law.
Although the State Supreme Court upheld the action
of the Local Boundary Commission,[17] the commission
has not since extensively exercised this authority
in trouble areas.

It may be that the Local Boundary Commission
has been effective in handling localized, perhaps
neighborhood, issues. So far as I am aware, it
has no broad view nor does it seek broad solutions.
As a government tool, it is a small one. I would
judge that its usefulness in the future would,
therefore, be limited to smaller and more localized
issues. The heat generated by annexation or incorporation, particularly when it is done by executive fiat, is very intense.[18]

Perhaps the commission could afford to make
enemies one by one, bit by bit, but it could never
maintain itself in the face of a barrage of criticism which was statewide. The legislature would
destroy it.[19] By the very nature of the political
organization, the commission is not in a position
to defend itself. The problems of annexation and
incorporation of local government are political
decisions which should be made in a manner permitting public political debate.

The first legislative attempt to define

boroughs occurred in the 1960 session with House
Bill No. 298, which was referred to the Local
Government Committee and never again saw the light
of day. It would have provided for the mandatory
creation of some fourteen boroughs, several of
which followed closely the boundaries ultimately
used in the 1963 Mandatory Borough Act. The bill
perhaps could have provided a point of departure,
but it was so rudimentary as to be only suggestive
of an idea that we should have boroughs of some
type, as the State Constitution later provided.

The 1961 session of the legislature was more
productive and actually defined the legal structure
of a borough--how it was to function relative to
special service districts, assemblymen, representation from cities, etc. The law (Chapter 146, SLA,
1961) provided for the formation of boroughs on
local initiative in much the same manner as State
and Territorial law provided for the incorporation
of cities on local initiative. The fact remained
that local initiative involving serious tax reform
would no more work in the instance of boroughs
than it had worked in the instance of school
districts or cities. The result: no boroughs.[20]

During 1961 and 1962 there were a number of
borough study groups organized by civic-minded
persons throughout the State.[21] These groups addressed themselves to the various practical and
constitutional problems. It seemed, however, that
they had little chance of successfully creating
boroughs if the boroughs exceeded the areas of the
cities and the independent school districts. That
is, the moment the borough was extended into unincorporated areas, or, in other words, the moment
it began to have an immediate tax equalization
feature,[22] the borough had two chances for suc-
cess--slim and none. The result was that the
various borough study groups were tending toward
incorporation of boroughs along the geographic
lines of the independent school districts. These
districts were quite small.

There was considerable conflict in the minds
of persons studying the problems as to whether
boroughs should be primarily metropolitan in nature,
that is, encompassing one community and its surrounding suburban area, or whether boroughs should
be regional in concept, that is, encompassing
several communities with the boundaries to be determined by major resource areas and geographical
features such as mountain ranges, major bodies of
water, etc. I personally favored the regional
concept and felt it would, in most instances, be
undesirable to create small geographical units.
Because of the distances involved in the State of
Alaska, the rural areas cannot be readily administered from the State capitol. I therefore
favored the tying of rural areas to the urban
areas and linking various cities with common interest into a regional government. The only way
regional government would come about through the
local initiative of the various borough study
groups was in some manner to eliminate legislatively the tax equalization problem.

The 1961 legislature had created a curious
deadline. It stated that existing school districts
and public utility districts could continue to
function until July 1, 1963. Unfortunately, the
law did not state what would happen if areas did
not incorporate into boroughs or cities by that
time.* It was generally assumed by persons discussing the problem that school district and

---

*Editors' Note: In reference to this point,
Roger W. Pegues, director of the Local Affairs
Agency in 1961 and a drafter of the Borough Act,
remarks: "There was no intention of letting the
time elapse. The deadline was, in a sense, advisory. The legislature was saying that it would brook
little further delay. . . . It was generally believed [by the drafters and supporters of the original Borough Act of 1961] that the 1963 legislature
would adopt a mandatory incorporation law." Letter
from Pegues to Cease.

public utility district properties would escheat to
the State if the districts were abolished, and that
the State would then operate the schools and possibly perform the functions of the utility districts.
This section of the law would have had a disastrous
effect if it had been permitted to operate. It
would have increased greatly the tax inequity by
permitting all of those outside of incorporated
cities to escape any contribution to local government. People living outside cities but in the old
Territorial school districts would even be relieved
of local taxes for their schools.

THE GENESIS OF HOUSE BILL NO. 90

My experience as the Anchorage City Attorney
and the State Attorney General led me to believe
that the greatest unresolved political problem of
the State was the matter of boroughs.[23] As near as
I could see, no reasonable solutions were being
propounded. A great opportunity to create something of value could be lost. A state of the size,
population density, and distribution of Alaska
makes State administration of local problems impossible. Anyone who had ever worked in Alaska on
the local level or on the State level could see
the frustrations of honest attempts repeatedly
failing because of the simple fact that there was
no governmental structure upon which to hang necessary governmental functions. I therefore decided
to do what I could.

During my campaign for the State legislature
in 1962,[24] I had occasion to mention the need and
the desirability of instituting borough government
in my own district, which included the entire
Anchorage metropolitan area. There was an unincorporated portion of the area in which the State
operated an extensive school system without contribution from the residents. I attempted to emphasize what I thought would be the advantages of
a regional government which would encompass an
area much larger than the Anchorage election

district. Such a region would have an economic,
resource, and political base which I felt could
truly function for the benefit of the people of
the entire area.

Prior to the convening of the legislature in
January, 1963, I formulated in broad outline what
I felt to be the basic requirements of a borough
bill which would:

1. Encourage local initiative and the voluntary formation of boroughs.

2. Provide for tax equalization. However,
if tax equalization was to be meaningful, it could
not be piecemeal. Mandatory incorporation of
boroughs would be necessary in all areas which
could feasibly be included within a borough and
which did not incorporate on local initiative.

3. Give each borough a meaningful responsibility and interest in the development of natural
resources within its boundaries. Under the Alaska
Statehood Act, the State of Alaska will receive,
over a period of twenty-five years, in excess of
one hundred million acres of land to be selected
by the State from the federal public domain. I
felt that it would give local residents a stake in
the development of their borough if they were
given some portion of the State lands which were
vacant, unappropriated, and unused.[25]

4. Encourage the formation of large boroughs.
I hoped that the land grant provision would encourage the urban areas to reach out and assume
some of the responsibility for the rural areas
which could hardly support themselves or schools
on their own tax base. I hoped that the boroughs
might be the catalyst causing the wealth of the
cities to react favorably with the opportunity for
development of the rural areas.

5. Delay the operation of the act long
enough for local initiative to come into play and

for borough study groups to formulate and put into
effect their own desires since those desires might
be stimulated by the bill.[26]

   6.   Provide initial funds so that the boroughs
created could set up rudimentary government and
prepare to levy their own taxes and develop their
own sources of income.[27]

   7.   Turn over to the newly formed local governments not only responsibilities but also assets
which had previously been committed to the discharge
of these responsibilities. In this respect, I had
hoped to turn over to the boroughs certain road
equipment, together with shops, buildings, and
other assets. Although this was abandoned later
in the actual drafting of the bill, I had intended
to follow the precedent set by the United States
when it granted Alaska statehood.[28]

   8.   Get the boroughs created with their officers elected and functioning prior to the 1964
legislature. There were two reasons for this:
(a) The same legislature which created the boroughs
could correct any oversights or errors which might
be shown to exist in its earlier work, and (b) when
the tax equalization features of borough organization came into effect, those who had heretofore
avoided taxes would form a powerful force to destroy the effectiveness of the reform, much in the
same manner as they had destroyed the territorial
property tax. For this reason, I felt that election of borough officers prior to the convening of
the legislature would create a group with a vested
interest in retaining the boroughs. Because they
would be elected representatives of the people,
the legislature would be highly persuaded by the
very fact of their existence.

   9.   Prevent, if possible, the formation of
boroughs from becoming a partisan issue. I felt
this to be desirable for two reasons: (a) The
Territorial property tax had been repealed apparently because it became a Republican campaign

promise. I didn't want the same thing to happen
to the boroughs, and (b) the House of Representatives of the 1963 legislature was composed of
twenty Democrats and twenty Republicans. It was
painfully obvious that if any issue became a hard
and fast party issue, it would be stalemated.

10. Provide for a self-executing clause
calling for the election of borough officers without any further finding by a court, the legislature, or any agency in the executive branch of the
government. In other words, the bill should be
written in such a manner that when the legislature
adjourned that which still remained to be done
would be ministerial in nature and not force
painful decisions and action upon anyone. If
the job was to be done, it had to be done by the
legislature and not delegated to the courts or the
executive. For that reason, an election procedure
was set up whereby the Secretary of State would,
upon the happening of certain events, step in, call,
and conduct the election of borough officers in the
various boroughs without further ado.

11. Provide for definite boundaries. In the
event the boroughs were not formed on local initiative, the geographical lines had to be certain.
This decision on lines should likewise be made by
the legislature and not delegated. The reasoning
on this was the same as on the immediately preceding point.

THE ORGANIZATION OF THE LEGISLATURE

The legislature met in Juneau in the last
week of January, 1963, with no public demand for
the solution of unresolved borough issues nor any
apparent self-imposed pressure. It was customary,
prior to going to Juneau, for the Anchorage area
legislators to meet with the Anchorage City Council
and the school board. We met. Although we specifically raised the problem of boroughs and borough-
city relationships, the city council exhibited only
polite interest.

The school board was another matter. Although
generally the school board concerned itself only
narrowly with the problems of the community, in
this instance it was aware of the impending problems. A majority of the board favored retention of
the special district deadline date of July 1.

At the time there was a borough study group
operating in the Anchorage area which was proposing
a first-class borough. The members of the school
board seemed to think that the Anchorage area would
voluntarily vote to incorporate. However, no
alternative was proposed as to what would happen if
the voters rejected the proposed borough.

When the legislature met in Juneau, the twenty
Democrats and twenty Republicans in the House of
Representatives could not agree on a method of organization. The Republican caucus wanted to share
with the Democrats the responsibility for the organization and the operation of the House of Representatives by giving each party an equal number of
important committee assignments and chairmanships.
The House Democratic caucus resolved at an early
stage that one party or the other should have
responsibility for the organization of the House
and, therefore, the "flow of business." After approximately a week of stalemated debating and
voting, a Republican was elected speaker of the
House and, therefore, the Republicans organized the
House as the majority party, controlling all committee chairmanships, as well as having a majority
of members on each committee. For convenience
they were designated the majority party and the
Democrats the minority. After organization I
served as Democratic minority leader and caucus
chairman.

My fellow legislators were somewhat bored with
my apparent interest in boroughs. One of the most
intelligent, and probably my closest confidant in
that session of the legislature, expressed amaze-
ment at my interest and gave me cause to wonder
about it myself. There is traditionally a general

feeling among legislators that it is certain political death to become involved in local government
problems.

What interest there was in boroughs at this
precise moment appeared to be negative. Typical
was a letter to the editor written by an energetic
citizen active in a number of organizations and the
president of the Sons of the American Revolution in
Anchorage. His letter concluded:

> I might say that the First
> Class Borough as presently
> constituted and as interpreted
> by the local affairs committee
> without amendatory action, is
> one of the cleverest and most
> subtle pieces of Legislation
> devised by man to enslave a
> free people. . . .
>   Are we going to allow our-
> selves to be bound by the chains
> of increasingly dictatorial lo-
> cal governments until we have
> completely lost our American
> heritage of over three hundred
> years as free men?[29]

The Democratic representative from Emmonak, a native village at the mouth of the Yukon River, and
the representative from Kotzebue, an Eskimo village
north of Nome on the Arctic Coast, were both reported as "antiborough."[30]

A Senate bill to extend the deadline for dissolution of special districts from July 1, 1963, to
July 1, 1970, was introduced. This bill (Senate
Bill No. 17), amended to extend the date by only
one year, passed the Senate, on March 15, without
a single dissenting vote.[31]

THE EXECUTIVE PROPOSAL

There was one encouragement. In the Governor's State of the State message on February 4, approximately two pages of his twelve-page address were devoted to the problems of the borough and local government. The Governor said:

> Local government problems continue
> to be [the] subject of deep and
> understandable concern. Many
> areas need improved school sys-
> tems, sanitation, fire protection,
> planning and zoning, water and
> flood control, community water
> and sewer systems. Organized
> boroughs can provide these local
> government services.[32]

The Governor also promised to submit proposals to accomplish the ends stated.

At the earliest moment after the Governor's address I contacted the director of the Local Affairs Agency and asked him if he could possibly give me a preview of what was coming. My enthusiasm was dampened somewhat when he cautioned me that he knew of no executive proposals of the scope indicated by the Governor's message. Although the signs of spring appeared in the Governor's address to the legislature, summer never came.

The Governor's disappointing proposal, House Bill No. 62, was substantially the same as the Territorial school incorporation legislation which had never been used successfully. The "new proposal" was a result, according to the Governor's transmittal letter, of a study of the problems of school districts by the Department of Education, the Board of Education, and the Local Affairs Agency.[33] It was specifically based upon draft legislation submitted by the State Board of

Education. The bill provided for the creation of
second-class boroughs "for school purposes" [em-
phasis added]; these would be organized either by
local option or by the Board of Education. Similar
to the old Territorial law, House Bill No. 62 provided that the board "may provide for the incorporation" [emphasis added] of boroughs. The board
was to investigate the ability of a community to
support school functions and to incorporate the
area if it met certain criteria. The Governor did
not even put the force of his own office behind the
bill. The transmittal letter stated that he was
submitting it "at the request of the Alaska Board
of Education."

THE CREATION OF HOUSE BILL NO. 90

Pending a view of the Governor's position, I
held back on finalizing my own proposal. As soon
as the Governor's bill came down, I met with the
director of the Local Affairs Agency and key members of his staff. We commenced a feverish but
unofficial activity which extended from that day
until House Bill No. 90 was introduced precisely
seven days later. Key members of the staff worked
late into the nights and through the weekend debating, discussing, and putting together the various sections.

The Governor's proposal had been referred to
the House Local Government Committee, of which I
was a member. The committee agreed to withhold
action until I could submit my own proposal.

One of the first problems was whether to define the borough as metropolitan or regional government. Most of the borough study groups throughout the State had viewed the boroughs as a means
to solve the problems of urban and suburban development around a single community. This approach was particularly strong in southeastern
Alaska, where the major communities were separated
by extensive bodies of water.   It seemed southeastern

Alaska could be considered a single region tied together with certain common transportation, resources, and other assets and problems. But I became convinced from talking with representatives
from Ketchikan, Sitka, Wrangell, Petersburg, Haines,
and Juneau that a proposal embracing the entire region would receive little support and considerable
opposition, and would probably at that time serve
no useful function.

To the west, however, things appeared to be
different. For example, the Kenai Peninsula representatives viewed themselves as having a broad
community of interest, and ultimately, Kenai,
Soldotna, Homer, Seldovia, and Seward were all
made part of a single borough.

I personally viewed the Anchorage area, my
election district, as fitting into a regional government, consisting of the upper Cook Inlet and the
Susitna-Matanuska Valley-Palmer areas. I discussed
this concept with the representative from the
Matanuska Valley, who personally agreed with the
desirability of joining the areas together, but who
cautioned against it at that particular time. It
was his idea that if the proposal came from the
Matanuska Valley instead of from Anchorage or the
legislature, it had more chance of success.

Fairbanks, like Anchorage, had outgrown its
city limits. In trying to define a feasible unit
for Fairbanks, we explored the possibility of using
the school district boundaries; however, upon examination, it seemed that the school district represented a much smaller unit than was desirable.
The Fairbanks delegation in the House was sharply
divided.

We thus decided that the defining of a borough
as being either metropolitan or regional would be
detrimental. It would be necessary to use the
borough in different areas as a different form of
government, even though there was a danger that the
smaller metropolitan boroughs would be actually

serving the function of a city. We were, in effect,
perhaps exhausting one of our constitutional governmental tools to duplicate what could be done by
city government.[34] However, a new unit of government without assets, liabilities, or personalities
could be useful.

As a practical legal matter, a bill which provides ultimately for mandatory incorporation must
state boundaries with precision. We considered
definitions in terms of mountain ranges, shore-
lines, rivers, and watersheds, and in terms of
longitude and latitude. Finally, we settled on
election district lines, which were precise and
known to everyone. In many instances, election
district lines seemed to be closer to the lines
proposed by the local groups, or at least considered by the local groups, than any other existing definitions of area. I considered, as a
general proposition, that the election district
lines in most areas covered too small a geographical area for regional government. I hoped that
when the tax equalization problem was overcome
there would be a tendency for adjacent boroughs to
consolidate. In other words, when talk was commenced concerning the joining of boroughs, the only
question would be whether or not the area could
best be governed by one or two boroughs. This combined with the land grant incentive, I thought,
resulted in a good formula which would bring the
rural and urban areas together.

We considered many areas as possibilities for
mandatory borough incorporation. However, after
looking over the available information on taxable
wealth, I concluded that the areas we proposed as
boroughs, together with cities such as Nome,
Wrangell, Petersburg, Cordova, Valdez, and others
not included in any borough, encompassed roughly
90 per cent of the taxable wealth in the State and
approximately 80 per cent of the population. These
cities had not outgrown their corporate boundaries
and did not have significant suburban development.
Nor was it necessary to the tax equalization

features of the bill that they be within a borough.
It appeared to me that very little would be gained
by expansion of the boundaries or the creation of
additional boroughs under the circumstances.

The main source of revenue for the borough
would probably be the property tax, both real and
personal. In very sparsely populated areas the
costs of administration would exceed the revenues
derived or the other social benefits which might be
achieved. When consideration is given to charter-
ing small airplanes to assess cabins, trap-lines,
one-man gold mining operations and similar activities, the conclusion is reached that the taxes
could not maintain the bureaucracy necessary to assess and collect them.

House Bill No. 90 had the distinction of being the most debated bill in the House of Representatives during the 1963 session. In the early
stages of the bill I had hoped to have the boroughs assume functions in addition to taxation,
planning and zoning, and education. I felt it
desirable that, if boroughs were not incorporated
on a local initiative basis and if mandatory boroughs were to be created, they should have sufficient authority to satisfy the local government
needs of their area without a referendum on each
new power. For this reason I had hoped that the
mandatory boroughs would all be first-class. In
the course of debate, however, amendments were
adopted which permitted the voters to opt for
either first- or second-class.

As mentioned, I had originally planned that the
borough provide services covering such areas as police, health, roads, and fire, and that it have the
general authority to build and operate docks and to
participate in economic development. However, on
closer consideration, it seemed to me that time would
not permit us to explore these items to the extent
necessary to convince legislators of the desirability of turning over State assets such as repair
shops, road maintenance equipment, police

facilities, etc. For example, if we were going to
force on the boroughs road maintenance, I wanted
to make certain that all State equipment dedicated
to the functioning of local roads would be turned
over to the borough. However, the Department of
Highways viewed this as being the dismantling of
its own organization, the destruction of its hoard
of equipment and personnel. I asked the department
for inventories, descriptions of local roads, and
costs of maintenance in various areas. In reply to
my request, I received bland answers that were not
calculated to be helpful. I decided that if I
pursued this and the other matters, I probably
would increase the size of the problem so greatly
as to make it insoluble. I therefore decided that
we should hang a minimum of functions on the structure. Education, by far the largest function of
local government in Alaska, was essential. The tax
equalization feature could be applied to the educational problem and made more palatable. The
planning function proportionately would involve
a very small amount of money and yet I felt it was
absolutely necessary to the future development of
the boroughs.

House Bill No. 90, once enacted, would create
a mechanical procedure which would call for the
exercise of a minimum of discretion. If the areas
involved were not incorporated prior to October 1,
1963, the Local Affairs Agency would direct the
Secretary of State to hold elections for officers
in each of the areas before December 1. Each
area would formally be incorporated as a borough
on January 1, 1964.

The time sequence was very important. I felt
that it would be impossible to maintain the tax
equalization features of the Borough Act unless,
prior to the 1964 meeting of the legislature, local officials had already been elected and were in
a position to exert their influence to keep their
boroughs, their offices, and their sources of
revenue. Additionally, if the local elected officials were in office before the next legislature,

they could advise the legislature on necessary cor-
rections relative to area of the borough and other
factors which might affect the feasibility of the
unit.

The bill did not force the immediate dissolution of existing school and public utility districts, but rather left it to the boroughs to as-
similate these units more or less at their convenience, but with an ultimate transfer date.[35] The
reason for this approach was simple. I felt that
some school boards and school board members would
be less than human if they did not resist final
transfer of authority to the borough. In a political contest between the established school boards
and the newly created boroughs, the boroughs would
certainly lose. And possibly the school boards
could delay interminably the actual functioning of
the boroughs as intended. This, of course, involved not only school systems but also public
utility districts, which were functioning with
water systems, sewer systems, road equipment, fire
protection, etc. Therefore, the bill contained a
final cut-off date by which functions would be
automatically transferred and the old utility districts would cease to exist if they refused to cooperate. The transition could be relatively pain-
less if the governing bodies were made aware that
they could not save their own little empires by
refusing to cooperate.

With the bill, I submitted what I thought to
be some of the pertinent historical background and
a statement in some detail of the intent of the
legislation. I concluded as follows:

> Our present system of local government
> is inadequate and cannot be made ade-
> quate because of constitutional limi-
> tations. Because of the vast size of
> Alaska, local government is even more
> important than in the smaller states.
> State government invariably forces
> administration from great distances.

This is expensive, undesirable and, in
fact, impractical when it comes to the
solution of local problems. People
should be encouraged to form local
government on boundaries which they
draw themselves. Local government
must be attractive, not only as a political theory, but as a practical
reality. This demands the giving of
funds, assets and revenues to local
governments so that they can truly
participate in the development of
their own areas.

Existing local government units,
i.e., public utility districts and
school districts, will be integrated
into constitutional forms of government. If there is no succeeding governmental entity, the properties of
school districts and public utility
districts would escheat to the state,
and if local functions were continued,
they would have to be administered by
the state. The net result would be
great damage to local programs.

If, because of confusion, lack
of knowledge, error or oversight, there
is no borough incorporated by local
initiative in the populated areas of
the state, then the bill provides that
the election district lines in which
the populations are located are the
temporary borough lines, until adjusted either through local initiative
or the state boundary commission in
the Legislature.[36]

Omitted was any mention of tax equalization.
I tried to sell House Bill No. 90 on the abstract
principles of local government and the desirability
of home rule. Obviously the question of who was
going to pay would sooner or later come up, but I
felt that if we got into price too quickly we would
never get to the consideration of the desirability

of the product. If some of the study groups and
then, perhaps, the press would support the bill, I
felt we would be in a position to discuss costs and
taxes with legislators. In short, if I could get a
few of the legislators committed through grass roots
pressure to the desirability of local government,
it would only be natural to later consider costs of
home rule and tax equalization.

THE POLITICAL HOMEWORK
ON HOUSE BILL NO. 90

Six days after the Governor had introduced his
bill, House Bill No. 62, I called a House Democratic caucus. There were several unresolved items of
business to be handled. However, my main purpose
in calling the meeting was to see what type of support I might get for House Bill No. 90. As in many
legislative bodies, it is customary in Alaska to
have several cosponsors on major legislation. I
doubted very much that I would actually find any
cosponsors, but I wanted to help form the legislators' first impressions. I also wanted to make it
clear that I did not propose that the bill be a
party issue at that time.

I explained the contents of the bill. One member of the caucus, although sympathetic to the bill,
took a newspaper from his desk and read to the caucus an editorial which concluded that the Senate
bill to delay consideration of mandatory boroughs
until 1970[37] was desirable in order to permit public opinion time to form: "This takes time under
the normal democratic process."[38]

Another member of the caucus raised the question of the conflict between my proposal and the
Governor's. I told him that the bills were not
harmonious and that the proposals dealt with parts
of the same problem, but not in the same way. The
caucus was interested, but from the questions asked,
I felt that it would be a mistake to go into detail
at that time to persuade the members on the merits

of the bill. I closed off the discussion by saying
that I had reasonable hopes for the final adoption
of the bill. I intended to circulate it to the
borough study groups throughout the State and see
if I couldn't generate some interest. I asked that
anyone who was interested in cosponsoring the bill
contact me after the caucus. The caucus adjourned.
Nobody contacted me.

The largest newspaper in the State, the Anchorage Times, had a special representative in Juneau
to report on legislative proceedings. I took the
bill and the explanation to this reporter. The
Times, probably more than any other paper in the
State, had shown interest in the problem of boroughs and local government. I, therefore, thought
that some substantial mention would be made of the
bill and the explanation if I gave the Times reporter an edge. This I did. I told her that I did
not intend to release the bill to the other media
until the following day. I had hoped that the reporter would have a story ready for immediate release when the bill was filed. She didn't. The
Anchorage Times report of the legislative activity
for February 21, the day the bill was introduced,
had nothing from its special correspondent concerning the bill, and the Associated Press dispatch
dealt with such items as refund of pinball machine
tax money to certain communities. For example, it
considered newsworthy that the City of Pelican was
to receive $64, the City of Skagway $97, and the
City of Girdwood $24.

Within hours after the bill was introduced, a
very prominent Republican leader in the House of
Representatives made inquiry as to the contents of
the bill and its purpose. After I explained the
bill to him in detail, he became most confidential.
"Rader," he said, "I'll have to beat your head off
with that bill if you push it." I had discussed
the tax equalization features of the bill with him
frankly and he told me in no uncertain terms, but
as one friend to another, that the bill would kill
me (which he didn't want to see happen) and the

Democratic Party (which he would like to see happen) if it became law. I told him that I felt basically that there was support for the bill in many areas. Although there would be a lot of complaining by those who were going to have to pay taxes, I felt that the bill could be defended politically. At any rate, I told him he could never make it a real issue in the next election unless it passed. By the time the conversation was over, without saying so, I understood that he would vote against the bill but that he hoped it would pass so that in the next election he could debate the issue as he hoped to frame it: The Democrats were to be the tax-raisers and the money-spenders and he was to be the money-saver and the representative who voted against that terrible bill imposing taxes for local government.

After the press failed to mention the bill when it was introduced, I contacted the sympathetic Republican chairman of the House Local Government Committee. I asked him to schedule hearings. He picked a date approximately two weeks away and announced hearings on both House Bill No. 90 and the Governor's bill, House Bill No. 62. Announcement of these hearings was noted in the press. I obtained the names of the persons in the various borough study groups throughout the State and sent them copies of the bill and the explanation: perhaps fifty to seventy copies in all.

Approximately a week after the bill was introduced, the press began to take some note of its contents. By and large, it wasn't favorable. Typical were such statements as "the compulsory borough, large or small, would be obnoxious . . ."; "some legislators have proposed a deadline in 1970. That seems desirable. Within seven more years the people should be able to crystallize their opinion if the borough has any merit at all."[39]

I wanted to develop some legislative support for the bill prior to the public hearings if possible. I had received word that a number of citizens

prominent in the borough study groups planned to
attend the hearings to testify favorably. I went
to work on members of the House Local Government
Committee; I did not try to get commitments of support but only to remove active hostility.

I first contacted certain members of the "ice
bloc"--this is a term used to denote the cadre of
representatives from the rural Arctic and sub-
Arctic areas, most of whom were in whole or in part
of Eskimo extraction.

One of the "ice bloc" members was having a
problem in his area with dog teams running loose.
Some of the reindeer herders were having a difficult time protecting their herds, and frequently
stray dogs would get within the tether of the con-
fined dogs, resulting in vicious fights. On occasion a child would be attacked. I recall vividly
this discussion, for even in the Anchorage environs
a pack of dogs, many of which were of Husky blood
and considered to be pets by their owners, had attacked and killed a child. I discussed with this
representative the fact that outside the City of
Anchorage there was no one to license the dogs,
confine the dogs, and protect the people except the
State police, and they could not do it. We talked
of this and other aspects of local government as
applied to my area and his. We found common ground.
When we were through talking, while he had not committed himself to the bill, I felt certain he would
vote for it. As it turned out, in a later "ice
bloc" meeting he persuaded some of the other rural
representatives who were hostile to vote for the
bill also.

I contacted the antiborough "ice bloc" representative from the lower Yukon who had been a personal friend since we had served together in the
first State legislature. He had been the chief of
his unincorporated village as well as the chairman
of an association of chiefs on the lower Yukon. He
was in a way a super-chief of what might be called
a regional government of the lower Yukon Eskimos.

Although he appeared to be 100 per cent Eskimo, he
was one quarter Norwegian and a great lover of the
Finnish sauna bath. A small bath was operated by a
grandmotherly Finnish woman in her home across the
street from the major hotel in Juneau. As he threw
water on the hot rocks, we talked. I couldn't take
the heat as well as he, and therefore when I began
to feel faint I would take a cold shower or leave
the room for a few minutes. We discussed the problems of local and regional government on the lower
Yukon. We discussed the same problems as they applied to Anchorage and to the Kenai Peninsula. He
supported the bill.

The House contained a conservative group, primarily, though not exclusively, Republican. My
discussion with members of this group revolved
around the desirability of home rule and the decentralization of our State government. In Alaska,
local governments customarily are controlled by
Republican businessmen and professionals; the State
government had been customarily controlled by Democrats. Though I did not view the bill as a dismantling of the State government, firmly in the
hands of the Democratic Party, some of my Republican colleagues did so view it and supported it for
that reason.

Throughout my discussions it was implicit that
my intent was to create a governmental framework on
which to hang any number of future functions, such
as fire and police protection, health services, etc.,
in addition to the mandatory functions of education
and planning.

I made it clear that I considered that we were
creating a governmental tool by which the people of
a particular area could provide themselves with a
minimum governmental structure necessary for civi-
lized group living. I tried to plant seeds which
would grow in the various types of soil on which
they were sown; some others planted seeds which I
considered to be weeds. I didn't argue about it;
at least it was vegetation on an otherwise barren
field.

I awaited word from the mining and fish processing industries, the agricultural areas, the
logging and timber interests, and especially the
oil industry. Remarkably, the industry opposition
I expected never developed in either the House or
the Senate. The only industries which maintained
active lobbies were the fish processing and oil interests. To my recollection, I never discussed the
matter with the fishing people, but I did with the
oil lobbyist. He ended the conversation with the
statement that his clients didn't object to paying
their fair share of local taxes for schools, roads,
fire and police protection, and health services.
They would object to paying what they considered to
be more than their fair share. He observed that
there was nothing in the bill to indicate that they
were going to have to pay more than their share and
that, therefore, they wouldn't oppose it. A great
and powerful industry had consented to local taxation where it had previously been exempt. I was
pleased and surprised.

If the other industries affected even knew of
the bill, it would be my supposition that they considered passage remote. The fact that I was the
Democratic minority leader of the House may have
also helped keep the opposition to a minimum. If
that were the case, I would have to say that the
industries were more impressed with my position
than were my colleagues in the legislature.

Besides, various industries had other bills of
importance to them on which I could be personally
helpful or hurtful. As a general proposition, what
is everybody's business, is nobody's business in
legislative matters. For example, the timber industry was expending its efforts in the dispute it was
having with the fishing industry relative to the destruction of salmon spawning streams. It was con-
centrating its efforts on bills which had a direct
and immediate and singular effect on the industry.

Several legislators offered to trade votes with
me on House Bill No. 90. Although a "holier than

thou" attitude was not a completely satisfactory position, I advanced the arguments that the bill was
of broad significance, that it was not of unique
importance to my election district, that I had no
more to gain from passage of the bill than any
other representative, and that as a matter of fact,
I considered the bill to be a liability to me, at
least in a political sense. I didn't want to engage in trading unless it was necessary. The bill
passed the House without these side commitments.

Since in all probability most of the witnesses
who would appear at the hearings would be friendly,
it would be a good time to give the Senate a little
education on the problem. I contacted the chairman
of the House Local Government Committee who issued
an invitation to the Senate Local Government Committee to meet with us jointly for purposes of the
hearing. A number of the Senators were present.
The hearing went well. People from Anchorage,
Fairbanks, Ketchikan, Sitka, and Juneau were in attendance. There was a general atmosphere of help-
fulness and cooperation created in no small part by
Senator Harold Hansen's[40] stimulating questions.
The only citizen opposition to the bill came from a
Ketchikan borough study group member who stated he
was afraid that the bill might take the steam out
of the formation of a voluntary borough which was
underway at the time. It was his position that a
majority of people in his community wanted a borough and that they would probably incorporate even
if nothing were done legislatively.

The director of the State Division of Lands
testified relative to the land grant provisions and
suggested a return of 10 per cent of the revenue
from the sale of State land to the boroughs rather
than the selection of 10 per cent of the land. I
opposed this suggestion. The land grant was much
more than a revenue measure. I viewed it as having
importance as a resource and community development
tool.

At about this same time the representative
from the Matanuska Valley, a Republican, and I spent

many hours discussing the possibility of combining
the Matanuska Valley and Anchorage areas into a
single borough. I proposed to him that we offer a
joint amendment to that end. Already, the legislators from the Kenai-Cook Inlet and Seward election
districts had agreed to jointly sponsor an amendment combining their two areas into a single Kenai
Peninsula borough. However, the legislator from
the Matanuska Valley wanted to get some sampling
from home before actually committing himself. I
suggested to him that he let me "leak" to the Anchorage Times a statement that such a move was
under consideration. He agreed. Following our
discussion, I telephoned long distance to the Anchorage Times. As so often happens, either I
didn't say what I intended or the reporter misunderstood me. The March 6 issue contained an article to the effect that: "A move to establish one
big borough including Anchorage, Palmer, Wasilla,
Talkeetna election districts was to be made in
Juneau today by [the representative from Palmer]."
When I read the article, I was appalled and immediately contacted the representative concerned. He
took it most graciously, but the damage had been
done. He was receiving from home almost unanimous
opposition and it was vehement. It was so bad that
he set up a meeting in Palmer and flew back for
several days to meet with his constituents. When
he returned to Juneau, there was no question about
it: The Matanuska Valley wanted no part of a borough which included Anchorage.

The House Local Government Committee reported
the bill favorably, made a few minor changes and
improvements, and called it Committee Substitute for
House Bill No. 90.[41] On March 14, three weeks after the bill was introduced, it was on the House
calendar and up for passage.

THE HOUSE DEBATE

The Alaska House of Representatives in 1963
was a truly deliberative body in which persuasive

debate actually affected the outcome of legislation.
This was in marked contrast to the State Senate at
the same time. The House resolved itself into a
committee of the whole. This is a procedure which
permits free and informal exchange. We took the
bill section by section, making frequent reference
to the original explanation,[42] and the subsequent
sectional analysis on the Committee Substitute.[43]
The director of the Local Affairs Agency, in a very
rare procedure indeed, was invited to the floor of
the House where he participated. After several
hours of this informal debate, the House resolved
itself into a formal House of Representatives and
we began to debate and vote on specific amendments.

A number of geographic areas were taken from
the operation of the bill. For example, the Annette
Island Indian Reservation was excluded as was the
Haines-Skagway area. The military reservations
were excluded from the boroughs in which they were
located, because certain federal funds pertaining
to schools would have been adversely affected if
the areas were incorporated into local units of
government.

Tax equalization was discussed thoroughly.

A vigorous dispute developed around the land
grant provision. Some extraordinarily political
speeches were made. Using the phraseology common
among the members at the time, a colleague would
"wrap himself in the American Flag and shoot himself out of a cannon."

Special interests were voted at various times
on the amendments. One member, having very extensive real estate holdings in an area which had been
heretofore tax-free, debated skillfully. Somewhat
as an aside, but typical of certain portions of the
debate, was his conduct on the second day, March 15.
The press was seriously understaffed. Frequently,
hours would go by with no member of the press in
the gallery. However, because of deadline considerations and time zone differentials, all the press

would be in the gallery between 11:00 and 11:30
A.M., this being the latest the members of the
press could leave the legislative halls, compose a
story, and get it on the wire in time for the af-
ternoon papers in Western Alaska. Legislators were
aware of this. This particular member made it a
point to say what he had to say between 11:00 and
11:30 A.M., no matter what the status of the debate
or the bill under consideration. We used to call
his dissertations "11:30 specials." True to form,
promptly at 11:00, on March 15, the legislator took
the floor and, as I recall, stated:

> The people in my area don't want more
> government, they want better govern-
> ment. This bill is completely unnec-
> essary. This legislation was intro-
> duced simply because ambitious poli-
> ticians don't want to face up to
> providing adequate government for
> those areas without local government.

He made his point, and the press left the room to
file the story, which made front-page news. As the
debate progressed, however, he was somewhat at a
loss to tell us how the State was to provide sewers
and water, garbage collection, and dog control to
the areas in question. He failed to tell us how it
would be better government to have these functions
administered from Juneau, 500 or 1,000 miles distant from the local cesspool. Only scraps of the
debate were carried by the press. It seemed the
more outlandish the statement, the greater the
prominence given the story. Generally speaking,
the people of the State did not know what was going
on in the House of Representatives.

Legislators from rural areas not affected by
the bill became a problem. The tax equalization
features of the bill obviously did not apply to the
areas left out. I was accused on a number of occasions of leaving out these rural areas for purely
political reasons, that is, in order to obtain the
votes from their representatives. It is probably

true that many of the rural representatives who
voted for the bill would have voted against it had
their areas been included. Actually, most of these
areas could not possibly have supported or operated
a borough successfully. Surprisingly, even though
I had therefore omitted great expanses of rural undeveloped areas, the representatives from these
areas still feared the bill because they realized
that it provided for a general tax equalization and
that they were the only ones who were not being
"equalized." They were easily persuaded by some of
the opponents of the bill that they would be "equalized" by the next legislature. This was particularly true in the Senate, where one of my strong supporters on the last day on the last critical vote
switched his vote from "Yes" to "No" after being
persuaded that the next step would be further
equalization affecting his area. The people who
were continuing to benefit from the inequity of
taxes recognized that if the bill passed, they
would have a hard time politically maintaining the
inequity in the future because their numbers would
be diminished substantially. People benefitting
from tax inequities do not like to discuss tax re-
forms; they never know when reform will finally
reach home. As it finally ended up, however, these
rural representatives almost to a man supported the
bill, and the main opposition came from the urban
areas.

Newspapers, with some exceptions, remained primarily hostile. The Anchorage Times editorialized,
on March 15, against the bill. Unfortunately, I
was seriously misquoted by the Associated Press,
which attributed these remarks to me: "We must act
in the best interest of the State and in the best
interest of the people--in that order." (The AP
reporter apologized profusely to me for this error
and offered to print a retraction. I declined the
offer because I felt the damage had already been
done and didn't want to have it dwelt upon further.)
Understandably, I began to receive furious tele-
grams, phone calls, and letters. "Letters to the
Editor" referred to me as a junior Hitler, a person
with a Napoleonic complex, etc.

The bill passed the House because it made good sense--better sense than the status quo and better sense than any of the alternative proposals. It passed on a vote of twenty-seven yeas; six more votes than needed--a safe margin. The next problem would be the Senate.

THE DEBATE IN THE SENATE

In 1963, it was customary for the members of the House of Representatives to refer to the Senate as "that place where good House members go when they die." The same epitaph sometimes applied to good House bills. I feared for the good health of House Bill No. 90. It was transmitted and received by the Senate on March 18th. Within hours, the power of the "third house"--the Joint Senate-House Finance Committee--was exerted. The chairman of the most powerful committee in the Senate, the Senate Finance Committee, moved to return House Bill No. 90 to the House of Representatives because it had allegedly been improperly processed.[44] On a voice vote it was ordered returned to the House of Representatives.

The whole maneuver caught me by surprise. I had not gone to any great efforts to prepare the Senate for the bill. What happened here is somewhat typical of the 1963 Senate and might be called a casebook example of its method of operation.

First to be noted is that the move to return the bill to the House was made by the Democratic chairman of the Senate Finance Committee. Since I was the Democratic minority leader in the House, one might suppose that the most powerful Senate Democratic committee chairman might treat my personal bills more kindly. Although this inclination no doubt existed, it was not sufficient to overcome the power structure of the "third house."

The Joint Finance Committee was an institution which had existed from the first State legislature

in 1959. It had become the custom for the finance
committees to choose either the House or Senate finance chairman as the chairman of the Joint Committee. When the Republicans organized the House of
Representatives, they of course chose the House Finance Committee chairman. When the House and Senate Finance committees met as the Joint Finance
Committee, remarkably enough, they also chose the
House Republican chairman as the chairman of the
Joint Committee, although the Joint Committee had a
majority of Democrats. The Joint Finance Committee
became the "third house." It conducted proceedings
at the same time that the House and Senate were in
session.

This arrangement suited the convenience of the
Republicans in the House because it assisted their
legislation through the Senate, and the Democrats
in the Senate as it assisted their legislation
through the House. The House Democrats were badly
left out. I had occasion to observe on the floor
of the House that I would like to have the same
privilege of voting in the "third house" as the
members of the "third house" had of voting in the
other two. There was no "right to be heard" in the
"third house," and the courtesy extended by the
committee seldom exceeded that required by proto-
col. This power structure was meaningful. The
legislature was _de jure_ bicameral, _de facto_ tricam-
eral.

The House finance chairman, also chairman of
the "third house," was vigorously opposed to the
bill. During debate in the House of Representatives, he had attempted to get it into his committee for purposes of destroying it. He did so on
the basis that, according to the Uniform Rules of
the legislature, the bill involved appropriations
and therefore must be referred to the finance committee.[45] I argued that it was an authorization
bill. I informed the House that if House Bill No.
90 passed, I would introduce an appropriation measure which would be referred to the finance committee in due course. The House of Representatives

appropriately adopted my argument during debate and
did not refer the bill to the finance committee.
However, members of the "third house" were doing
their work. Republicans controlled the House of
Representatives and also the "third house." The
House finance chairman, it appeared to me, could
also control the Senate on this bill unless the
signals were switched.

A second instructive item concerning the return of the bill to the House was the fact that it
was done on a voice vote with no record. This was
no accident. There was a group of Senators who did
not want to be recorded because this was a controversial bill. The nature of the Senate was such that
controversy was what it wanted to avoid. The Senate also wanted to avoid responsibility for either
passing the bill or defeating it. The fact that it
intended this action as final disposition of House
Bill No. 90 was acknowledged by a prominent Senator
some six months later when he said: "We sent this
borough act back to the House knowing full well we
had killed it."[46] This truthful statement was made
during a Legislative Council meeting to consider
calling a special session of the legislature to repeal House Bill No. 90.

When I heard of what the Senate had done, I
contacted Senator Harold Z. Hansen, a member of the
Senate Local Government Committee. Hansen had been
the architect of the Voluntary Borough Act of 1961,
and his knowledge and wise counsel were essential
to the passage of the bill. We discussed the problem and he agreed that he would ask the Senate to
rescind its action in returning House Bill No. 90
to the House. He went back onto the Senate floor,
made the motion, and was promptly ruled out of order by the president of the Senate. Another Senator then gave notice of reconsideration, which was
accepted by the presiding officer as being proper.
In both instances the ruling was clearly wrong.
There can be no motion of reconsideration on a
voice vote. For such a motion to be made there
must be a record that the mover was on the

prevailing side when the earlier vote was taken. The record did not exist. Senator Hansen's motion to rescind was correct. The _Uniform Rules_ of the Senate and the House had been ignored for the third time in as many hours in the treatment of House Bill No. 90.[47]

All of this occurred on March 18. That night I contacted both friendly and unfriendly Senators hoping that I could keep the bill in the Senate when the reconsideration motion was to be voted on the following day. When I found that those opposed to the bill were using the excuse that it was an appropriation bill, I decided to show how shallow this excuse was by introducing an appropriation bill which would in truth and in fact accomplish the payment of funds authorized by House Bill No. 90. The Legislative Council, at my request, worked into the evening hours of March 18 preparing House Bill No. 216, the appropriation bill.

I contacted the chairman of the House Local Government Committee. An emergency committee session was held on the morning of March 19, and the bill was introduced as a Local Government Committee bill. All of this occurred before the Senate debate of the same day. I took a copy of the bill to a supporter, Senator Nicholas Begich, for his use in the Senate debate. Then I went to the Senate chambers to observe this example of "responsible" government in action.

Senator Begich handled the debate very well. He asked the purpose of returning the bill to the House. The chairman of the Finance Committee answered that the absence of a referral to the House Finance Committee violated the joint rules. Another Senator, a Democratic committee chairman, came up with the somewhat preposterous idea that if the Senate didn't send the bill back to the House, there would be a taxpayers' suit filed. A third Democratic Senator observed: "Neither House can unilaterally ignore the rules." A Democratic leader of the Senate stated that he had been informed

reliably that the House had rejected two attempts
to get the bill into the House Finance Committee.
"Surely," he said, "we should send this bill back
to the House and to the House Finance Committee."
Senator Begich rose with the copy of the appropriation bill in his hand, and asked the gentlemen of
the Senate if they were aware that an appropriation
bill had been introduced in the House that morning
and was properly lodged in the House Finance Committee at that very moment. Under the circumstances
there was no need whatsoever to return House Bill
No. 90. He in effect showed the Senators in black
and white the difference between an appropriation
and an authorization bill.[48]

Black and white was not what the Senate was
looking for that day. The question was addressed
to the president of the Senate who, even in the
face of what seemed to me to be an obvious fact,
took it upon himself to rule that House Bill No. 90
was an appropriation bill. A prominent Republican
arose and allowed as how the Senate should support
"their Democratic President." It was done--the
vote was 11 to 8.[49]

The bill left the Senate on March 19, and was
received back in the House on March 20. The Republican majority leader of the House, a gentleman in
every respect, as a matter of courtesy asked me
what I wanted to do with the bill. This was early
in the business of the day. I asked him to have it
set over on the calendar until later in the day. I
wanted to wait until the press had left, as I knew
they would at 11:30. Additionally, I wanted to
discuss with several knowledgeable House members
what I planned to do and to get their reactions.
The delay gave me the time I needed.

I decided to blast the Senate for its callous
disregard of the rules. To do this, I decided to
criticize the Democratic leadership of the Senate
and to say openly what I knew a lot of the members
of the House felt to be the case: that basically,
although there were some excellent Senators, the

Senate was not operated in a competent manner. The
Republicans, on occasion, had gently suggested
this, but they had never permitted themselves to
say it as loudly and as strongly and as publicly as
I proposed. The only way to get the bill into the
House Finance Committee and out again was to make
the whole matter an issue of an incompetent
Democratically-controlled Senate returning a bill
to the competently-controlled Republican House.

Under normal procedures, once the bill was returned to the House Finance Committee it would not
be returned to the floor except by a majority vote
of the committee. The chairman firmly controlled
the majority of the committee and he was absolutely
dedicated to the destruction of the bill. Therefore, rather than leave it up to the committee to
return the bill, I resolved that the same action
that returned the bill to the House Finance Committee should also contain within it the words which
would bring it out. This would prevent the committee from killing the bill, yet would permit it to
make such analysis as it wished and propose amendments.

The press left at 11:30. (I did not want my
remarks to create any more of a problem than was
absolutely necessary and, therefore, felt I should
address them primarily to the House of Representatives and not to the general public or the Senators.) I took the floor and outlined to the House
what had happened in the Senate. I read to the
House the joint rule in question and cited Mason's
Manual.[50] After complimenting the House on its
orderly procedure, I moved that House Bill No. 90,
in order to conform to the erroneous demands of
the Senate, be returned to second reading, referred
to the finance committee, and taken up as a special
order of business at 10:30 A.M. the next day.[51]
The Republican majority leader asked unanimous
consent.

The bill was reported back to the floor of the
House as specified in my motion. When the House

Finance Committee attempted to delete the land grant provisions, a most vigorous debate ensued. The House Finance Committee had come into possession of an inter-office memorandum between the commissioner of Natural Resources and the director of the Division of Lands which contradicted some of the material they had presented at the hearings and which I had used earlier in the debate. A friendly source in the finance committee had informed me of this contradictory memo. At about eight o'clock in the morning of the debate, and before the House assembled, I went to the Governor's office to outline the whole matter to him. He summoned the commissioner of Natural Resources, who verified the existence of the contradictory document. The commissioner then dictated an additional memorandum concerning the land provision. It was signed and delivered to me. When the land debate developed on the floor of the House, the House Finance Committee chairman produced the contradictory memorandum which postdated that which I had earlier submitted to the House. I had now another contradictory memorandum which postdated his contradictory memorandum and reestablished the position of the department, as stated in the original document. No matter how undesirable it seems, such were the conditions under which the legislature operated.

House Bill No. 90 again passed the House, on March 22, and was again transmitted to the Senate.

On several occasions I discussed briefly with the Governor the contents of House Bill No. 90. The Governor seemed friendly toward the bill and I felt that in all probability I could call upon him for help in the Senate. I had resolved that the best way to get it through the Senate was to make it a party issue if possible.

It was customary in the closing days of a legislature for the Governor to send a message to the House and Senate, or at least make a public statement through the press, urging passage of what he considered to be priority and necessary bills. On

March 28, the Governor listed his priority bills
and notified the speaker of the House and the president of the Senate. He listed his "borough bill,"
House Bill No. 62, as being a priority measure. He
omitted any reference to House Bill No. 90.

So that, again, the legislative climate can be
understood, it must be recalled that Senate Bill
No. 17 as amended, which extended the status quo,
passed the Senate unanimously on March 15. The
Senate viewed the whole problem of local government
as a political thicket. Besides, it was too much
work.

It was absolutely necessary that I reach an
understanding with the Governor concerning the
bill. I obtained an appointment with him and spent
several hours going over the historical background
and, finally, the tax equalization features. I told
him that on the last test vote on the bill in the
Senate it lost 11 to 8. Now I thought I had ten
favorable votes if I could get it to the floor. I
did not think I could get it out of the Senate Finance Committee, whose chairman had sent it back to
the House. Further, the bill needed eleven votes
to pass.

I am not certain what the Governor did, but I
attribute to his efforts the fact that the next day
the bill was reported out of the Senate Finance
Committee with a "do pass" recommendation.

I contacted the Senate Rules Chairman and
House Bill No. 90 was on the calendar for passage
on April 2. I again counted the votes and felt
safe. I was busy in the House and did not plan to
attend the Senate debate.

When the bill came up, the provision requiring
the incorporation of boroughs on January 1, 1964
(before the meeting of the next legislature), was
amended to July 1, 1964. Deferral meant the bill
would never become effective. The only way to keep
the bill from being repealed in the second session

of the third State legislature was for it to go into effect before the session met. This change from
January to July[52] would have killed the bill and
yet was innocent to all appearances. There was no
chance at all that the next legislature would let
that date stand, or let the bill go into effect on
the eve of upcoming elections. This amendment was
deleted the next day when the Senate reconsidered
the bill.

Yet, even with the amendment, when the question was put--shall the bill pass the Senate--there
were only nine yeas and eleven nays. Actually, the
vote had been ten and ten, but a Senator who was a
proponent of the bill had changed his vote from yea
to nay in order to give notice of reconsideration.
Thus the bill held over another day and gave us a
chance to muster one more vote.

When I was apprised of the situation, I contacted the Governor somewhat despairingly. I told
him we had two apparent problems: One was to keep
the votes we had and, the second, to get at least
one more.

The lines were hard. I had not been successful in making the bill a partisan issue in the Senate and therefore getting party support. That evening, I contacted a number of Senators. I put the
issue on a personal basis. I cajoled, coaxed, offered assistance on certain pieces of legislation
that individual Senators were interested in, and
used every argument I could think of to persuade
them--every argument, that is, except the merits of
the bill. I had already tried that argument. It
had been persuasive with some of the Senators who
were early supporters of the bill; however, it soon
became painfully obvious that the merits of the
bill were not sufficient to command the vote of
most Senators. It may be said that the bill was
not meritorious and therefore could not command the
support of the Senators. I do not accept that explanation. One Senator who voted for the bill con-
fided that had it not been the first year of his

four-year term, he would have opposed it, though he
believed it to have merit. This is typical of the
fear that legislators have of controversial bills.
Also, it was toward the end of the session and the
Senators were not interested in listening to the
merits of the bill. The appropriations bill was in
the wind and pet projects were at stake. The power
of the Joint Finance Committee over specialized and
localized appropriations was even more substantial
at this point and gave it an even greater voice
than it had before.

The next morning the bill was up for reconsideration. There was a thirty-minute debate of no
substance. The Governor had persuaded the Senate
Finance Committee chairman to support the bill, but
the latter did so with tongue in cheek and brought
no votes with him. One Senator stated that he had
reached a conclusion that this was the most important piece of legislation that he had wrestled with
in his several terms in the Senate and that his
conscience would not permit him to vote for the
bill. I was in the gallery. I knew the Senator
well, knew that he understood the bill well, and
knew that his words were nonsense and his stated
reasons only for publication. I recall that immediately after the vote, he walked from the chambers
and I walked out from the gallery. We went into
the coffee room and I said, "Senator, you remind me
of a story about the man who wrestled with his conscience and lost." We both laughed.

The bill passed with a majority of one vote.[53]

KEEPING WHAT WE PASSED

The Governor signed the bill. Later, some of
the voluntary local initiative petitions for borough incorporations were defeated. When this occurred, there was a great cry for a special session
of the legislature to repeal the Mandatory Borough
Act. Although I had not expected the problem of a
special session, I had recognized that the session

of 1964 would be under great pressure to repudiate
everything we had done. I resolved that the best
protection for the act at this time was to try to
make it a partisan issue. To this end, in a speech
before the State Democratic Convention, I made it
clear that the major support for the bill was Democratic and the major opposition, Republican. The
Governor then began to sell the bill. In speeches
before municipal associations and other groups, he
commented upon it favorably.

The moves in October, 1963, to call a special
session were rejected by the Legislative Council.
Court cases which were filed to test the constitu-
tionality of the act terminated favorably. House
Bill No. 90 went into operation as scheduled. On
October 1, the Local Affairs Agency directed the
Secretary of State to set up election procedures.
Borough officials were elected in December and for-
mally took office on January 1, 1964. The boroughs
were established facts.

The legislature reconvened the last week of
January, 1964. The borough chairmen were encouraged to meet in Juneau for legislative committee
hearings early in the session. It so happened that
most of the borough chairmen were Republican, although they were elected in nonpartisan elections.
When the Republican chairmen got together with
their Republican colleagues in the House of Representatives, the steam of the movement to repeal
House Bill No. 90 dissipated.

NOTES TO CHAPTER 2

1. SLA, 1923, chap. 97; Alaska Compiled Laws Annotated (1949), sec. 16-1-1. Hereafter cited as ACLA.

2. SLA, 1923, chap. 97, sec. 51, p. 215; ACLA, 1949, sec. 16-1-22.

3. See Town of Fairbanks v. USSR & MCo., 186 F2nd, 126, 13 ALASKA 75.

4. 128 F. Supp. 717, 15 ALASKA 67.

5. Occasionally it would be the most civic-minded who would present the greatest obstacle to the extension of the city limits; i.e., those in a particular neighborhood who made arrangements for snow removal in driveways and roads, or perhaps organized a neighborhood garbage service or a volunteer fire department with its ladies' auxiliary and neighborhood social club.

6. As a result of the elections held, some of the area was annexed--the rest remained outside.

7. A similar finding, relative to Fairbanks was judicially noted in 1950 by no less a jurist than Chief Judge Denman of the Ninth Circuit, U.S. Court of Appeals, 13 ALASKA 75 at 79; 186 F2d 126 at 128.

8. 129 F. Supp. 551, p. 554; 15 ALASKA 504, p. 509.

9. At one time during this period of growth approximately 40 per cent of the land located within the city limits was owned by the Federal Government, was untaxed, and largely undeveloped. These federal properties had the effect of creating a dam to the flow of municipal utilities and services to the areas beyond.

10. See Town of Fairbanks v. USSR & MCo.

11.   The Alaska Constitutional Convention was held in 1955-56.

12.   In a combined annexation incorporation proceeding reported in 146 F. Supp. 98, 16 ALASKA 519, November, 1956, the question was raised as to whether or not the United States District Court had the authority to hear incorporation and annexation proceedings. The judge decided that the Congress of the United States had specifically granted to the court the power to supervise incorporation of cities, but that it was only the Territorial legislature that had given the court supervisory authority in regard to annexation. In a lengthy opinion, the judge declared that the delegation of authority from the legislature was not valid. Actually, incorporation problems developed largely in response to annexation petitions; therefore, the court, by taking itself out of the annexation field effectively took itself out of the incorporation field. The District Judge observed, "Three of the four District Courts for the District of Alaska are years behind in the disposition of their work. This is principally caused by two factors. One factor is the delegation by Congress and the Territorial Legislature of non-judicial functions upon the District Courts. Until recently the courts were required to issue liquor licenses. . . . The court and personnel also had the responsibility to supervise the Territorial elections."

13.   SLA, 1951, chap. 72.

14.   Ibid., 1957, chap. 88.

15.   Ibid., 1959, chap. 64.

16.   Relying upon an Attorney General's opinion, the acting governor stated that the existing law could not be changed as it pertained to special districts, since Article V, Section 3, of the Constitution required that special districts remain static as of the date of statehood.
      In his veto (the veto was overriden) the

acting governor said, "It would appear that, as I
suggested in my message, the Legislature, instead
of amending existing law, should have been spending
their time during this session of the Legislature
implementing the several provisions of the Constitution. I trust that, when the Legislature returns
for its second session, this will be given your
priority attention." Letter from Hugh J. Wade,
Acting Governor, to President of the Senate, Alaska
State Legislature, Juneau, Alaska, April 10, 1959.

17. Fairview Public Utility District #1 v.
City of Anchorage et al., 368 P2d 540 (Alaska Supreme Court, 1962).

18. Executives and administrators may find
the Boundary Commission to be useful as a buffer
between themselves and the public.

19. This problem was foreseen by the Constitutional Convention which gave the commission constitutional status (Art. X, sec. 12) to protect it.
Despite this, the legislature could effectively
limit the commission, e.g., by statutory definitions and by withholding appropriate staff and
other necessary support.

20. A notable exception was the Bristol Bay
Borough, located on the Bering Sea, which was created by the enterprising fishermen of Bristol Bay
in an attempt to solve an educational problem.

21. The creation of borough study groups was
stimulated and assisted by the Local Affairs Agency. In May, 1961, the Agency published a Borough
Incorporation Manual to assist persons interested
in establishing borough government.

22. The borough also had a tax equalization
feature in the incorporated areas because ultimately citizens would begin to support services previously furnished by the State free of charge.

23. As a personal matter, my primary interest
as a member of the first State legislature and as
Attorney General was organization of the State government.

24. I resigned as Attorney General in 1960 to
return to private law practice in Anchorage.

25. As the bill was finally drafted, I used
language almost identical to that contained in the
Alaska Statehood Act. This permitted the borough
to select 10 per cent of the State lands on approximately the same terms and conditions as the State
was permitted to select federal lands.
          The concept of turning over land to local
governments was not new. In the development of the
West it was not unusual to set aside at least one
section in every township for school purposes.
This method of parceling out land was not feasible
in Alaska because of the nature of the lands, survey costs, and other factors which were considered
but need not be reviewed here.

26. As the bill was finally prepared, it provided that mandatory incorporations would result
only if by October 1, 1963, designated areas were
not in whole or in part already incorporated as
boroughs by local initiative.

27. The bill authorized an initial grant of
$10 per voter.

28. For example, the United States turned
over to the State of Alaska all of the equipment
and assets of the United States Bureau of Public
Roads when Alaska assumed the functions heretofore
performed by the Federal Government. Another example may be cited in the area of fisheries. The
Federal Government had managed and controlled the
fisheries of Alaska throughout its Territorial existence. The Statehood Act provided for the turn-
over of airplanes, boats, houses, cabins, hatch-
eries, and all related assets of fishery management
to the State when the State assumed the management
of its fisheries.

29. Anchorage Times, February 7, 1963.

30. Ibid., February 9, 1963.

31.   Alaska, Legislative Council, Senate Journal, March 15, 1963, p. 298.

32.   Alaska, Legislative Council, Supplement to House Journal, February 4, 1963, p. 6.

33.   Ibid., February 12, 1963, p. 11.

34.   Purely as a practical matter, however, city boundaries could not be extended by the legislature. Such a proposal would not have the support either of cities generally or of the areas surrounding them. Most cities would have reasoned, and properly so, that the new areas attached to the city could not pay their own way in taxes for a great number of years. This was a burden which most city councils would not voluntarily place upon themselves.

35.   ". . . within two years after the date of the borough's incorporation." AS 07.10.130-140.

36.   "An Explanation of A Bill for the Incorporation of First Class Organized Boroughs," Supplement to House Journal, February 25, 1963, p. 7.

37.   Senate Bill No. 17, before amendment.

38.   Anchorage Times, February 15, 1963.

39.   Editorial in ibid., February 28, 1963.

40.   Harold Z. Hansen was chairman of the House Local Government Committee during 1961-62 and is often called the Father of the Borough Act of 1961.

41.   House Journal, 1963, p. 279.

42.   "An Explanation of a Bill for the Incorporation of First Class Organized Boroughs," Supplement to House Journal, February 25, 1963, p. 2.

43.   "A Sectional Analysis of Committee

Substitute for House Bill No. 90," in *ibid*., March 14, 1963, p. 1.

44.   *Senate Journal*, p. 319.

45.   Alaska, Alaska State Legislature, Legislative Council, *Uniform Rules*, Rule 25(d) (Juneau: March 11, 1963), p. 10.

46.   *Anchorage Times*, September 20, 1963.

47.   *Senate Journal*, pp. 319 and 320.

48.   Most legislation involves expenditure of public funds as did the $10 per capita distribution authorized by House Bill No. 90. It would not be inappropriate to refer such a bill to the finance committee--but it certainly wasn't required.

49.   *Senate Journal*, p. 332.

50.   The "Rules of Parliamentary Practice" comprised in *Mason's Manual of Legislative Procedures* implement and govern the *Uniform Rules* of the legislature in all cases not covered by the *Uniform Rules*.

51.   *House Journal*, p. 345.

52.   *Senate Journal*, p. 446.

53.   *Ibid*., p. 454.

CHAPTER **3** THE LAW AND THE
ATTORNEY GENERAL

by Theodore E. Fleischer

In the years since Alaska achieved statehood
and embarked on its experiment in metropolitan government, the State Attorney General has played a
key role in the development of boroughs into viable governments. As these units struggled to
gain a place for themselves, borough administrators and State officials called on the Attorney
General to interpret or clarify applicable law.
Since requests for legal opinions usually arise
out of actual or anticipated conflicts, the Attorney General's opinions provide a record of the
trials and tribulations faced by boroughs during
their formative years.

It is the purpose of this chapter, by examin-
ing some of these opinions, to show the kinds and
variety of legal problems which arose during the
initial years of Alaska's experiment in metropolitan government. The experiment in Alaska, as
mirrored in the opinions of the Attorney General,
may prove valuable as a guide for other areas attempting some form of metropolitan government.

GENESIS OF ATTORNEY GENERAL'S
OPINIONS ON THE BOROUGH

A brief examination of the procedure by which
Attorney General's opinions on local government
are normally requested and issued will serve as an
introduction to the opinions themselves.

AS 44.23.020(4) provides that the Attorney General is legal adviser to State agencies and officials. Although the law is silent about the giving of legal advice to the State's political subdivisions, it is the Attorney General's policy as a rule not to issue legal opinions directly to municipal governments or officials. This is a sound policy. It is not possible or desirable for the Attorney General to be involved in the legal problems of every municipality in Alaska. Moreover, most municipal legal problems can best be solved at the local level.

Even so, it early became necessary for the Attorney General to get involved in interpreting the laws which govern boroughs. Boroughs did not have full-time staff attorneys during their initial years of operation. Except for matters referred to local attorneys retained by the boroughs, the only person to whom borough administrators could turn for legal advice was the Attorney General. Further, it was State policy to assist boroughs to develop and take on the responsibilities prescribed in the Alaska Constitution. In fact a State agency, the Local Affairs Agency, was created by constitutional mandate and statutory law to advise and assist local governments.

The Local Affairs Agency, while providing technical assistance to Alaska municipalities, also served as a sort of liaison between boroughs and the Attorney General. The agency, through its contacts with borough administrators throughout the State, was aware of legal problems faced by boroughs. And as a State agency the Local Affairs Agency was entitled to request legal opinions from the Attorney General. When the agency believed that a borough was involved in a legal problem which required the Attorney General's attention, it would request an opinion. As this procedure became standard, borough administrators began to request the agency to use its good offices to obtain opinions from the Attorney General. The Attorney General depended on the agency to screen requests from borough administrators and to

request opinions only on those matters of general
interest to all or most boroughs. In addition, the
Attorney General expected the agency to provide,
either in its request for the opinion or through
informal conversation with him and his staff, background on the problem, including the fact situation which gave rise to the problem. Normally the
agency would also present its opinion as to the desirable result.

After reaching a decision the Attorney General
would either issue a "formal" numbered opinion
which would be published and widely distributed, or
send his opinion to the agency in the form of an
"informal," unnumbered and unpublished memorandum
(or letter). Although an "informal" memorandum is
not included as part of the year's collection of
Attorney General's opinions or otherwise published
by his office, it has the same status as a published
"formal" opinion.

Many opinions considered by the Attorney General to be of narrow interest and not deserving of
"formal" status proved to be of general interest to
borough administrators. The Local Affairs Agency
reprinted many of the memorandum opinions on borough matters in bulletins,* which it distributed
to all municipal government officials. As this
practice became standard procedure, the Attorney
General began to designate most of his opinions
which dealt with boroughs as official, published
opinions, so they would immediately receive wide
circulation.[1]

Opinions on borough law were, and still are,
requested by State agencies other than the Local
Affairs Agency and by State legislators. In a few
exceptional cases the Attorney General has forwarded

_____

*Editors' Note: The agency carried a number
of both formal and informal Attorney General's opinions in its monthly publication, Alaska Local Government.

a letter opinion directly to a borough administrator. In a few other cases the Attorney General has
become aware of a problem and, even though neither
borough administrators nor the Local Affairs Agency
sought an opinion, he issued one.[2]

The opinions which best exemplify the type and
scope of legal problems which faced boroughs during
their formative years fall in the following categories: (1) boundaries, (2) organizational problems,
and (3) jurisdictional disputes.

BOUNDARIES

The coming of statehood in January, 1959,
raised the question of who would determine boundaries for borough governments. Section 3, Article X,
of the Alaska Constitution directs that the State
be divided into boroughs, organized and unorganized,
and provides that borough boundaries be developed
according to standards to be established by the
legislature, taking into consideration such factors
as population, geography, economy, and transportation.

Section 12, Article X, requires that a local
boundary commission or board be established. This
State commission has authority to propose any
"local government boundary change" to the legislature. Unless a majority of both legislative houses
resolve to veto a boundary change proposed by the
commission, the proposal automatically becomes effective. As explained by the Alaska Supreme Court
in Fairview Public Utility District No. 1 v. City
of Anchorage, 368 P 2d 540, 543 (Alaska, 1962),
the drafters of Alaska's Constitution gave broad
control over local government boundaries to a
State commission because:

        . . . boundaries should be established
        at the State level. [Footnote omitted]
        The advantage of the method proposed,
        in the words of the [convention's
        local government] committee, ". . .

> lies in placing the process at a level
> where area-wide or statewide needs can
> be taken into account. By placing
> authority in this third-party, argu-
> ments for and against boundary change
> can be analyzed objectively."

The first session of the Alaska legislature,
meeting in early 1959, did not establish standards
under which boroughs could be formed. Instead the
legislature gave the newly established Local Boundary Commission the power to develop "proposed
standards" for changing local boundary lines.[3]
In addition, the legislature restated the commission's power, granted by the Constitution, to propose local government boundary changes. The legislature also purported to give the commission authority to present proposed boundaries, presumably meaning initial boundaries of yet unformed boroughs.

The first chairman of the Local Boundary Commission was understandably perplexed. His commission's power to change boundaries of boroughs was
unambiguous, but there were then no boroughs and
no boundaries yet in existence. The first problem
was the formation of boroughs and the establishment
of initial boundaries. Until the legislature enacted some standards under which borough boundaries
might be established, the problem was whether the
Local Boundary Commission, guided by its own concept of appropriate standards, could propose boundaries to the legislature.

Against this background the chairman of the
Local Boundary Commission asked the Attorney General for an opinion on the commission's authority
to propose borough boundaries. In an unpublished
opinion dated November 25, 1959, the Attorney General told the commission that it was "not restricted to a consideration of boundary changes,
but may present proposed local government boundaries which are being established for the first
time."[4] As it turned out, the Local Boundary Commission did not propose boundaries for boroughs.
Instead, the Borough Act of 1961 provided standards

for incorporation of boroughs and gave the Local
Boundary Commission authority to adjust proposed
borough boundaries to conform to statutory standards.[5] This authority the commission has exercised on a number of occasions.*

It is interesting to note that the question of
the Local Boundary Commission's authority to propose initial boundaries was raised again in 1964
(after nine boroughs had been incorporated). This
time the question, posed by the Local Affairs Agency, was whether the Local Boundary Commission could
on its own initiative propose incorporation or dissolution of boroughs and cities. The Attorney General ruled that the Local Boundary Commission has
constitutional authority to propose borough and
city incorporation and dissolution, as well as
other traditional boundary changes such as merger
and annexation.[6] He reasoned that a boundary
change, which the commission has authority to initiate under Section 12, Article X, includes incorporation and dissolution. While "boundary change"
in its strictest sense does not perhaps include
the initial setting of boundaries or their obliter-
ation, the Supreme Court's broad interpretation of
the Local Boundary Commission's authority in Fairview Public Utility District No. 1 v. City of
Anchorage (cited above) gives the Attorney General
a basis for this interpretation.

The heart of Alaska's system of metropolitan
government is, in one sense, the Local Boundary
Commission, which has control over local government boundaries and thus over the life or death

---

*Editors' Note: The commission may alter
boundaries of local option borough proposals and
"the Local Affairs Agency may combine petitions
for incorporation from the same general area
whether all or part of the same area is included
in the petitions." (AS 07.10.080[b]) Although
the effect may be the same as initiating boundaries, the commission may not act until the State
receives a borough proposal and the Local Affairs
Agency has investigated the proposal and made a
report.

of local governments.* While the Attorney General
has not often been called on to clarify the commission's authority over boundaries, it is clear from
the nature of the questions raised that control
over borough boundaries has been, and will continue
to be, crucial to the development of metropolitan
government in Alaska.

ORGANIZATIONAL PROBLEMS

A number of Attorney General's opinions relate
to the procedural and mechanical problems associated with formation of boroughs as new units of government. Not unexpectedly, just getting the machinery going raised numerous questions which, while
not of great long-term consequence, had to be answered before boroughs could effectively assume
their responsibilities.

Elections

Before boroughs could begin to function, incorporation elections** had to be held and the
first borough assemblymen and borough chairmen
elected. An early question directed to the Attorney General asked whether the voters could at the
time they voted on borough formation also pass on
the establishment of sections (assembly districts)
from which future borough assemblymen would be
elected. The Attorney General replied that from
both a legal and practical standpoint the task of
carving up the borough into legislative districts
was best left to the borough assembly.[7] The implication was that it was enough to expect the

---

*Editors' Note: For a politician's view of
the Local Boundary Commission, see the observations
by John L. Rader in Chapter 2.

**Editors' Note: Boroughs created under the
Mandatory Borough Act were automatically incorporated on January 1, 1964.

voter to decide whether or not to accept borough
government; it would only heap confusion upon confusion to ask him also to pass on a legislative
apportionment scheme. Until the borough assembly
decides to set up sections (which was and still is
optional), assemblymen must be elected at large.

Election problems ranged from the length of
the terms of the first borough assemblymen and
chairmen to the question of who was to pay the
cost of incorporation elections. The Attorney General decided that the first elected borough officials should serve a full term rather than merely
serve until the next election, which would be held
within a year after the initial election.[8] On the
mundane question of who would pay for borough incorporation elections, the Attorney General ruled
that, although AS 07.10.120(h) required boroughs
to reimburse the State for the cost of incorporation elections, it could not constitutionally be
applied to those boroughs mandatorily incorporated.[9]
In 1965 the legislature subsequently repealed AS
07.10.120(h) and thus released all boroughs from
an election debt to the State.

Integration of Existing
Governmental Entities

Perhaps the most significant procedural problem concerned the orderly transfer of governmental
functions from the entities exercising those functions to the new unit. AS 07.10.130 and AS
07.10.140 provide a schedule for integrating existing governmental entities and functions into
newly incorporated boroughs. A borough is allowed
two years after incorporation in which to assume
the rights and obligations of school districts and
public utility districts. Although the statutory
provisions are detailed, the Attorney General was
called on to resolve a number of problems arising
out of the transfer of special districts and their
functions to the boroughs.

Borough assumption of the education function,

formerly spread among various species of school
districts, produced many birth pains. For example:
Does a teacher who has attained tenure in a rural
or district school retain this status when the
school or district becomes a part of an organized
borough? Yes, replied the Attorney General.[10] Can
the creditors of a city school district, which has
lost its functions to a borough, recover the debt
from the borough? Yes, said the Attorney General.[11]
When does the borough take over responsibility for
State-operated schools located in the borough? Immediately, held the Attorney General: The two-
year transition period for assimilation of special
district functions is not applicable to schools operated by the State Department of Education.[12]

    Transfer of the education function to the new
borough governments was difficult. Existing school
districts and boards had managed to achieve a good
deal of independence over the years. In many cases
they were among the most potent forces in their
communities. Any diminution of the powers of these
well-entrenched and often highly respected bodies
was bound to be controversial. The borough could
not simply wish the existing school board well and
cut all ties with the past. Basically the Borough
Act allowed the borough assembly that power over
education granted by law to a council of a first-
class city.[13] While an aggressive borough government can have a great deal of influence over the
school system, the school board backed by the local
school administration can also hold its own and
better. In several boroughs the battle between
the borough assembly and administration on one
side and the school board on the other has raged
hotly. In some boroughs the conflict has resulted
in a stand-off and the maintenance of an uneasy
status quo; in others, one side or the other has
gained the upper hand. Personalities have played
an important part in these struggles.

    Sometimes the questions asked by fledgling
borough administrators indicated a need for aid in
the most basic areas of government operation. For

example, AS 07.20.080(a) provides that "those acts
of the [borough] assembly shall be by ordinance
which . . . levy taxes." Since, however, it is the
usual practice of Alaska's cities to adopt both a
general tax ordinance and a resolution fixing the
annual mill rate each year, it was desirable to
issue a formal Attorney General's opinion, which
stated that "the borough assembly may levy taxes
only by means of an ordinance."[14]

To those not familiar with the situation in
Alaska, it might seem strange that the Attorney
General would bother with matters which could presumably be easily solved at the local level. Often
questions about parliamentary procedure or the
mechanics of law-making are asked by municipal
officials, not out of ignorance as to the letter
of the law,but for confirmation that the procedure
to be followed is technically correct and will not
be subject to challenge. Routine questions about
the procedure to be followed, for example, in
levying taxes would, in the ordinary situation, be
referred to the municipal attorney. The attorney
would settle such matters by checking the law and
talking it over with the official who raised the
question. Often a written opinion would not be
considered necessary either by the attorney or the
requesting official. However, in the early days
of borough government full-time staff attorneys
were not available for this kind of consultation.
In many cases the only alternative was to seek advice from the Attorney General. Thus the Attorney
General found himself serving, through opinions
nominally prepared for the Local Affairs Agency,
as legal adviser for the new boroughs.

This situation had at least one valuable by-
product. By issuing opinions on routine procedural
matters the Attorney General encouraged a uniform
approach to many borough matters. Although a situation in one borough was the immediate cause for
issuing an opinion, the Attorney General wrote the
opinion with all other boroughs in mind, expecting
to set a precedent which would be followed by all

boroughs. Even the most basic questions were
raised time and time again, in one borough after
another. As this pattern became clear, the Attorney General found that, rather than handling each
individual problem on an informal basis as it arose,
it was better to issue a formal opinion which could
be distributed to all boroughs. A borough was usually quick to adopt the Attorney General's interpretation on matters of procedure, especially when it
had not yet established its own conflicting precedent. The Attorney General served a valuable function in acting as a clearing house and decision-
maker on these routine but vexing procedural matters and by establishing precedents which boroughs
could follow with confidence.

There is no question that the boroughs needed
their own attorneys. However, if they had been
able to obtain local legal advice, the Attorney
General would not have been as influential as he
was in shaping the course of borough development,
and very probably borough operations would not
have achieved the uniformity they now have.

JURISDICTIONAL DISPUTES

In addition to giving assistance on incorporation and initial operational problems, the Attorney
General has rendered opinions on controversial
questions concerning the boroughs and other local
governments (and the school system). The creation
of boroughs meant death for some existing local
government entities and an uncertain future for
cities within organized boroughs. The Attorney
General could not avoid being thrust into the midst
of the conflicts that arose out of this situation.
The result is a series of legal opinions outlining
the authority of boroughs in sensitive areas involving actual or potential conflict with other
local government entities.

Boroughs vs. Obsolete
Governmental Units

Boroughs first had to contend with the dying gasps of governmental entities, such as public utility districts, which were slated for eventual dissolution under the Constitution. These units desired to continue business as usual for as long as possible. An important question was whether such units still had authority after the effective date of the Constitution to contract indebtedness or issue bonds. The question came to the fore in 1961.[15] Senate Bill No. 137 provided that public utility and school districts could continue to incur general obligation and revenue bonded indebtedness. Some legislators were concerned that granting such authority to these districts, which under the State Constitution could not indefinitely continue their independent existence, might be unconstitutional. State Representative Harold Z. Hansen asked the Attorney General for an opinion on the constitutionality of Senate Bill No. 137. The Attorney General replied that the bill was unconstitutional.

After noting that Section 2, Article X, of the Constitution provides that all local government powers are vested in boroughs and cities, the Attorney General pointed out that the only provision supporting the continued existence of public utility and independent school districts was Section 3, Article XV. This section provides that such units continue to exercise their powers and functions until the legislature enacts laws implementing the constitutional provisions on boroughs. At the time the Attorney General wrote, the legislature had not enacted such laws. The Attorney General held:

> The grant of further power to incur debt constitutes an expansion of the powers of a subdivision of government whose power can only be diminished if the constitution is to be

> complied with. . . . Accordingly, it
> is our opinion that because S. B. 137
> calls for an increase in the powers of
> public utility and school districts it
> is contrary to the provisions of the
> Alaska Constitution, and must be con-
> sidered unconstitutional.[16]

Despite this opinion the legislature passed the
bill. However, during the same session the legislature also enacted the Borough Act. The Act made
explicit provision for the integration of public
utility and school districts into the borough structure, but permitted these units to continue to exist for a maximum of two years after borough incorporation.[17] The district's authority to contract indebtedness during this transition period
was limited by AS 07.10.140; under subsection (c)
a district within a borough cannot, after incorporation of the borough, assume new bonded indebtedness, make any contract, or transfer any assets
without the consent of the borough assembly. In
light of this provision, the only effect of the enactment of Senate Bill No. 137 was to ensure that
the districts had authority to contract indebtedness during the transition period, but only if the
borough assembly gave its approval. The ultimate
effect was that public utility and other districts
could continue to operate within a borough only
with the approval of and subject to the desires of
the borough, which was eventually to assume their
functions and obligations.

In another unpublished opinion issued later
that year (June 13, 1961), the Attorney General re-
iterated his view that special districts existing
on the effective date of the Alaska Constitution
were not permitted to expand their powers. The
Local Affairs Agency asked whether a public utility district could expand its territory by annexation. To begin with, replied the Attorney General,
there was no statutory provision permitting annexation. Even if there were, annexation would be
prohibited by the section of the Constitution which

vested all local government power in boroughs and cities. The Attorney General reasoned:

> It is evident from a reading of Sec. 3, Art. XV, that the framers of the constitution wished to freeze school districts, health districts, public utility districts and other local subdivisions of government, other than boroughs and cities, as they were on the effective date of the constitution. The purpose of this was to insure that eventually all local government powers would be vested in boroughs and cities. A public utility district or school district, by increasing its area, would defeat this policy.[18]

This approach was vital to the successful launching of boroughs. Boroughs had difficulty enough establishing and protecting their jurisdiction against onslaughts by coexisting units of government such as cities. If boroughs also had to fight rear-guard actions with stubbornly dying special districts which were scheduled to lose their functions to the boroughs, borough development might have been fatally retarded.

Borough Administrators vs. School Boards

Governmental units and bodies which would continue to exist within boroughs, that is, cities and school districts,* resisted the assertion of

---

*Editors' Note: The reference is to borough school districts created by absorption by the borough of the independent school districts. In seven of the nine boroughs the "new" borough school superintendents and a majority of the school board members had previously been officials of the old independent school districts. They had

borough jurisdiction. Boroughs have three mandatory areawide powers--education, planning and zoning, and property tax assessment and collection--
and may acquire additional areawide functions such
as health, library, parks and recreation, by transfer from a city or by an areawide vote of the
people.[19] A city within a borough, even if it is
a home rule city, may not exercise any areawide
power exercised by the borough.[20] A brief review
of borough powers shows that the possibilities of
conflict between boroughs and cities, and between
boroughs and school boards, are virtually unlimited,
especially when one considers that prior to statehood cities and school boards themselves exercised
the powers now granted to boroughs.

     Some of the most intense conflicts arose be-
tween school boards and borough administrators.
Conceivably the Borough Act might have allocated
all control over borough schools, both fiscal and
administrative, to the borough assembly and executive. Instead AS 07.15.330 originally provided
that a borough must operate its school system "in
the manner provided by law for city school districts, except as otherwise provided by this title
[the Borough Act]."[21] In order to find out how to
run its school system, a borough official or school
administrator must refer to the Education Code[22]
under "City School Districts." Wherever he found
reference to the city council, he had to substitute
"borough assembly"; wherever the city school board was
referred to, "borough school board" was substituted.
The relationship between the borough administration
and borough assembly and the school board was
theoretically to be the same as that between the
city and its council and the city school board.*

_____

difficulty understanding why their authority should
be different from what it had been.

     *Editors' Note: However, the "except as
otherwise provided by this title" made some important differences.

The manner in which the Borough Act incorporated
by reference all of State law on city schools into
the provision covering the borough school system
was confusing. The drafters obviously were attempting to make matters simple by adopting for boroughs
a ready-made set of laws. The problem was that the
laws under which city school districts operated
were obsolete and far from satisfactory even for
city school districts. The city districts had,
however, learned to live with inadequate laws,
sometimes by ignoring them. In some cases this
resulted in city councils abdicating their responsibility to school boards as a matter of convenience and comity. It was a different matter
with the new boroughs.

Most borough assemblies and administrators
took seriously their responsibility for fiscal control of their school system, and made efforts to
exercise the control required by law. As a result
neither the school boards, which controlled the
day-to-day administration of the school system,
nor the borough assemblies, which had control of
the purse strings and capital improvements program,
were happy with the relationship. The school
boards thought that boroughs were attempting to
usurp authority which the boards had traditionally
enjoyed; boroughs, as newly formed governments
with a mandate to establish an areawide general
purpose government, often looked upon school boards
as thorns in their side whose primary purpose was
to thwart progress. As relations deteriorated,
each side tended to exaggerate and caricature the
other's position.

The Attorney General advised the two State
agencies which had vital interests in the outcome
of the borough-school board encounters. The State
Department of Education tended to sympathize with
the school boards and school administrators. The
department had worked with the boards, was familiar
with their methods of operation, and now found the
brash young boroughs threatening to upset this
smooth working relationship. The borough

administrators found support in the small but effective Local Affairs Agency in the Governor's Office. The Department of Education and the Local Affairs Agency, as might be expected, acted as spokesmen within the State administration, as well as before the legislature, for their respective "clients." As borough problems erupted, these agencies, if legal questions were involved, as was usually the case, would seek the Attorney General's advice. Each agency could be expected to present and, more often than not, to support the viewpoint of its "clients."

The Attorney General could usually expect the State agencies to be more objective about school board-borough administration conflicts than the borough agencies themselves. While interested in the outcome of each local conflict, the Department of Education and Local Affairs Agency had state-wide responsibility, which allowed them to be more dispassionate about each individual situation than the local participants. As a result of the dialogue between the State agencies, with the Attorney General's Office tending to act as an umpire, the Attorney General was able to gain insight into the problems and arrive at legal opinions which often helped reconcile conflicting views.

The Attorney General's opinions do not reveal the extent and intensity of some of the school board-borough administration conflicts. One reason is that these were local disputes, often involving personalities, which ultimately had to be resolved at the local level. While the State agencies might be interested and the Attorney General aware of what was happening, the problem did not always lend itself to solution by the Attorney General. After extended dialogue and consultation with the parties involved, a dispute could often be resolved (at least temporarily) by truce or compromise. The Attorney General's role in such situations was that of a combination umpire-arbitrator. Occasionally a problem could be settled by the Attorney General's indicating informally to all

parties what would probably be his official opinion
if his advice were to be formally requested. The
lack of major opinions on school board-borough administration conflicts is the result of the peculiar
manner in which the State agencies acted in these
conflicts, and does not reflect a lack of concern
or involvement by the Attorney General's office.

The Attorney General did issue a number of
opinions which touched upon the conflict. One published opinion set out in detail the fiscal responsibilities of the city council and the city
school board in administering a city school system.
This opinion was applicable to, and possibly intended primarily for, boroughs, which by law were
required to operate their school systems in basically the same manner as first-class cities. The
opinion examines the law in detail and, in so doing, emphasizes the glaring inadequacy of the law,
whether applied to cities or boroughs.[23] A later
unpublished opinion deals briefly with a question
which became one of the rallying points of the con-
tending parties in the school board-borough administration conflict: the centralized borough treasury.[24] City school law applicable to boroughs
provided that money appropriated by the borough
assembly for schools could thereafter be expended
only under authority of the school board by direction to its treasurer, who was "custodian" of the
funds.[25] For a number of reasons discussed elsewhere, borough administrators decided it would be
more efficient to have all borough monies, including school monies, held in one central treasury.*
In his opinion the Attorney General held that a
central treasury, subject to the school board's
right to withdraw its appropriated funds, was permissible. The opinion did not discuss the question of who would establish and administer this
central fund.[26]

---

*Editors' Note: See Chapter 4, written by
Robert J. Dupere, and Chapter 7, written by Claude
Millsap, Jr.

With the principle of a central treasury for
holding general borough and school funds now established, the next logical step for boroughs was to
seek a central accounting system for school and
general borough operations. Borough administrators were soon pursuing this goal as well.

Foreseeing opposition from the school boards,
some boroughs threatened to take unilateral action
to establish centralized systems. With the school
board-borough administration conflict very evident
on the local political scene, the controversy eventually reached the legislature. The situation was
partially resolved in 1965 with the passage of
several amendments to the education provisions of
the Borough Act.[27] Among these amendments were
provisions permitting establishment of centralized
treasury and accounting systems. However, no
sooner were the amendments enacted than the boards
and administrators began asking questions about
the meaning of the clarifying amendments and, in
addition, raised new questions on entirely different matters. In 1966 these amendments were amended
to further clarify school board and general borough
responsibilities. Until relations become more
stable, it seems that each legislature will be
faced with the task of attempting to further clarify and detail the allocation of powers between
school boards and borough assemblies and chairmen.

Boroughs vs. Cities

While the conflict between the school boards
and borough administrators and assemblies probably
received the greatest publicity and produced the
most fireworks, the most significant conflicts
were those between boroughs and cities. Although
controversy was aroused by the transition to
borough-controlled school systems, education was,
by the Borough Act, firmly within the control of
the borough; the difficulty was the split of
authority between the borough school board and
the borough assembly and administrators.

Cities are constitutionally part of the boroughs in which they are located. However, they
are also separate units of local government.
While excluded by law from authority in the areas
of property tax assessment and collection, education, and planning and zoning (except for the
board of adjustment function) over which boroughs
have mandatory areawide control, cities retain--
until acquired by boroughs--the other powers or-
dinarily possessed by municipalities.

City-borough conflict has generally centered
on the following: (1) scope of the borough's areawide authority and the extent to which borough
authority limits or excludes city authority, and
(2) control of the apparatus of borough government.

One of the earliest questions posed to the
Attorney General was whether a city within an organized borough has authority to initiate, finance,
and execute an urban renewal project. At the time
boroughs assumed the planning and zoning function,
many cities were involved at one stage or another
of federal urban renewal projects. Some had contracted with the Alaska State Housing Authority
for various services, including planning for proposed projects.*

In an unpublished opinion,[28] the Attorney
General pointed out that in 1964 the legislature,
in recognition of the borough's exclusive planning authority, amended the law to provide that
the Housing Authority could perform planning services within a borough only at the request of the
borough. After a borough assumes the planning
function, cities within boroughs are precluded
from planning whether for an urban renewal project

---

*Editors' Note: The Alaska State Housing
Authority is the public corporation responsible
for administering "701" planning, public housing,
and urban renewal programs for municipalities
throughout the State.

or otherwise. If a city desires to prepare an
urban renewal application, it must obtain the borough's approval of its contract with the Housing
Authority for planning services and of any plan to
be carried out by an urban renewal project. Actually, from a practical standpoint, it would generally not be difficult to obtain approval of the
borough assembly for such action by a city, since
AS 07.20.070(d) gives to the assembly representatives of a city with the majority of the borough's
population the weighted vote on planning and zoning
matters.

Somewhat anomalously, a borough did not necessarily have authority to carry out urban renewal
projects, even though it had final authority on
proposed renewal projects of cities within the
borough. Under AS 18.55.950(10) the Housing
Authority could contract with cities to execute
urban renewal projects, but could similarly contract only with those boroughs which acquired
urban renewal functions or with second-class boroughs "within disaster areas adversely affected"
by the March 27, 1964, earthquake.

Thus, cities in all boroughs may initiate and
finance their own projects, but only subject to
approval by the borough assembly of the project
itself. As the Attorney General commented:

> This is a system which provides the
> borough with a final check on city
> planning and allows it to act as a
> regional planning authority, while
> leaving much of the initiative for
> financing and carrying out the
> project in the hands of cities.[29]

In 1965 the legislature removed the limitation on
the Housing Authority's power to contract with
boroughs. The Housing Authority may now carry
out urban renewal projects for all boroughs in
the same manner as it does for cities.[30]

Service Areas

The Alaska Constitution provides that "service areas to provide special services within an organized borough may be established, altered, or abolished by the assembly." (Art. X, sec. 5) However, the Constitution also provides that a new service area may not be established by the borough assembly if the needed service can be furnished or performed by a city through annexation of the area.[31]

Borough supporters view the service area as a useful vehicle for expanding services to noncity parts of the borough on an "as needed" basis and, at the same time, for limiting the cost of providing services to those persons who receive them. Cities, however, view the establishment of service areas as a severe limitation on the city's annexation potential. Thus the question was put to the Attorney General: May a borough establish a service area near a city, even if the city wants to annex the area included in the proposed service area and provide the services itself? The Attorney General's reply shows understanding of the practical politics behind the question. He stated:

> Since the borough assembly has power to establish a service area, it must also make the initial decision as to whether a city can in fact annex an area and provide services. If this were not so, a city could prevent or delay establishing of a service area simply by indicating that it can provide the needed services.[32]

If a borough decides to create a service area over a city's protestations, the city may challenge in court the borough's action as unauthorized.

The Building Code

Another opinion of the Attorney General deals with a borough's authority to adopt and

enforce building codes on an areawide basis. The
Borough Act expressly grants boroughs areawide
planning, platting, and zoning authority.[33] Even
after boroughs assumed the planning and zoning
function, they did not immediately become concerned
with whether their planning and zoning power included authority to adopt and enforce building
codes. The Borough Act provides that after the
assumption by a borough of an areawide function,
city ordinances and procedures then in effect remain in effect until superseded by borough action.[34] Thus, as long as the borough does not enact its own building code, city building codes remain in effect. However, the provision does not
make it clear whether the city or the borough enforces these codes under such circumstances. Failing any direction from the borough, cities simply
continued to enforce (or failed to enforce) their
building codes, as was their custom.

A number of factors forced boroughs to take a
close look at their planning and zoning authority
as related to building codes. First, it became
apparent that in order for a borough to qualify
for various Federal aid programs, specifically
urban renewal grants, it had to satisfy the pertinent Federal agency that satisfactory building
codes had been adopted and were vigorously being
enforced throughout the entire borough (as required by the "Workable Program"). From a practical standpoint, this goal could be achieved only
if the borough had areawide authority to adopt and
enforce its own building codes. The only alternative would be for each city in the borough to
adopt and enforce its own codes and for the borough
to enact and enforce codes for the area outside
cities. However, this alternative is not available
in second-class boroughs, because such boroughs do
not have general municipal powers in areas outside
cities, as do first-class boroughs.[35] In addition,
the alternative is unsatisfactory even for a first-
class borough, because of the unlikelihood that it
would result in uniformity in the codes and their
enforcement.

Another factor contributing to concern about
a borough's authority to adopt building codes
arose from the increasingly obvious need to provide and enforce building codes in areas outside
of cities. Thus, unless the areawide planning and
zoning power includes the authority to adopt and
enforce building codes, second-class boroughs have
no authority to establish building codes even in
areas outside cities.*

Cities are particularly loath to concede to
the borough authority to adopt and enforce building codes. Even a city which has conscientiously
enforced its building code might be concerned that
its special needs and problems would receive little
attention from a borough intent on qualifying for
grants under a Federal program. The cities' argument was simply that the planning and zoning function does not include authority to adopt building
codes. The cities believe that even though borough planners may want control over building codes
in order to ensure success of their planning and
zoning schemes, the Borough Act explicitly re-
stricts borough administrators to control over
"planning and zoning."

The problem was finally put to the Attorney
General by the Local Affairs Agency, which argued
that the areawide planning and zoning authority
did include power to adopt building codes. A combination of factors convinced the Attorney General
that the boroughs do have this authority.[36] Most
significantly, the borough's planning and zoning
responsibility is tied to that of a first-class
city. Under municipal law a first-class city is
given power to establish building codes,[37] apparently as part of the city's planning and zoning
authority.[38] The Attorney General reasoned that
the legislature, in granting boroughs the same

---

*Editors' Note: However, building codes would
be provided outside cities _if_ the voters approved
acquisition of the power.

planning and zoning authority as first-class cities, intended to give boroughs, as part of their
comprehensive planning and zoning authority, the
power to enact building regulations. Legal precedents on the question of whether the planning and
zoning authority includes the power to enact and
enforce building codes are virtually nonexistent;
the Attorney General cited two cases in support of
his conclusion. To bolster his interpretation he
referred to the trend among municipalities to link
planning and zoning and building code regulation
and enforcement. This trend, he pointed out, is
reflected in both organizational and legislative
changes. Some municipalities have placed their
planning, zoning, and building code enforcement in
one agency, sometimes called the urban development
department. Another approach, sometimes combined
with the first, is to consolidate zoning, subdivision, and building codes in one ordinance. The
purpose of citing this trend was to indicate the
reasonableness of assuming that the legislature,
in granting to the borough areawide planning and
zoning power, viewed the authority to enact and
enforce building regulations as an adjunct of that
power.

The conflict between boroughs and cities over
borough and city jurisdiction tended to follow a
pattern in each borough. It was almost certain
that a major conflict which arose in one borough
would eventually arise in others. Thus the Attorney General preferred, as did the Local Affairs
Agency, to deal with a question as soon as it
showed signs of developing into a problem of concern to all or many of the boroughs. Although
Attorney General's opinions are often resented by
the party which seems to lose the most by a particular opinion, there are surprisingly few cases
in which a city or a borough has ignored them.

The Weighted Vote

The second category of opinions on the city-
borough conflict deals with control over the

machinery of borough government. Here two areas
are the ground of intense dispute between cities
and boroughs: use of the weighted vote and apportionment of assembly votes.

The weighted vote is important to cities. In
five of the nine boroughs a single first-class
city[39] has the majority of the borough's population and thus has the advantage of a weighted vote
on areawide functions (including planning and zoning and property tax assessment and collection).

AS 07.20.070(d) limits use of the weighted
vote to an assembly vote on an "ordinance or resolution" related to exercise of one of the enumerated areawide powers. As might be expected, this
reference to use of the weighted vote is not lucid
enough to prevent parliamentary hassles over whether the weighted vote must be used in a particular
situation. For example, the weighted vote applies
when the assembly votes on an ordinance adopting
the borough budget for carrying out an areawide
function such as education.[40] It is not clear,
however, whether the weighted vote applies to a
motion to strike an item from the proposed budget
ordinance. Cities contend that it is obvious that
such a matter is closely related to the adoption
of the ordinance itself and that the weighted vote
applies; noncity representatives answer that such
a preliminary motion does not strictly call for a
vote on an "ordinance or resolution" and the
weighted vote does not apply.[41] Although the
Attorney General did not issue an opinion on this
question, he did rule on an equally significant
question about the applicability of the weighted
vote to decisions made by the borough assembly
when it sits as a board of equalization or board
of (zoning) adjustment.

When borough assemblies began to sit as
boards of equalization and adjustment, the question arose whether the weighted vote applied to
decisions made by the assembly when sitting in
such a capacity. Naturally, said city representatives, the weighted vote applied to such decisions,

as they concern areawide functions clearly covered
by the weighted vote provision. Borough administrators retorted that the assembly sits as a board
rather than as the assembly, and thus it makes no
sense to apply the weighted vote. The director of
the Local Affairs Agency sent the problem to the
Attorney General.

The Attorney General first analyzed the various roles which are played by the borough assembly.
The assembly may act in at least two different
capacities. At various times it is: (1) a legislative body,[42] or (2) an administrative or quasi-
judicial board.[43] Whether the weighted vote applies to the assembly's decisions, reasoned the
Attorney General, depends on the nature of the
role which the assembly is filling at the time of
the decision. The statute makes it clear that when
the assembly functions as the borough's legislative
body, the weighted vote applies on the enumerated
functions. The very purpose of the weighted vote
is to ensure that borough citizens are fairly represented on the borough assembly when it acts as a
legislative body. When the assembly functions as
a board of equalization or board of adjustment,
however, it is not acting as a legislative body;
a board of equalization or board of adjustment is
an administrative body.* This leads inevitably to
the conclusion that:

> . . . when the assembly functions as
> an administrative agency which adju-
> dicates the rights of parties, the
> reason for using the weighted vote
> disappears. Members of an adminis-
> trative agency are to examine the
> facts objectively and reach a fair,
> non-political decision based on the

---

*Editors' Note: Despite the theory, boards
of adjustment and equalization throughout the
country are indeed "political" entities.

> evidence presented. Thus the
> weighted vote, . . . is inappropri-
> ate and inapplicable to the action
> of the borough assembly when it
> sits as a board of equalization or
> board of adjustment.[44]

The Attorney General found support for his interpretation in the practice in other states. Generally members of boards of equalization and adjustment are selected for their expert qualifications
in the area of the boards' activities and do not
achieve their positions by virtue of election to
the local municipal governing body, as is the case
in Alaska. Where this is the practice, pointed
out the Attorney General, "the separation of the
legislative and administrative functions is perhaps
clearer than it is under Alaska's system."[45] This
was a not too subtle hint that the legislature
might consider establishing independent, appointed
boards of equalization and adjustment rather than
forcing borough assemblymen to develop split per-
sonalities--one as legislator, the other as objective fact-finder and adjudicator. The Attorney
General sums up the borough assemblyman's position
as an ex officio member of an administrative board:
"He then has one vote only, whatever the matter
under consideration."[46]

     This opinion left intact the right of city
representatives to exercise their weighted vote
on all enumerated areawide functions when the
assembly sits as a legislative body. An opinion
issued just one month earlier, however, opened up
the possibility the cities might not retain even
this advantage. The weighted vote is given to
council-assemblymen only if the first-class city
or cities have the majority of the borough's population. If the area outside first-class cities
has or gains this majority, the weighted vote is
not given to city representatives.

Reapportionment

Over the last several years city annexation
has almost come to a standstill, while suburban
population has grown steadily. As the population
trends became clearer, demands for "reapportionment of votes" began to be heard in a number of
boroughs. The section of the Borough Act of 1962
establishing the weighted vote did not specify a
method for determining (between official decennial
censuses) whether first-class cities have a majority of the borough's population. Anticipating
that at least one borough assembly would soon be
faced with a demand for "reapportionment of votes,"
the Local Affairs Agency requested an interpretation of the law from the Attorney General. In his
opinion the Attorney General cited the Borough Act
provision which establishes the mechanics by which
seats in the borough assembly may be reapportioned.[47]
The procedure is simple: Whenever its apportionment does not meet the standard provided by the
Borough Act, the assembly is to reapportion itself;
assuming, as is most likely, that this will not
occur, fifty voters may petition either the assembly or the Local Affairs Agency to reapportion the
assembly. If conflicting reapportionment plans
are promulgated, that of the Local Affairs Agency
prevails over the assembly's.

Reapportionment of seats in the assembly is
not the same as "reapportionment of votes." The
former refers to a reallocation of seats to first-
class cities based on changes in the cities' population.[48] "Reapportionment of votes" refers to
determining whether the population of first-class
cities represents a majority of the borough's
population (entitling city representatives to the
weighted vote) or whether first-class cities have
lost the majority of the borough's population and
the weighted vote as well. While conceding that
AS 07.20.030 deals expressly only with reapportionment of seats in a borough assembly, the Attorney General concluded that the legislature apparently intended that this section would also provide the mechanics for reapportionment of votes;

that is, for determining whether first-class cities have the majority of population and are entitled to the weighted vote. His reasoning: "The
[reapportionment] section is not expressly limited
to reapportionment of assembly seats, and the law
specifies no other method of reapportioning votes."[49]
The Attorney General also held that the Local Affairs Agency, if it were petitioned to determine
whether cities were entitled to the weighted vote,
can make use of population data other than official decennial census figures. Since it is obviously the intent of the law that reapportionment
take place whenever population changes demand, and
not merely once every ten years, it would be impossible to conclude that only official census data
could be used for reapportionment. With this
opinion the way was opened for loss of the weighted
vote by the cities in some boroughs. If they do
not lose the weighted vote before 1970, they will
lose it then when the decennial census confirms
the growth of population outside cities.

However, the demise of the weighted vote concept itself may be nearer at hand than 1970. During the summer of 1966 the City of Juneau filed
suit against the Greater Juneau Borough asking,
inter alia, that the weighted vote provision be
declared invalid under the one-man, one-vote,
principle.[50] It is interesting that the city, not
the borough, has asked that the weighted vote be
thrown out. Normally the weighted vote has given
the city a slight majority in the assembly on most
areawide items. The city hopes to persuade the
court to replace the weighted vote system, which
is cumbersome and often an illusory benefit to
cities, with one even more advantageous to the
city. What the city desires is reapportionment
of the assembly on a pure one-man, one-vote,
principle. Relying on population figures of 1960,
the City of Juneau calculates that the two first-
class cities in the Greater Juneau Borough should
be entitled to a majority of the assemblymen on
the borough assembly, not just a majority of votes
on enumerated areawide functions.

In rebuttal, the borough argues that the weighted vote is constitutional because it insures the majority of the borough's population a majority of the votes on almost all matters of concern to them, that is, on areawide functions; on matters that are of little or no concern to city voters, it is only fair that the representatives of borough residents outside first-class cities, who alone are affected by the decision, have a majority of votes. Although a unique system, the borough contends that weighted voting is not unconstitutional and serves well the interests of the borough residents, both city and noncity. What is unconstitutional under the one-man, one-vote, principle, contends the borough, is the Alaska constitutional provision (Section 4, Article X) granting every first-class city, regardless of size, at least one representative on the borough assembly. Further, the borough challenges the constitutionality of that part of the same constitutional provision which requires that a city's representative on the assembly be appointed from among members of the city council, rather than designated by voters. Finally, the borough argues that if weighted voting is declared unconstitutional, then the court should use the most recent available population data in reapportioning assembly seats, rather than the obsolete 1960 census figures. (A privately conducted census by an independent consultant made in 1966 shows that the population of the area of the borough outside the city of Juneau has grown to the point where it nearly equals the population of the City of Juneau.)

Even if the city wins the legal battle on all points, straight population representation may eventually shift control to suburban and other borough areas anyway. Whether by court decision, shifts in population, or act of the legislature, boroughs will probably be required in the near future to adjust the existing method of allocating seats on the assembly. The weighted vote is almost certainly on its way out as a means of allocating power between city and noncity areas of the

borough. More significant in the long run than
loss of the weighted vote will be a decision by
the court on the constitutionality of the provisions under which every first-class city is entitled to at least one representative on the assembly and city representatives are appointed by city
councils. If the court holds that a first-class
city is not entitled to a representative on the
assembly unless eligible for one on the basis of
population and a city council cannot appoint representatives to the assembly from among its members
but voters must make the choice, the influence on
borough assemblies of city councils and city administrations will be seriously reduced. Some argue
that such a result would fatally upset the balance
which the drafters of the Constitution intended
between cities and noncity areas in the borough.
Others contend that this would free borough assemblies from a kind of built-in conflict of interest
which the constitutional authors did not anticipate
would be the result of appointing city council members to borough assemblies. At present it does
not appear that victory for the city in the legal
battle over the weighted vote will produce anything
more than a short-term advantage, if that.

CONCLUSION

A succession of capable Attorneys General
have greatly influenced the development of Alaska's
new unit of metropolitan government. Working closely with the Local Affairs Agency, the Attorney General was involved in most of the significant problems and controversies surrounding the birth and
early development of the boroughs. In a number of
opinions the Attorney General made significant decisions which will affect boroughs for many years
to come.

A unique situation existed when Alaska's boroughs came into existence. The fledgling boroughs
had no full-time staff attorneys and few experienced administrators to guide them through their

first difficult days. The Attorney General provided boroughs with legal advice and guidance in
policy formulation. He was able significantly to
influence development of Alaska's boroughs because
he worked from a strong position of central authority and was backed by the resources of a State administration dedicated to establishing a metropolitan form of government. Further, boroughs looked
to the Attorney General for aid and accepted his
advice when it was given. Other states and communities that consider metropolitan forms of government should be aware of the role played by the
Alaska Attorney General in the development of the
boroughs of Alaska.

NOTES TO CHAPTER 3

1. In this Chapter "formal" numbered opinions
are designated by number; "informal" opinions which
were not officially published (though they may have
been reprinted in a Local Affairs Agency bulletin)
are listed as "unpublished."

2. An example of the latter was an opinion
which held that a first- or second-class borough
has no authority to require that voters "pre-
register" as a condition to voting in a borough
election. (1965 Opinions of the Attorney General,
No. 9) This opinion was issued just before the
1965 borough elections and aroused the ire of borough officials who had been requiring "preregistration." While heartily disagreeing with
the opinion, boroughs nevertheless repealed or
suspended the operation of ordinances requiring
preregistration, and allowed borough citizens
who had not "preregistered" to vote.

3. SLA, 1959, chap. 64, sec. 7.

4. Compare the Alaska Supreme Court's decision in Fairview Public Utility District No. 1 v.

City of Anchorage, 368 P 2d 540, 543-45 (Alaska, 1962).

5.   AS 07.10.110.

6.   Unpublished opinion of the Attorney General to Dennis E. Cook, Acting Director of the Local Affairs Agency, July 13, 1964.

7.   Unpublished opinion of the Attorney General to Roger W. Pegues, Director of Local Affairs Agency, July 9, 1962.

8.   1963 Opinions of the Attorney General, No. 25.

9.   1964 Opinions of the Attorney General, No. 3.

10.   1964 Opinions of the Attorney General, No. 11.

11.   1965 Opinions of the Attorney General, No. 1.

12.   1963 Opinions of the Attorney General, No. 23.   However, AS 14.17.210 provides that State schools that become borough schools are considered State schools for purposes of financial support until the expiration of a complete fiscal year after borough incorporation.

13.   AS 07.15.330.   [Editors' Note: This section of the Borough Act was amended in 1965 and 1966 to reduce the powers of the general borough government over education.]

14.   1963 Opinions of the Attorney General, No. 25.

15.   See the discussion above by John L. Rader, in Chapter 2, concerning Senate Bill No. 89, 1959, which concerned the powers of public utility districts.

16.   Unpublished opinion of the Attorney General to State Representative Harold Z. Hansen, March 15, 1961.

17.   AS 07.10.130.

18.   Unpublished opinion of the Attorney General to Roger Pegues, Director, Local Affairs Agency, June 13, 1961.

19.   AS 07.10.130.

20.   AS 07.15.310.

21.   AS 07.15.330 was amended in 1965 and 1966. The reference to city school districts was removed.

22.   Title 14.   This title was substantially revised in 1966.

23.   1962 Opinions of the Attorney General, No. 24.

24.   Unpublished opinion of the Attorney General to Dennis E. Cook, Acting Director of the Local Affairs Agency, August 4, 1964.

25.   AS 14.15.300, 14.15.330.   References in this chapter to AS 14 (the Education Code) are from the code prior to revision in 1966.

26.   Somewhat incongruously, the opinion also held that a provision of city school law must be applied literally to require the State to pay all State support funds for borough schools to the school board treasurer, presumably even if a centralized treasury were established.

27.   AS 07.15.330, as amended.

28.   Unpublished opinion of the Attorney General to Dennis E. Cook, Acting Director, Local Affairs Agency, September 29, 1964.

29. *Ibid*.

30. <u>AS</u> 18.55.950, as amended by chap. 44,
<u>SLA</u>, 1965.

31. "A new service shall not be established
if . . . the new service can be provided by an existing service area, by incorporation as a city,
or by annexation to a city." (Art. X, sec. 5)

32. Unpublished opinion of the Attorney General to Representative E. N. Orbeck, March 19, 1965.

33. <u>AS</u> 07.15.340(a).

34. <u>AS</u> 07.10.140(a).

35. <u>AS</u> 07.15.710, 07.15.720. At this writing
the only first-class borough in the State was the
Greater Juneau Borough.

36. 1966 Opinions of the Attorney General,
No. 5.

37. <u>AS</u> 29.10.213.

38. <u>AS</u> 29.10.207-243.

39. However, population growth outside the
cities in these boroughs is outstripping the cities.

40. It should be noted that some specialists
in borough law, such as the attorney of the Greater
Juneau Borough, maintain that the weighted vote
does not apply on budgets for enumerated areawide
functions, since the budget function itself is not
enumerated.

41. The Local Affairs Agency early advised
borough officials that the terms "resolution,"
"motion," and "order" were legally equivalent.
<u>ALG</u>, January, 1964.

42. <u>AS</u> 07.20.010.

43.   The assembly sits as a board of equalization pursuant to AS 07.15.320(a) and AS 29.10.402(a),
and as a board of adjustment under AS 07.15.340(b).

44.   1965 Opinions of the Attorney General,
No. 7.

45.   Ibid.

46.   Ibid.

47.   AS 07.20.030.

48.   Whenever the assembly seats of first-
class cities are enlarged or reduced, the number
of representatives from the borough areas outside
first-class cities must be adjusted so that such
areas have one more seat than first-class cities.

49.   1965 Opinions of the Attorney General,
No. 5.

50.   City of Juneau v. Greater Juneau Borough,
Civil Action No. 65-317, Superior Court, First
Judicial District, Juneau, Alaska.

CHAPTER **4** FISCAL
OPERATIONS
AND PROBLEMS

by Robert J. Dupere

The State, the borough, and the city are the
only governmental units in Alaska. They form a
network of general purpose government. However,
before boroughs came into being, the Alaskan local
scene was characterized by special purpose governments, including independent school districts and
public utility districts. These units were forceful, viable, and indeed, extremely necessary. Today, however, they are inimical to unified local
government under the borough concept.

The hegemony of special purpose governmental
units is extremely disruptive, particularly during
the transitional period, when boroughs are strug-
gling to become fully established.[1] Officials of
the school districts, fighting to hold on to their
power, have been unwilling to accede to the philosophy of general purpose government. Indeed, they
have been actively working against it.

BOROUGH-SCHOOL BOARD RELATIONS

While a general purpose form of government may
exist by law, the consistent and widespread lack of
cooperation with (and opposition to) the boroughs
by the school boards and school administrators
points out that it may be years before the full
benefits of this form of government are actually
achieved. The basic fact that the school function

is an explicit responsibility of the general purpose
form of government, the borough, is still resisted.
Aside from the impetus that any on-going organization develops over time, part of the difficulty may
come from the illusion that a five-man or seven-man
elected school board is the head of a system so
unique that it must be separate and distinct.

Failure on the part of the school board to recognize or accept its altered role as part of borough government is typified in the position of one
school board president who claimed that "they were
like two separate corporate units, and that the
school board was indeed independent from this borough form of government." Independent, that is, in
all fiscal matters and decisions. He felt that the
board still had independent legislative authority
as in the "olden days." (And he is an attorney!)
Instead of working to create one administrative arm
that could serve the needs of both the borough and
the school board, he insisted that the accounting,
business, and purchasing activities of the school
district be kept separate and apart from the general borough government. Duplication of effort was
fostered to "prove to the people that these boroughs are a waste of money."

Another school board condescended to permit
its members to be part of a joint borough assembly-
school district committee to discuss the advisabil-
ity of centralizing the accounting procedures. After $4,500 worth of study and recommendations from
a leading national accounting firm, the attitude of
one school board member was, "Where do they [the
accounting firm] get off indicating you could save
$24,000 a year by centralizing the accounting sec-
tions?" Even after a lapse of two years, there is
still no centralization. Ironically, the same
school board has undertaken another $5,000 study to
find out what's wrong with its bookkeeping!

The Greater Juneau Borough, the first borough
government to initiate an integrated fiscal program,

had a trying time.* The "revolutionary" concept of
a single treasury was introduced after a bitter
struggle which resulted in an Attorney General's
opinion pointing out that it was not illegal to
have a centralized treasury, not illegal to institute sound budgetary checks and balances, and not
illegal to specify just what the total monetary authorization of the school board was via appropriation from a central treasury.[2] Although a centralized treasury results in higher yields from interest earnings on temporarily idle cash balances, and
brings the advantage of having a single administrator responsible for financial management of cash,
and the ancillary benefit of lower insurance costs,
many school officials have vigorously opposed the
implementation of such a system and have in fact
made strong representations before the State legislature against it.

Special purpose governmental advocates are appalled that under the Borough Act the chairman, the
elected chief administrative officer of the borough,
is responsible (once the assembly appropriates money) for school construction. Moreover, following
the assumption by the borough of the areawide planning and zoning power, school construction must fit
into the comprehensive plan of the borough. Thus
it was legislative intent that the school district
be integrated into the borough, ending the separation of education from other governmental functions.

However, the educational establishment's concept of the borough is for the assembly and the
chairman to raise the taxes, assess the property,
and turn the money over to the school board, which,

_____

*Editors' Note: Greater Juneau Borough Reso-
lution No. 23-64 (See Appendix B) called for both
centralized accounting and a centralized treasury.
The centralized treasury was adopted, but centralized accounting never went into effect. See Chapter 7, written by Claude Millsap, Jr.

in its wisdom, will do the best job for all concerned, and will build schools where, when, and how
the board felt proper.

Conversely, one of the borough assemblies at
one point had an opposite and equally extreme concept of general purpose government involving comprehensive control of schools down to detailed elements of administration. This concept was summarized in what was called an itemized budget. The
"comprehensive control approach" implied that the
assembly would determine the number of teachers to
be hired, as well as the number of administrators,
janitors, etc. Not surprisingly, such an extreme
concept of fiscal control raised violent objections
from the particular local school board.

At the time of this writing, one observes the
general borough government-school board relationship in various stages of transition. In one borough there is essentially no change in school operations from the old autonomous independent school
district. In another, only the central treasury
has been initiated. In yet another borough, not
only is the treasury centralized but also the bookkeeping, accounting, and business office (yet the
record-keeping is such that the concept of two independent units is maintained).

INSURANCE AND PENSION PLANS

Some progress has been made to induce municipalities to take advantage of cooperative insurance
purchasing and health insurance and to join the
State's pension plan. However, the State itself
has not always vigorously presented these programs
or stressed their advantages, and the municipalities sometimes appear to prefer to be independent
in these matters and make their own arrangements.

The Greater Juneau Borough is the first municipality to take advantage of AS 39.35.010 et seq.,
which allows political subdivisions to join the

State Public Employees Retirement System. State
officials were of assistance in helping the borough
to join the plan.

The advantages of a single retirement system
for the State and its political subdivisions are:

1. Only one technical staff is needed to supervise the retirement programs throughout the
State, thus reducing the per person administrative
cost.

2. Small pension programs are eliminated.
These are often expensive and the individual employee loses accrued benefits if he transfers to
another local governmental unit, or to the State.

3. Personnel mobility between governmental
units is increased. There is a greater interdepen-
dence of governmental units, especially in regard
to certain personnel categories. Specialized personnel in various fields may transfer as required
between governmental units without losing their accrued retirement benefits.

4. A uniform level of benefits for all employees can be obtained, ending the extremes of no
retirement plan in one governmental unit and an extensive plan in another.

TAX ASSESSMENT AND COLLECTION

The transfer of governmental powers and functions from cities to boroughs has been made with
mixed emotions. This is seen in the transfer of
the assessment and collection power, which under
the law is exclusively within borough jurisdiction.

Many of Alaska's home-rule and first-class
cities are within organized boroughs. Although
most are no bigger than small villages in other
states,[3] they have broad governmental powers. Here
again, the acceptance of the new form of government

was sporadic in nature.[4] Some of the more advanced
and larger cities had well-organized tax assessing
and collection operations. Some of the smaller
communities only partially and haltingly exercised
their powers and had small tax assessing and collection operations.

The largest city of the State, Anchorage,
rather gracefully gave up the property tax assessment and collection function, including responsibility for collection of the prior year's taxes.[5]

In addition to transferring the property tax
function, the City of Fairbanks, which has a sales
tax, created a uniform sales tax form in cooperation with the borough under which the merchant
could pay sales tax receipts either at the city office or the borough office.* While the city administration desired to have the borough assume the
collection of city sales taxes and remit city taxes
to it, the city council persistently refused to
authorize the arrangement. The reason for the
council's refusal to authorize the borough to assume sales tax collections is rather tangled and
involves the internal operations of the City of
Fairbanks under a city manager since departed. But
the situation may shed some light on the kinds of
difficulties that create roadblocks in the stream-
lining of governmental operations.

Because it lacked faith in the borough tax
collection staff, the Fairbanks city council refused to authorize the borough to collect the city
sales tax. Ironically, this staff was composed of
essentially the same persons who had worked for the
city and who had transferred to the borough when it

---

*Editors' Note: The Borough Act provides for
an areawide borough property tax assessment and
collection function. It makes no such provision
for the sales tax. However, the Fairbanks North
Star Borough levies a 2 per cent areawide sales tax.

began operation. Before the borough came into being, however, the City of Fairbanks had developed
a rather substantial sales tax delinquency list.
This was due to the fact that the then city manager had shifted tax collection personnel from the
enforcement and surveillance of sales tax collections to other financial functions in an ill-
advised economy move. However, the city council
blamed the delinquency problem not on the false
economy move, but on the staff. This incident is
not atypical of the seemingly minor yet very important incidents which determine whether intergovernmental cooperation can effectively be achieved.

The City of Juneau, with a full-time professional staff, from which one would have hoped for
more rational leadership, used every legal techni-
cality it could find to avoid transferring its
property tax rolls of prior assessment years, and
proved most uncooperative in the collection of the
borough sales tax within the city. Evidently city
officials considered the new unit of government
such a threat to the city's existence that they
felt they could not cooperate with the borough
without jeopardizing the city's standing.

UNIFORM MUNICIPAL CODE

During the 1965 and 1966 sessions of the State
legislature, basic enabling legislation dealing
with municipalities (the Uniform Municipal Code[6])
was drafted, reviewed in much detail, and rewritten
in order to further clarify city-borough and school
district-borough relationships and to systematize
the basic law on municipalities. Some cities, anticipating a reduction in authority, prerogatives,
and power, successfully sought to defeat this
needed legislation. Interestingly, a review of
their current tax levies would show increased rates
reflecting the cost of overlapping government and
just plain bickering.

Unfortunately, it is the attitudes of local
officials that assist or hinder the setting up of

even simple fiscal techniques and achieving intergovernmental coordination.

SIMPLE FISCAL TECHNIQUES

The size of most local governmental units in
Alaska rationally precludes anything other than a
central accounting section serving the general government and school activities. However, a central
accounting section is not now possible unless the
school board approves centralization of the accounting system. Legislation permitting a veto on
this issue was sought and gained by school officials during the 1965 legislative session.

The school superintendents fought centralization of accounting on the ground that it would not
satisfy their need for "finger-tip" information required to enable them to effectively perform school
functions. Yet many of the heretofore independent
school districts did not publish monthly reports
concerning the status of funds for the information
of the borough administration and the school board
anyway; nor do some of the decentralized accounting
sections of the borough school boards provide this
information at present. School officials also argue against centralizing accounting by maintaining
that only school-controlled accounting personnel
can properly perform the detailed bookkeeping necessary to comply with the procedures outlined in
the financial accounting manual of the U. S. Department of Health, Education, and Welfare.[7] In my
opinion, the underlying reason for resisting the
centralization of accounting is that the school
people erroneously believe that he who controls the
accounting section controls the education function.

A central treasury system may be established
by ordinance of the assembly without the consent of
the school board. Better cash management is possible with a central treasury than without one.
However, without central accounting, delay in the
daily and monthly information necessary to make

timely investment of idle cash balances may result
in maintaining excessive cash on hand. The best
practice is to implement both central accounting
and central treasury systems, and to thereby
achieve optimum benefits from both of these excellent management tools.

In establishing simple fiscal techniques, the
guidelines of the National Committee on Governmental Accounting[8] concerning funds and multiplicity
of funds should be utilized. The Fairbanks North
Star Borough, the Greater Juneau Borough, and the
Matanuska-Susitna Borough have implemented a general ledger program. Where the school boards demand a decentralized accounting system, a simple
transmittal document is used between the school accounting section and the borough general control
section. This transmittal is used when checks are
drawn on the treasury subject to the signature of
the treasurer and when monies are deposited in the
treasury. The school administration in Fairbanks,
however, has refused to use a "control" document,
thus causing year-end accounting difficulties. Its
continued refusal to cooperate lends further cre-
dence to the view that this school district views
itself as a totally separate governmental entity
with no need to inform anyone of its daily accounting activities or of anything else. The borough,
as far as the Fairbanks school district is concerned, might just as well not exist.

Rather than assume its financial responsibility for the total governmental unit, the Greater Anchorage Area Borough has delegated back to the
school board essentially all the powers that the
school board had as an independent governmental
unit before the borough was incorporated. The
consequences which logically develop from such a
delegation of power are many. Instead of maintaining a central treasury, funds when collected are
disbursed by the general government to the school
system, which then in turn sets up an operating
bank or bank accounts. This multiplicity of funds
--not normally recommended by the Municipal Finance

Officers Association--is the rule. The resulting
multiplicity of bank accounts results in more idle
cash in local banks. The extent of this separation
is emphasized by the 1966 annual financial report
of the borough,[9] which fails to include the assets,
liabilities, and operating details of its most important and largest component, the school system.
In my judgment, the largest and potentially most
sophisticated borough in the State is not providing
positive leadership in this important field.

A basic fiscal ordinance used by those boroughs which have centralized the treasury calls for
preparation and submission of budgets, establishment of a general treasury management plan, and creation of a central accounting office. It provides
for post-audit procedures, and further provides for
a review and audit by a committee of the borough
assembly.[10] This basic ordinance could potentially
be a model for all boroughs, and did indeed serve
as the pilot for a fiscal procedures and accounting
manual which was published and distributed in October, 1966, by the State Local Affairs Agency.[11]
The manual is an informational and educational document, which, if followed, will hopefully lead to
substantially improved financial practices.

THE BUDGET PROCESS

At this time, three of the nine boroughs (Fairbanks North Star, Juneau, and Matanuska-Susitna)
have essentially identical budget documents reflecting uniform charting of accounts for the general
ledger, expenditure ledger, and revenue ledger.
Even at this early date, administrative personnel
and assemblymen have found it useful to compare the
budget documents of these three boroughs. (It is
possible that three boroughs will soon adopt the
State's pay classification schedule as their basic
salary plan. The grade structure outlined in the
State plan is uniform, thereby providing the important factor of comparability.)

The budget and capital program called for in
the basic fiscal ordinance requires submission of a
comprehensive budget and a message by the chairman
outlining the programs in detail. This comprehensive budget also includes the budget for the school
system.

Contained as part of the budget are an appropriation ordinance and a tax-levying ordinance. In
some of the boroughs a single ordinance makes the
appropriation and sets the tax millage rate. Other
boroughs find it preferable to use one ordinance
for appropriation purposes and another for tax-
levying purposes. In other instances, when dealing
with nonareawide functions, a separate ordinance
is used for these functions and for the respective
tax levies.

The fiscal ordinance normally requires the
chairman to submit annually a five-year capital
program three months before the date for submission
of the operating budget. This capital program must
include a clear general summary of its contents and
a list of all capital improvements which are proposed to be undertaken during the period. Supporting information, cost estimates, methods of financing, and recommended time schedules for each improvement, as well as the estimated annual cost of
operating and maintaining the facilities to be constructed or acquired, are also required. This
writer has been advocating that these capital programs be adopted by an ordinance which outlines the
projects approved, the completion dates desired,
the method of funding, and the responsibilities of
the borough chairman.

The borough assembly's procedures in adopting
an operating budget are outlined in the fiscal ordinance, clearly pointing out the role of the
policy-making body in the budget process. Appropriations should normally be lump sum by department
or major function. Lapse of appropriations are
provided for so that on June 30, the last day of
the fiscal year, the unexpended balance of the

operating budgets are lapsed back to the general
fund regardless of the function of government.
Transfer from one appropriation to another must be
by ordinance.[12]

The basic fiscal ordinance also provides for
treasury management, central accounting, and post
audit. The treasury management plan sets up a central treasury, with the borough chairman specifically given the responsibility for its management.
A schedule of permissible investments is outlined.

Although central accounting is provided for in
each ordinance, this provision, as previously stated, does not go into effect until the school board
passes a resolution accepting central accounting.

The assembly is the body that engages the post
audit. This audit covers the school board and all
the other governmental functions of the borough.
Some of the first borough audits were felt to be
unsatisfactory by the respective assemblies and
chairmen and by the various users of the reports.
This was a result of the local belief that the final annual report should be prepared by the post
auditor. However, the commercial public accountants in many cases had no specific knowledge or
comprehension of the desirability of following the
financial reporting format outlined by the National
Committee on Governmental Accounting. A recommended contract and agreement form between the boroughs
and the post auditor has now been developed which
should greatly assist in providing a standard reporting format, as well as in defining the responsibilities of each party concerned.[13]

PERSONNEL

The success of any community fiscal program
depends to a large extent on whether or not the
governmental unit has trained personnel from the
top echelon through the detailed clerical operations. In larger communities the direction normally

comes through the efforts of a finance director
who is trained and experienced in this area.

The role of a finance director is to plan,in
the fiscal management sense of the word. He must
not only consider the annual budget, but also the
possible effects of today's decision-making on the
budgets that will come before the legislative body
or chief administrator five years hence. He must
also organize his finance department into working
units: the accounting division, budget division,
assessment division, purchasing division, and treasury division.

The services of a capable finance director are
essential to most political subdivisions. In Alaska, however, this important financial administrator
is missing in even the larger cities and boroughs.
A local administrator--often without policy guidelines or financial management experience--is left
to his own devices. As might be expected, the budget document often serves only as an outline of
monies to be spent, rather than as an outline of
services and work to be performed. Any direction
by the legislative body is interpreted merely as an
authorization to spend, rather than as a mandate to
provide a certain level of services.

Though the smaller political subdivisions cannot afford the services of a qualified finance director, they should at least have guidelines from
the Local Affairs Agency as to what constitutes
good fiscal management practice. These guidelines
would include model ordinances, model budgets, and
model fiscal reports.

Some political subdivisions, recognizing the
need for financial and fiscal expertise, have attempted to rely on their independent post-auditor
for some of the services normally expected of a finance director. Others have contracted for consultant services either on an "as-needed" or on an
annual basis.

Even the State of Alaska, which has funds to employ fiscal management personnel, has had a difficult time recruiting. This is even more serious in the small political subdivisions.

Another important technician found in a larger governmental unit is the budget officer. Though he may have the same qualifications as the comptroller, he is often specialized in the administration of budget activities. The problems experienced in recruiting a budget director are similar to those of obtaining a finance director. The budget director often is qualified to serve as a comptroller and may have such a dual function in the smaller political subdivisions.

Even those boroughs that perceive the necessity of having highly skilled and trained financial management personnel cannot recruit them. Comptrollers, trained and experienced government accountants, purchasing officers, treasurers, and even local assessors are simply not available. Yet these skilled people, so essential in any governmental operation, are even more vital to a new, fledgling governmental entity, such as the borough.

Lacking trained administrative personnel at the top, one cannot expect the personnel on the operational levels to perform efficiently and effectively even if well trained in their particular areas of endeavor. Personnel with commercial bookkeeping experience can be adequately trained in the field of governmental accounting; however, in Alaska even trained bookkeeping personnel are in short supply. It is, therefore, not unusual to find the political subdivision attempting to perform all the functions of the above-listed specialists with a local person with inadequate training and background. This is particularly so when the accounting function is split in two, and the school board and the general government end up competing for the only one or two qualified bookkeepers in the community.

Boroughs which have adopted the recommended fiscal procedures and policies suggested by the Local Affairs Agency (in <u>Municipal Fiscal and Accounting Manual</u>) have the same difficulty in hiring trained personnel. However, this is somewhat compensated for by implementing the procedures contained therein, which are specifically designed for unsophisticated users, and devised to assist in training them.

GETTING THE BOROUGH KNOWN
ON THE BOND MARKET

Investors in municipal bonds are for the most part cautious and conservative. These people know what a city is, and have an idea what a county or even a special service district or school district is. But what is a "borough"? An inadequate answer will cost the taxpayers of the borough an "initiation fee" in the form of higher interest costs on their bonds.

One of the avenues for getting the borough known on the bond market is through the rating bureaus. One Alaskan stated that the new governmental unit can be introduced to the bond market by merely saying that it is a county form of government, thus allaying the fear of the unfamiliar. However, the borough is a regional or metropolitan form of government, and as such has all the fiscal benefits of scale, efficiency, and effectiveness of larger governmental units.

In my extensive personal conferences with rating bureau personnel, it is quite apparent that the written message as to what the borough is had not gotten across. It is necessary that those boroughs that have centralized their accounting and treasury and put into effect an organization which saves on manpower and resources should present such achievements through the rating bureau to the investors.

It is important that rating bureaus receive annual reports which are along standard and recommended lines. This is now practiced by some of the boroughs.

Prior to the establishment of boroughs, many of the independent school districts and cities received bond consultant services from investment bankers predominantly from the Seattle area. These investment bankers would, in many instances, negotiate local issues with their own firms while acting as consultants. When an issue was prepared for competitive bid, the mailing prospectus printed was often limited in number and distribution. Indeed, it is quite evident that in some instances rating bureaus did not receive background information on a timely basis. No specific evidence is available that any of the consulting firms who were also interested in purchasing the bonds did extensive public information work concerning the borough.

In May, 1966, the combination of a tight money market, earthquake disaster memories, and too many bonds authorized but unsold resulted in extremely high bids and only one bidder in each case for six bond issues of the Greater Anchorage Area Borough and the City of Anchorage. For example, the $6 million general obligation bonds for school purposes received an extremely high bid of 4.8355 per cent. Contributing to this high bid, in my judgment, was the fact that the single bidder was also the borough's bond consultant. This unfortunate incident was interpreted by a financial analyst in one of the country's leading banking firms as an indication of the erosion of Alaskan credit. Only after a personal discussion of the factual background did this analyst understand that simple erosion of credit was not the sole reason for this high interest bid. The problem was effectively summarized by the Anchorage Daily News as follows:

Both the City of Anchorage and the Greater Anchorage Area Borough suffered serious setbacks this week.

Only one bid was received on each of
six bond issues totaling $19,970,000.
And all of the six bids were astro-
nomically high even considering the
tightness of the national municipal
bond market.

The City Council reacted by
rejecting three of the bids on the
general obligation bond issues and
accepting bids on two revenue bond
issues totaling $5.4 million. The
Borough Assembly rejected its lone bid
on $6 million of school bonds. . . .

Up to now bond selling by the
City of Anchorage, the former Anchorage Independent School District, and
now the borough, has been a sometime
job. It was a job undertaken only
when a bond sale was imminent. It
was, in short, like the farmer going
to the banker, hat in hand, saying:
"I don't really know how to go about
it, but I would like to make a
loan." . . .

The borough, in fact, has a compound problem. One expert in Alaska
municipal finance says he is frequently asked during visits to New
York, headquarters for the money
market, "what is a borough?"

His facetious answer is, "El
burro es un animal."

THE POINT is not lost. The
borough has a tremendous selling job
ahead if it is to become accepted in
the bond market at anything but outlandish rates. It is a selling job
which should--indeed, must--be a
year round project.

And such a selling job is not a
matter of sending out glossy travel
literature telling what a wonderful
place this is. It is a matter of
providing detailed financial and

> growth statistics on a continuing ba-
> sis. It is also a matter of reporting
> the good with the bad. . . .[14]

The Anchorage borough has allowed the school
board to hire a financial consultant to sell general obligation bonds when the bonds pertain to
schools.

One positive effort to provide the investment
field with information about borough functions, responsibilities, and organization took place in 1965
when the Greater Juneau Borough sold one-year bond
anticipation notes for a school construction program. Information was furnished relating to the
following: administrative organization, the financial status, economic base, borough powers vis-a-
vis the State, and the advantages and implications
of areawide powers. A second effort was an orientation program for insurance and banking officials
in Hartford, Connecticut, conducted in late 1965.
These are, however, isolated instances and much
greater effort will be required.

FISCAL ADVANTAGES OF BOROUGH GOVERNMENT

As yet the potential of areawide government
has not been fully realized. Though the basic constitutional provisions and the implementing statutes and ordinances reflect a model local governmental unit, people in various competing areas of
authority have not allowed the fruits of this governmental unit to ripen.[15]

Some immediate fiscal advantages have resulted
from the use of capital improvement budgets and
programs as implementing tools of the comprehensive
planning process. Advance land acquisition for future school sites, as well as recognition of future
general governmental needs, are now being considered. A review of the total long-range capital
needs of the community also serves notice to those
concerned that these capital improvements will

cause pressures on tax levies in the future. Therefore, marginal items of expenditure may be reviewed
and considered more seriously regardless of the interest groups involved. In addition, more awareness of the need to gain Federal and/or State financial support for projected programs on a timely
basis is acquired.

PROBLEMS

A basic problem in fiscal management at the
local level is the lack of an up-dated municipal
code which fully reflects the intent of the Constitution of the State. Many of the present fiscal
and municipal procedures predate statehood (1959).
While modern and recommended fiscal policies and
procedures can and should be utilized in the State
of Alaska, many of our older State statutes and municipal charters utilize the antiquated and inadequate fiscal procedures of the Pacific Northwest.[16]

Another problem is the lack of trained finance
directors, governmental accounting personnel, assessors, and budgetary personnel. This lack, coupled with inexperienced legislators and administrators, has caused a problem in actual implementation
of progressive financial procedures.

Fortunately, many of the borough officials are
quick to comprehend the myriad advantages of sound
governmental fiscal policies, and this knowledge,
along with the outstanding potential of the borough
as a form of local government bodes well for the
future of Alaska.

NOTES TO CHAPTER 4

1. This applies to the old special districts
and their officials and particularly to the new
borough school districts and their officials.

2. Memorandum opinion of the Attorney General
to Dennis E. Cook, Acting Director, Local Affairs
Agency, August 4, 1964.

3. The 1960 Census populations of the larger
cities were: Anchorage--44,237; Fairbanks--13,311;
Juneau--6,797; Ketchikan--6,483; Sitka--3,237;
Kodiak--2,628; Seward--1,891; Petersburg--1,502;
Wrangell--1,315; Palmer--1,181; Cordova--1,128;
Douglas--1,042. All are home-rule cities except
Nome (2,316) and Homer (1,247), which are first-
class cities. U.S., Bureau of the Census, United
States Census of Population--1960: Alaska--Number
of Inhabitants, PC(1) 3A, pp. 3-10, 3-11.

4. Not all of the State's home-rule and
first-class cities are within organized boroughs.

5. See Appendix C for Greater Anchorage Area
Borough ordinance establishing taxation structure
and procedure for assessment, levying, and collection of taxes.

6. The code was first introduced in 1965 as
Senate Bill No. 101. The final version was 2d Committee Substitute for Senate Bill No. 101.

7. U.S., Office of Education, Financial Accounting for Local and State School Systems,
OE-22017 (1964).

8. Municipal Finance Officers Association of
the United States and Canada, Municipal Accounting
and Auditing Series No. 14 (September, 1951).

9. Office of the Comptroller, Greater Anchorage Area Borough, Greater Anchorage Area Borough
Audit Report, June 30, 1966.

10. See Appendix D for fiscal management procedures ordinance.

11. Alaska, Local Affairs Agency, Municipal Fiscal and Accounting Manual (Juneau, October, 1966). Hereafter cited as Municipal Fiscal and Accounting Manual.

12. For these and the following facts on fiscal management procedures, see the ordinance in Appendix D.

13. See Appendix E for sample of post-audit contract.

14. Ed Isenson, "The City Beat," Anchorage Daily News, May 6, 1966.

15. For instance, in the treasury management field: The Greater Juneau Borough earned $48,000 interest on its idle operating cash for the fiscal year ending June 30, 1966, on an operating budget of $3,199,215. The $48,000 is in addition to the approximately $106,000 earned on the bond construction funds.

The last reported earnings of interest on idle funds by the old Independent School District for 1964-65 was only between $4,000-$6,000, on an operating budget of $2,296,000.

The audit report to the City of Juneau for the fiscal period ending June 30, 1965, reflected earnings of a little over $42,000 from its bond funds, but did not indicate earnings on its operating funds. The City of Juneau also has approximately twenty independent bank accounts, which is wasteful. Yet the City could, if it wished, adopt the central treasury and accounting system, with savings and efficiency the result.

16. Two of these inadequate procedures are: (1) limitations on bonded indebtedness tied to property values, which causes the use of revenue bonds, and (2) special assessment or special district bonds.

CHAPTER 5 EDUCATION AND
THE BOROUGH:
INTEGRATION

by Billy G. Berrier

The borough <u>is</u> the school district in Alaska.

Provision is made by statute for city school
districts and for State-operated schools outside of
organized boroughs, but within a borough the school
district is an arm or agency of the borough government. School districts therefore have no corporate
identity of their own and are dependent upon the
borough, of which they are a part, for their local
support money. This relationship is simple and
rather straightforward, but it is not popular with
some of the education groups in the State--a fact
scarcely surprising.

In analyzing borough-school relations it is
necessary to briefly summarize the origins of the
organization of the State inasmuch as the organization of local government fits into a similar pattern of operation, administration, and responsibility.

The Alaska Constitutional Convention in setting up the framework for government in Alaska was
given a great opportunity to avoid problems that
the rest of the states were facing. It seized this
opportunity and framed a concept of a simply organized State Government with direct responsibility
in the elected executive and the elected legislative body.

There are only two elected State Government officials in the executive branch--the Governor and the Secretary of State, the official who directly succeeds the Governor. All State department heads are appointed by the Governor and are directly responsible to him. The Governor can be held directly responsible by the people, since he has real power to operate the State Government.

The Commissioner of Education is appointed by the Governor from a list of names submitted by the State Board of Education. The appointment is subject to legislative confirmation. The Commissioner is the chief administrative officer of the Department of Education and may be removed only by the Governor. The members of the Board of Education are also appointed by the Governor subject to confirmation.

The State Board of Education is not an independent board, although this fact has not been accepted by educators in the State. In 1965, the Legislative Council held statewide hearings on a bill revising the education code. Almost every presentation by school board members, superintendents, and other school-oriented organizations stressed a strong desire that the Board of Education be independent of the Governor.

The Constitutional Convention in considering local government was most concerned by the proliferation of special districts intended to render only a single, or at most a very small number, of governmental services. School districts, water districts, utility districts, fire districts, and even such far-out districts as mosquito-control districts exist in most states to provide a special service to the people within the districts. These districts have boundaries which do not necessarily conform to the boundaries of the general governmental units, cities, and counties, and they very frequently have power to levy taxes for the service they render entirely independent of each other and of the general governments.

This creates two basic problems: The citizen has great difficulty in knowing whom to hold responsible for services and how to hold them responsible; and it creates competition for the limited tax resources available for support of government on the local level. As long as such independent districts exist, there is no way in which community resources may be allocated to community needs with due consideration of the total resources and priority of needs, since no one body has control over resources and the determination of priorities.

The convention solved the problem for Alaska by providing in Article X, Local Government:

> Sec. 1.   PURPOSE AND CONSTRUCTION.
> The purpose of this article is to provide for maximum local self-government with a minimum of local government units, and to prevent duplication of tax-levying jurisdictions. A liberal construction shall be given to the powers of local government units.
>
> Sec. 2.   LOCAL GOVERNMENT POWER.
> All local government powers shall be vested in boroughs and cities. The State may delegate taxing powers to organized boroughs and cities only.

Mr. John H. Rosswog, the chairman of the Local Government Committee at the Constitutional Convention, in reporting the draft of Article X to the convention floor, said in part: "Of course, we have school districts and power districts and other authorities, and they should be under control of the assembly."[1] Later, in response to a question as to what would happen to the independent school district under Article X, Rosswog stated:

> Well, I believe it was the feeling of the Committee that the school districts should work <u>into the borough</u>

> government, that they should have
> their own possible governing body but
> it would be under the over-all super-
> vision of the Assembly.[2] [Emphasis
> added.]

Such a provision naturally met with great opposition from some members of the convention. Delegates with close ties to educational organizations,
such as school board members or school attorneys,
objected most.

The classic arguments were all used: Education is the most important service government gives
to the people and should therefore be independent
of the rest of government. The educational program
can be "dictated" if local government controls the
spending of school money. School boards should be
elected and should be composed of people who are at
least as competent as the elected officials of the
local general governmental unit. Education should
not be' in an "inferior" position to the general
government and its governing body.

Attempts were made to give school systems fiscal autonomy, representation on the assembly, and
full local governmental power as equals to boroughs
and cities.

These arguments were rejected by the convention, and schools were given neither corporate status nor fiscal independence. This should have
ended the question. But it, of course, did not.

Education is a State responsibility primarily
delegated to local governments. There is no legal
question that schools could be taken entirely out
of local control and operated and financed from the
State level. The several states uniformly choose
not to do this and Alaska is no exception. The
states, and again Alaska is no exception, uniformly choose to retain a greater or lesser degree of
control of schools and to provide certain financial
support. In fact, Alaska still maintains an

extensive State school system in the rural areas
outside of boroughs and cities, which is entirely
operated and financed by the State itself.

However, if the legislature decides to delegate school functions to the local areas (which it
has), it is bound by the constitutional provisions
relating to local government. Recognizing this,
the State delegated to the boroughs the school
functions, while retaining certain authority itself.
It generally provided that the law which had governed city school districts should remain in effect
unless altered by the Borough Act. AS 07.15.330,
Education, provided:

> EDUCATION. (a) Each organized borough
> constitutes a borough school district
> and the first and second class borough
> shall establish, maintain, and oper-
> ate a system of public schools on an
> areawide basis, and shall do so in
> the manner provided by law for city
> school districts, except as provided
> otherwise by this title.
>
> (b) The state law relating to teacher
> salaries and tenure, to financial sup-
> port, to supervision by the Department
> of Education, and other general laws
> relating to schools, govern the exer-
> cise of the functions by the borough.
>
> (c) The terms of office and member-
> ship of the borough school board shall
> be as provided by law for an indepen-
> dent school district. All school
> board members shall be elected at
> large, but school board zones for the
> representation of separate and dis-
> tinct areas may be established,
> altered, or abolished as provided by
> AS 07.30.110.

AS 07.10.130 further provided for the integration of school districts and other special districts

into the borough. The transition from the independent special districts to the borough was provided
in AS 07.10.140. The net effect was that the borough succeeded to all of the rights, powers and
duties, and all of the assets and liabilities of
the former districts within two years after borough
incorporation.

The political scientists' dreams seemed realized in this area. One unit of local government
was established whose boundaries were determined by
objectively sound standards. It was large enough
to be workable and to provide directly from the one
unit the needed services. Duplication was thus
avoided and the allocation of resources to needs
could be made on a community-wide basis. Therefore,
the borough was potentially the best form of local
government a body of dedicated men with good professional advice could create.

Paper organizations, however, need to be trans-
lated into real working organizations to be effective.

PROBLEM AREAS

Two major problem areas became immediately apparent when the borough actually began to function.
The ties of history and of vested interest did exist. The city had long existed as a unit of local
government in Alaska, and many cities resented the
interloper. School districts also had long existed, frequently as independent school districts with
full power on the local level, modified only by the
requirement that their budgets be submitted to city
councils. For reasons I find difficult to grasp,
both the cities and school districts felt that the
advent of the borough would make no meaningful difference in their operations.*

----

*Editors' Note: Opposition from city and
school officials to the passage of the Borough Act

The question of how schools fitted into the borough framework first came to a head in the Greater Juneau Borough. The general government took the position that the school system was a department of the borough, much like any other department, except that an elected school board existed to manage the professional aspects of education, such as curriculum and teaching methods. The school district took the position that the only changes resulting from the creation of boroughs were:

1. The board must submit its proposed budget to the assembly rather than to the city council;

2. The assessing and taxing function which was formerly performed by the school district for the areas outside the cities must now be performed by the borough;

3. School plant construction, formerly the board's responsibility, was now the responsibility of the borough.

The controversy was joined when the borough chairman proposed that all borough funds, including school funds, be held in a central treasury for management, and that all accounting be done by one central accounting group. The school board rejected this proposal, whereupon the borough

---

of 1961 would appear to indicate that they were much aware of the "meaningful difference" boroughs would make. "We [staff of the Local Affairs Agency and other supporters of borough legislation] were able, through personal contacts," states Roger W. Pegues, director of the Agency in 1961 and a drafter of the basic borough act, "to keep city officials quiet, but school officials kept up their fire all the way." Letter from Pegues to Cease.

assembly passed a resolution making it mandatory.*

Of course, this action set the stage for a battle royal, which soon involved other issues. The true issue here went well beyond the points ostensibly involved, since what really was at stake was the power relationships within the borough government.

Was the borough, as a general purpose government, superior to the school board? Or was the school board, itself an elected body, an equal? Was the school board charged with direct responsibilities by the State? The struggle to win over local public opinion continued, while the battle itself was taken to the State legislature. Unfortunately, a great deal of bitterness on both sides was generated.

The legislature ultimately passed a bill commonly known as "The Compromise Bill," Chapter 82, SLA, 1965. The bill title, House Committee Substitute for Senate Committee Substitute for Senate Bill 146, is indicative of the disagreement that developed. This bill dealt with the areas where quarrels over authority had arisen and explicitly delineated borough and school district authority. The net effect is that boroughs may require a central treasury, but may only provide a central accounting system with school board consent. The borough assembly determines the school board budget in total amount but not in line items. The borough determines the location of schools after due consideration of the school board recommendations. The borough chairman provides for major rehabilitation, all construction and major repair of school

---

*Editors' Note: For further discussion of centralized accounting and treasury, see Chapter 4, written by Robert J. Dupere. See also Appendix B for the Greater Juneau Borough General Treasury Management Plan and Central Accounting Office.

buildings, but the school board has the responsibility for design of school buildings, custodial
services, and routine maintenance for school buildings. The board also appoints, controls, and compensates school employees.

The philosophical question of what the exact
relationship of the school board with the general
borough government should be was not directly resolved, but the State legislature, by "settling"
these substantive issues, appeared to make philosophical determinations moot.

The officials of the Greater Juneau Borough
general government and the school district accepted
this clarification with a determination on both
sides to make it work. In my opinion, it has
worked, and the relationship is now close. It is
inevitable that some friction should arise, but
with good will and effort on both sides the problems that do arise are disposed of amicably and
well.

An example of a positive accomplishment is
voter approval of bonds for a five-year capital improvement program for the school system. The staff
work on the location of schools for the next five
years was done by the borough planning department
and the school superintendent working together.
The plan was presented jointly to the assembly and
school board by the superintendent and borough
planning director, approved by both bodies separately, and taken to the people for approval. By
being able to show that this plan had been considered from both standpoints--that of schools and that
of its effect on the over-all community--a cogent
case for approval was presented, and the bond issue,
in fact, carried by over a 2-to-1 majority. As a
result, needed school facilities can be constructed
in a planned manner which is less expensive as well
as more efficient than if constructed separately
without planning.

Unfortunately, near the close of the 1966

legislative session, an act was passed as Chapter 129, SLA, 1966, which became effective on July 1, 1966, without the Governor's signature. This act modified certain features of the "Compromise Bill" referred to above. It had long been thought that the Education Code of the State was outmoded to the extent that it needed revision rather badly, and in response to a widespread demand, a complete revision was drafted. Since this bill was basically in response to requests from educational groups, it was naturally drafted from their point of view. Most of the bill had no relevance to the power relationships within a borough, but was a much needed modernization of school law. However, sections were tacked on in an effort to alter the borough-school power relationships set up by the "Compromise Bill" of the previous year. The changes were in the direction of more autonomy for the school districts. After a great deal of controversy these particular sections were withdrawn from the proposed code and introduced as a separate bill. Although the bill passed the legislature, there was heated debate in the House, which accepted the final version of the bill by only a narrow margin.

The main modification is one that shows promise of generating a great deal of controversy and bitterness. It limits the borough assembly approval of the school budget to that portion of the budget made available from local sources. This amount furnished from local sources is, however, merely a residual amount depending in large part on the revenue raised from Federal and State sources. Since this can only be estimated at the time of budget submission, and since the estimates are based on complex factors, there can be large differences of opinion.

The focus on the budget could therefore change from the meaningful question of how much is needed for schools to the emotionally charged question of whose estimates are accurate. This can be avoided where an atmosphere of cooperation and mutual trust exists, as is the case in the Greater Juneau

Borough today. But the problem is there. The
temptation to the school people to secure real financial independence by juggling figures, and the
temptation for the borough to cut the school budget
without taking the responsibility for so doing are
also present. There is thus a great incentive to
present estimates based on other than the best
judgment, little check on doing so, and a resultant
serious danger to responsible government.

Both the Constitution and the State statutes
make the school district a part of the borough.*
The governing body of the borough is the assembly,
with the borough school system operated on a district basis under the management and control of an
elected school board. A degree of ultimate fiscal
control is vested in the borough: primarily the
right to determine the total amount of local money
to be made available for school purposes, and the
right of custody and investment of all school
funds. The general government does not have the
right to make line item cuts in the school budget
because of the fear that this could lead to control
of the content of education--something that neither
the general government nor school officials consider desirable. The school board has the right to re-
allocate funds within the total approved amount and
has exclusive control over expenditures subject to
budget limitations. Title to all school properties
is vested in the borough, and the responsibility
for construction, major repair, and rehabilitation
rests with the borough chairman. Routine operation
and maintenance is the responsibility of the school
board. The school board hires, fires, compensates,
and controls school personnel within budgetary

---

*Editors' Note: The State Constitution pro-
hibits the creation of special districts, such as
school districts. Although the Borough Act and
other State statutes refer to the "borough school
district," public education in organized boroughs
is a borough function.

limitations. Thus it has exclusive control of the
professional aspects of education, such as curriculum, teaching methods, and so on.

This arrangement is not ideal from anyone's
standpoint, and no one has yet advanced a system
considered ideal. Fiscal control, the most important single area, has not been workably solved so
there remains a potential for conflict and misunderstanding. The arrangement does, however, have
some very considerable advantages. Questions of
school finance, which play such a major part in the
total local government expenditure, may be decided
within the framework of the total needs of the community. Another advantage of this arrangement is
that the borough itself covers an entire economic,
geographic, and cultural area, and because the
school system is automatically borough-wide, the
problems created by numerous small and overlapping
school systems are not present.[3]

FUTURE RELATIONSHIPS

Where do we go from here? There are two extreme positions on this question: One, that the
school district should become a department of the
borough exactly like any other department, administered by a department head, the school superintendent, who would be appointed by and responsible to
the borough executive; the other, that the schools
be totally independent agencies, possibly utilizing
the assessment and collection facilities of the
borough as an administrative convenience.

Neither of these opposites seems likely to win
out, since the first involves giving up a cherished
tradition and putting educational methods and content directly under the local general government.
And the second is unconstitutional as well as contrary to the general trend in Alaskan local government which places a high value on general purpose
government. The most likely prospect for the near
future is that the current relationships will

continue essentially unchanged with minor adjust-
ments being made as problems of detail arise.

On a long-term basis the most workable concept
would seem to be a division of authority within the
borough government, whereby matters directly concerning education itself would be controlled exclusively by the school board; and matters of administrative and fiscal policy would be controlled
by the general government with advice from the
school board. Matters in which school needs do not
differ in kind from needs of other parts of the
general government would be controlled exclusively
by the general government. This approach is, in
my opinion, the most workable and the most economical since it requires centralization where such
centralization would be most efficient, and yet
recognizes that educational content and method pose
very special problems which should be solved by
persons dedicated to such problems.

This is not a difficult concept to state; it
will be a difficult concept to work with. It lacks
the essential simplicity of the extreme positions,
and leaves fuzzy areas where the authority is not
clearly defined. This concept, however, can be re-
fined over time to the point where major responsibilities would be clearly defined, and the unclear
areas would be worked out between the schools and
general government. It can be argued that this is
an impractical approach, depending as it does in
certain areas of minor importance on a reasonable
degree of cooperation and good will. Such an argument presupposes that the general government and
the schools will engage continuously in a dog-eat-
dog power fight with little or no regard for the
public good. Such an assumption is not justifiable
on the facts. The people involved on both sides
are almost always serving their community with ded-
ication; power questions are generally subordinate
to such service.

The best answer may be found in the Greater
Juneau Borough experience. We have had loud and

public controversy; we still have minor friction
and probably always will. However, both borough
and school spokesmen in the Juneau area were very
closely identified with the battles in the legislature and at home--a chastening experience for all.
The law was somewhat clarified, but the greatest
effect was that the two groups began to talk with,
rather than at, each other. Once this happened,
the bitter mutual mistrust which had existed tended
to disappear rapidly, since it was recognized that
each group was working toward what it really believed to be in the best public interest. When the
argument left polemics and became a discussion of
goals and methods of achieving goals, cooperation
became possible.

Laws clarifying power relationships are essential, but laws can never cover enough detail nor be
self-executing. The combination of law and good
will is essential for the borough general government and the schools to do the job expected of
them.

NOTES TO CHAPTER 5

1. Minutes, p. 2612.

2. Ibid., p. 2620.

3. The 1962 Census of Government, conducted
by the Bureau of the Census, shows there are 34,678
school districts nationally, although there are
only 3,043 counties. Most research on local government finds that the county, as generally constituted, is itself too small a unit. U.S. Bureau of
the Census, U.S. Department of Commerce, Census of
Governments: 1962, Vol. I, Governmental Organization.

CHAPTER **6** EDUCATION AND
THE BOROUGH:
AUTONOMY

by Donald M. Dafoe

Amidst the welter of conflicting opinions
over the Borough Act of 1961 and its effect on
schools, one point of general agreement stands
out--the provision that each borough is a school
district.*

Those who have lived and worked in states
which have harbored large numbers of small school
districts and have seen the trauma involved in
bringing about reorganization or consolidation
into larger, more effective school districts can
appreciate the wisdom of the Alaska legislative
action. In only a few other cases such as Utah,
Florida, and Virginia, have state legislatures
taken bold action to create larger school districts. Most of the states in the Midwest still
struggle with the problem of reducing the colossal
numbers of school districts.

Alaska in its Territorial days had developed
a good system of public schools, generally well-
financed and stressing the fundamental academic

----

*Editors' Note: It should be noted that the
school district is not <u>within</u> or <u>coterminous</u> with
the borough, but rather that it is the borough
which is the district.

skills. The schools enjoyed good public support--
both moral and financial--and the elected local
school boards took their jobs seriously.

The drafting of the Alaska Constitution in
1955 reflected the strong influence of advisors
from the Public Administration Service who, while
they gave lip-service to education as a function
of the State, really saw education as a subservient
arm of the municipal government. Their influence
pervaded the original acts organizing the State
government. This PAS political science philosophy
has been deeply imbued in the personnel of the
Legislative Council and the Local Affairs Agency,
both of which have had tremendous influence on
borough and school legislation and its interpretation.

There have been and still are some rifts between school people--board members and administra-
tors--and borough people. Some are honest philosophical differences, some may be caused by conflicting personalities, and some, perhaps most, by
lack of communication. There are ambiguities in
the statutes, and there are conflicting interpretations. There is evidence, however, that if all
concerned "lay their cards on the table" differences can be worked out.

In the following pages we shall briefly look
at the historical background, Territorial and
early statehood; we shall explore the 1961 study
of education in Alaska;[1] we shall review the 1961
Borough Act and subsequent amendments, and, finally, we shall look at some of the conflicts and
factors in school-borough relationships.

HISTORICAL PERSPECTIVES

The sordid story of the neglect of education
in Alaska by the Federal government for nearly
forty years following the Alaska Purchase in 1867,
the first steps toward establishment of schools in

incorporated towns in 1900 and 1905, and then the
farsighted and courageous act of the 1917 Territorial legislature in actually organizing a school
system are all well-treated by former Governor
Gruening in his definitive history, The State of
Alaska. In this work he speaks with considerable
pride of the years following 1917:

> But a system of public education was
> established which was to be unwaver-
> ingly cherished by the people of
> Alaska and would measure well up to
> standards by which any American
> public-school system might be judged.
> The territory had made itself wholly
> responsible for the conduct of the
> rural schools; it would furnish the
> greater part of the support of the
> schools in the municipalities. For
> the next thirty-five years primary
> and secondary education would be the
> principal item in every territorial
> budget, incurring its maximum biennial
> expenditure; and no request by the
> board for the education of Alaska's
> children would be denied or curtailed
> by any of the twenty-one legislatures
> which succeeded each other. . . .
> Thus there was early established a
> striking example of what the people
> of Alaska could do in an important
> field in which they had authority
> and responsibility.[2]

With the exception of a two-year period,
schools in Alaska from 1917 until statehood were
under the control of a Department of Education administered by a Commissioner of Education, appointed by and responsible solely to a Board of
Education. The board members, appointed by the
Governor with the consent of the legislature,
served six-year terms. (The two-year exception
noted above was in 1932 when statutes provided for
election of a commissioner, a provision which was

repealed during the next session of the legislature.)

There is ample evidence to indicate that the Territorial Board of Education was a respected and forceful body. The record of financial support for schools and constructive school legislation came about largely through the influence of this board and its commissioners. The system they developed was unconventional in many respects and over-paternalistic. For example, the system of Territorial support was deemed a "refund" system, wherein the Territory refunded a percentage (established by Territorial law) of approved expenditures by a district upon submission of vouchers to the commissioner, and the school district budget, besides being reviewed by the city council, was subject to further review and, possibly, cuts by the commissioner. However, the system served the needs adequately.

When statehood came in 1959 there were actually four types of public school "districts" operating in Alaska under the Federal Bureau of Indian Affairs. Three types of organized school districts had evolved under the Territorial system, each of which deserves some special mention. The fourth "district" under the Territorial system was, and still remains, the area outside of organized districts for which the State Department of Education serves as the local operating agency. The Bureau of Indian Affairs system involves day schools and boarding schools, both elementary and secondary, serving primarily native populations in more remote areas.[3]

CITY SCHOOL DISTRICTS

Local school districts in Alaska began with city school districts, which were formed in direct response to pleas from local organized groups-- literally the grass-roots--directly to their civil government. The statutes providing for city

school districts evolved over the years. But they
were basically little changed (to the date of their
repeal in 1966) after 1949 when they were annotated
in the 1949 compilation of Alaska laws.

Basically school law provided that "Each city
shall constitute a school district, and the council
shall provide the school district with suitable
school houses, and the necessary funds to maintain
public schools." Another section provided that
"City schools when established are under the supervision and control of a school board of five members."

Under the rather cumbersome system of Territorial financial support which ranged from 75-85
per cent of basic expenditures approved by the
Commissioner of Education, city school districts
enjoyed an average level of Territorial support of
over 70 per cent. Some small districts received
over 90 per cent Territorial support.

Many times, however, there was considerable
local controversy over providing the local share
of the budget. Sometimes the controversy centered
around choices as to what local needs should come
first, sometimes it raged around amounts being
paid to a particular employee. In a few cases,
there simply was little or no local tax base for
supporting the local share.

In six years as the last Territorial Commissioner of Education, the author on many occasions
participated as an arbiter in controversies between
school boards and city councils over budget problems, site locations, and judgments as to what constitutes "suitable school houses." Certainly
there were evidences that local "power struggles"
stimulated many of the controversies, and sometimes questions of nepotism and patronage were involved. Several court cases and administrative
rulings, however, had established the right of
school boards to employ personnel to handle and
spend budget funds once approved, and to otherwise

establish policy and manage the affairs of the schools. The statutes were in many respects ambiguous and inadequate but people had learned to work under them.

INDEPENDENT SCHOOL DISTRICTS

In 1935 the Territorial legislature authorized the creation of independent school districts in order to provide <u>unified</u> school districts which would embrace the central city and the clusters of suburban and rural residents in the vicinity. All of the larger school areas in Alaska became independent school districts before 1950.

The term "independent," however, was a misnomer. Although these districts received an average of over 65 per cent Territorial support, their budgets were still subject to review and approval by the city council or councils. The city council determined the amount of money to be made available by the city to the district; however, it could not reduce line items in the budget. The council decided the property tax rate to be levied within the city for school purposes, and the school board was bound by State law to levy the identical millage rate on real and personal property outside the city. Thus, a group elected by a portion of the school district, the city council, could determine the school budget for citizens whom it did not govern and to whom it was not answerable at the polls.[4]

In other areas of school management, however, the school board was sovereign. It had independent authority to request voter approval of general obligation bonds, issue the bonds, construct buildings, and staff and operate the schools.

Over the years there were various attempts, largely by school administrators and boards, to gain so-called fiscal independence for schools. Most of these efforts would have provided authority

to tax up to certain limits, with added taxing
authority by voter approval. These attempts largely stemmed from local budget fights and from the
experiences of people who had worked in states
where some measure of fiscal autonomy prevailed.
None of the attempts was successful, thwarted
mainly by a strong lobby--the League of Alaskan
Cities*--which no doubt believed that there should
be control of school budgets and felt that the cities, as major taxing units, could best exercise it.

Most school districts had learned to live
with the system. One school of thought, shared by
the author, holds that the budget review system in
Alaska provides in effect a public budget hearing,
and is to be preferred over systems in other states
which require various forms of voter approval.
Some of these "outside" systems appear simpler until one has to work under them. To the knowledge
of this writer, no school board in the country has
true and absolute fiscal independence--that is,
the authority to levy and collect any taxes it
sees fit or necessary.

The independent school district has a special
significance, however, when considering the development of boroughs. These districts were the
first to erase city lines and assume an areawide
function--that of education. Even though the city
councils within an independent school district
legally could exercise an unusual and undemocratic
budgetary control over the whole area, the record
shows that the independent school district boards
generally enjoyed the respect and support of their
areawide constituents and successfully transcended
sectional lines to provide strong educational programs. These boards pioneered areawide thinking.

---

*Editors' Note: The League of Alaskan Cities
is an earlier name for the Alaska Municipal League.

INCORPORATED SCHOOL DISTRICTS

From 1915 on, Alaska law provided for a form of organized school district designated as incorporated districts. Conceived for only those areas outside of towns, these could be formed where the people desired to tax themselves for a portion of their school costs and to manage their own schools. This type of district was the only true <u>independent</u> district, since its budget was not subject to review by another body.

So long as the Territory would provide and pay for schools in the unorganized (i.e., unincorporated) areas, there was little incentive for such areas to create incorporated school districts and thereby increase their tax burden. The establishment of independent school districts encompassed some suburban areas, which might otherwise have become separate incorporated school districts. For example, the Spenard area adjacent to Anchorage might well have been organized as a separate and smaller school district had not the Anchorage Independent School District been created in 1947.

Although the statutes provided incentives for incorporation of school districts and a form of "mandatory" incorporation was adopted in 1957, little was accomplished under this act largely because of adverse rulings of the Attorney General's office.*

CONSTITUTIONAL PROVISIONS
FOR EDUCATION

Without question the most penetrating and definitive study of education in Alaska was that

---

*Editors' Note: For a different view on State action under the mandatory school incorporation statutes, see Chapter 2, written by John L. Rader.

done in 1961 by a survey team headed by Dr. E. L.
Lindman, Professor of Education, University of
California at Los Angeles.   The study, financed
with Ford Foundation funds, came about through the
efforts of the State Board of Education and Governor William A. Egan.   While the study was prompted
by the need for a revision of basic school finance
laws, it had a broader purpose of reviewing public
school organization, particularly in the light of
problems incident to statehood.   An advisory council of Alaskans prominent in education and local
and State affairs helped to guide the study, and
at its conclusion issued a summary with recommendations independent of those of the survey team.
The entire survey report was published in September, 1961, under the title, A Foundation for
Alaska's Public Schools.   It should be required
reading for any person who speaks or writes of
Alaskan education.

The survey team records an intensive analysis
of the Alaska constitutional provisions for education (pp. 54-68 and 77-82 of the report).

It is clearly evident to me that the Constitution in Article VII mandated education as a State
function and that the legislature, while it was
free to modify, abandon, or continue existing patterns of school organization, did not have the
right to delegate education wholly to the uncer-
tainties of local government.   Analysis of the
tapes of the discussions on various parts of the
Constitution clearly shows that the intent of the
framers of the Constitution was to place the operation of school districts under legislative direction as instruments of the State, not as instruments of local government.*

---

*Editors' Note: Borough supporters were high-
ly critical of the school reorganization portion
of the Ford Foundation study and maintained that
the study's recommendations in this area ran counter to the provisions of Article X of the State
Constitution.

There is equally clear evidence, however, that the Local Affairs Agency of the State of Alaska held little regard for the constitutional mandate and intent. In its <u>Preliminary Report on Borough Government</u>, incorporated and independent school districts are labeled as "special service districts" of local government and the report proceeds to subordinate them to the plan for local boroughs.[5] The report suggests as one alternative that the borough assembly might take over the administrative control of local education and leave to the school board only the supervision and control of curriculum and teaching.[6]

Thus, it appears that the leadership of the Local Affairs Agency misinterpreted the Constitution itself and the expressed intent of its makers, and went beyond its authority in proposing drastic changes in the organization and control of public schools. The Borough Act of 1961 as adopted by the legislature shows this influence--an influence which apparently also was wielded on the Legislative Council, the advisory body and technical-professional staff of the legislature. Unfortunately, few, if any, watchdogs for public schools were aroused, probably because the leadership of the State Department of Education did not understand the ramifications of the direction being taken-- or perhaps were constrained from raising objections. Certainly there is no evidence that this department or the State Board of Education sought to inform local school boards of the implications of the Local Affairs Agency's advice and guidance.

THE "VOLUNTARY" BOROUGH
ACT OF 1961

Chapter 146, <u>SLA</u>, 1961, implementing certain constitutional provisions, is popularly referred to as the Voluntary Borough Act. The law itself, designed for boroughs and local governments, was not based upon educational issues but nonetheless involved the State school system in many ways.

For the unorganized borough,[7] particularly,
the act created more questions concerning schools
than it answered. Reference is made in the act to
"service areas" to provide special services which
may include schools. However, basic questions of
incorporation of areas for school purposes were
left untouched. The legislature apparently was
giving itself a statutory authority in the unorganized borough which was already mandated by the
Constitution.

The act provided that "special service districts" could continue to exercise their powers
and functions until July 1, 1963. It provided no
answers to the "ifs." If the voters rejected a
borough, then what? If July 1 came without a borough, were the school districts dissolved? The
act made no provisions for school planning by the
State Board and State Commissioner. Quite clearly,
people familiar with school problems and organization were consulted little, if at all, in the formulation of this act!

In regard to organized boroughs, the law shows
several inconsistencies. For example, AS 07.10.130
provides that an organized borough succeeds to all
the rights, powers, and duties of any school district within its boundaries. This automatic absorption of school districts is clearly contrary
to some ideas expressed at the Constitutional Convention which referred to leaving "the way open to
independent school districts" and providing for
"more than one within a specific borough."

AS 07.15.330 devotes itself to education,
stating that organized boroughs "shall establish,
maintain, and operate a system of public schools
on an areawide basis, and shall do so in the manner provided by law for city school districts"
[emphasis mine]. Thus, the legislature abdicated
its responsibility by shackling education in the
new State in the bonds of an archaic, ambiguous,
and controversial statute, preserving controls
over schools which are only present elsewhere in

the obsolete systems of county government--which
the boroughs were to avoid.*

Yet, the 1961 Borough Law made no attempt to
classify schools as a borough department. In this
regard, the 1961 report, A Foundation for Alaska's
Public Schools, notes that:

1. The borough assembly legislates
    by ordinance for borough depart-
    ments, but the state legislature
    legislates for schools by general
    law.

2. The assembly may "alter or abol-
    ish any borough department" but
    it cannot do so with schools.

3. The borough chairman shall ap-
    point all borough employees
    and administrators, but the
    school board performs this
    function for schools.

4. The assembly may provide for
    centralized supply and equip-
    ment management "for the bor-
    ough and for its departments,"
    but the school board determines
    its own separate policy for
    schools.

---

*Editors' Note: Apropos of this problem,
Roger W. Pegues comments: "The Department of Education had agreed that it would undertake a long-
needed revision of the Education Code. At the
time the Borough Act was drafted, it was assumed
by all concerned that the Legislative Council,
Local Affairs Agency, and Department of Education
would complete a revision of the Education Code by
the time the new borough had to take over the
schools." Letter from Pegues to Cease. The Education Code was not revised until 1966. The revised code became SLA, 1966, chap. 98.

5.   If the borough provides for a
     personnel system, the borough
     chairman serves as personnel
     officer, whereas the school
     employees are under state law,
     State Board of Education, and
     local school board personnel
     policies.

6.   The organized borough estab-
     lishes salaries for borough
     officers and employees, while
     teachers' salaries are gov-
     erned by the state salary
     schedule and local school
     board policies.[8]

The survey report indicates the need for
legislative review of the Borough Act to clarify
the State's policy in the delegation of its responsibility for education to local school boards.
It makes a strong statement in this regard:

A sovereign state must be prudent in
ignoring what has been learned from
experience over a period of 150
years.   Education is too important
to a free people to subordinate it
to incidental treatment in a search
for new patterns of local government,
however worthy and challenging these
may be; or to permit it to fall by
default into the controlled philosophy of any particular theory of
government.   It is not in the best
interest of a strong state system of
public education to delegate it to
local governments as a branch of
local affairs.   Section 3.33 [AS
07.15.330] in the Borough Law and
parts of other sections mentioning
schools should be repealed.   The
Legislature should retain control of
educational organization and programs

until, when boroughs prove themselves as desirable areas for state
services, an intelligent and informed adaptation can be made for
the benefit of both education and
local government.[9]

The survey report explicitly detailed its
recommendations with regard to local school organization. Those which are germane are excerpted below:

1.   The Alaska Legislature is obli-
     gated by Article VII, Section 1,
     of the State Constitution "by
     general law [to] establish and
     maintain a system of public
     schools open to all children of
     the state."

2.   The Legislature may elect to dis-
     charge this obligation by estab-
     lishing and maintaining local or
     regional educational agencies to
     operate public schools.

3.   The Legislature may place these
     local educational agencies under
     the administrative control of
     boards of education.

4.   Such local or regional educa-
     tional agencies may be cotermin-
     ous with boroughs or cities, but
     such coincidence of boundaries
     does not require the Legislature
     to place the administrative con-
     trol of local educational agen-
     cies under borough or city gov-
     ernment.

5.   To avoid duplication of effort,
     the Legislature may require
     borough or city governments to

> levy and collect taxes for local
> educational agencies and perform
> other ministerial services for
> them in the interest of economy.[10]

In addition, the survey report, which proposed
a "foundation" system of basic State support (the
major elements of which were enacted into law in
1962), recommended that local tax levies for school
purposes above determined amounts be subject to approval by a vote of the people rather than city
councils or borough assemblies. It proposed that
the council or assembly tax for schools as a separate entity rather than as a part of the city or
borough tax.

It is also interesting to note that the report
and recommendations of the advisory council to the
survey (pp. xvii-xxviii) strongly express the belief that elected local school boards should be
directly responsible for carrying out the State
educational function:

> The Council believes that under the
> Constitution, free public education
> is a function of the state. It be-
> lieves also in the traditional and
> uniquely American practice of vest-
> ing control of educational policy in
> lay boards of education as direct
> representatives of the people. The
> Council believes in a state policy
> of encouraging the active participa-
> tion of individual citizens in their
> reponsibilities for school affairs.
> It strongly endorses the election by
> popular vote of local school board
> members who serve without pay as a
> civic responsibility to their
> schools and the state.
>
> The Council recognizes the responsi-
> bility of the Legislature to estab-
> lish a plan for operating a statewide

system of public education. After
three years of statehood, the Legislature should now be encouraged to
proceed to enact into law a comprehensive school program in order to
implement Article VII, Section 1 [of
the Alaska Constitution], and to
clarify the organizational structure
of public education in Alaska.

The Legislature should by general
law create School Administrative
Units on the basis of criteria
adopted by the State Board of Education, the effective date of the
reorganization to be July 1, 1962.
To accomplish this, the 1962 Legislature should first repeal [cita-
tions omitted] and references to
schools and school districts in the
Borough Law [citations omitted],
and elsewhere. This action would
discontinue all types of local
school districts.

A board of school directors should
be provided by law for each school
administrative unit. The statute
should state specifically that such
boards are agents of the state and
are not local government officers.

UNEASINESS--BUT LITTLE PROGRESS

After the publication of the survey team report in 1961, school officials and school boards
began to realize that there were serious implications for their future in the 1961 Borough Act,
particularly because of the attitude of the Local
Affairs Agency, which wanted to subordinate education to local government and which apparently had
the "legislative ear." Although the State Department of Education, at the urging of the survey

team, did develop draft legislation detailing the
organization of separate local school districts
(introduced in the 1963 legislature), the suggested
legislation went nowhere for a variety of reasons.*

One reason for failure to consider seriously
the Department of Education's proposal was that it
lacked administrative "push." The administration
was pushing the foundation school support act, ad-
mittedly a good measure which deserved and received
firm support from the schools generally. No one
wanted to jeopardize its chances by alienating
legislators through intensive efforts on district
organization. There is no question that a State
Board of Education which has only advisory powers
and a State Commissioner who is a political ap-
pointee are not going to alienate either the governor or the legislature--hence, there was little
"push" from this direction.

Then, too, there is reluctance on the part of
a succeeding legislature to amend or repeal an act
of the previous legislature, especially when the
legislation is untested.** This writer had the experience of legislators telling him, "How do you
know it won't work--we've just adopted the former
laws by reference and you operated under them.
You've got to have faith and try to work these
things out!"

In several communications, including official
resolutions of their respective associations,
school officials and school board association

---

*Editors' Note: House Bill No. 62.   See Chap-
ter 1, written by Ronald C. Cease and Jerome R.
Saroff, and Chapter 2, written by John L. Rader.

**Editors' Note: In 1962 the legislature en-
acted a number of changes to the Borough Act (sometimes referred to as the Borough Act of 1962).
None of these changes, however, concerned education.

members recommended to the legislators, the Legislative Council, the Local Affairs Agency, the State
Department of Education, and even the Governor that:

1. AS 07.15.330 be repealed and all references
    to education be in the Education Code,
    Alaska Statutes, Title 14. They felt that
    misinterpretation and further confusion
    would be increased by having school laws
    in several titles.

2. If AS 07.15.330 were retained, the refer-
    ence to city school districts be deleted
    and the reference be only to Title 14, to
    which a new chapter should be added to
    specifically provide for school operations
    in organized boroughs.

3. The phrase "except as otherwise provided
    by this title" be deleted from AS
    07.15.330(a), since it was already becom-
    ing apparent that borough proponents
    would variously interpret parts of the
    general borough law to relate to schools,
    particularly AS 07.25.030, POWERS AND DU-
    TIES OF THE BOROUGH CHAIRMAN, and AS
    07.25.040, FUNCTIONS UNDER DIRECTION AND
    SUPERVISION OF BOROUGH CHAIRMAN. School
    officials felt that the borough would
    claim undue powers over schools.

The attitude of the Local Affairs Agency toward these suggestions was purely negative. Legislators generally reverted back to the argument
"You haven't been hurt yet--let things work out,"
or "You school people always want everything your
own way--the borough people who are going to be
responsible for all taxation need to have control
over schools."

THE 1963 MANDATORY BOROUGH ACT

From 1961 to 1963 there was only one borough
formed, the Bristol Bay Borough, an area in which

the three schools had all been State-operated.
Thorny questions of disposition of assets and liabilities did not arise because the State simply
turned the assets and liabilities over to the borough. However, almost from the beginning, controversies over budgets and fiscal control arose,
and discussions and correspondence with school
board members indicated that they received conflicting opinions and interpretations from representatives of the State Department of Education
and the Local Affairs Agency.

In the Anchorage area a borough study committee had worked diligently for over a year to determine whether to petition for a first- or second-
class borough. Although the first-class borough
was subsequently rejected by the electorate, the
study was most significant in that it served to
broaden public understanding. In particular, the
work of a subcommittee on schools set the stage
for a smooth transition in education when a mandatory borough came into existence.

Chapter 52, _SLA_, 1963, known as the Mandatory
Borough Act, squarely met the problem of organizing boroughs by providing that certain designated
areas, covering the major population centers of
the State, would become on January 1, 1964, organized boroughs. The die was cast!

In relation to schools, the Act provided that
the functions of city and independent school districts would have to be assumed by the borough
within two years from the date of borough incorporation.[11] However, State-operated schools within
a borough were to be turned over to the _full con-
trol_ of the borough _immediately_ upon incorporation.
As soon as a borough was formed no independent or
city school district could assume new bonded indebtedness, enter into contracts, or transfer
assets without the consent of the borough assembly.
Within the two-year limit permitted by law, the
borough assembly would decide when to assume the
school function for districts.

To the credit of the Local Affairs Agency and
the State Department of Education, both realized
the enormity of the transitional problems for
schools under the Mandatory Borough Act. They col-
laborated in the preparation of <u>Borough Manual No.
II--Schools</u>, [12] issued in December, 1963, which suggested transitional procedures, interpreted some
portions of the law, and set guidelines for borough
school operations.

In the meantime the Department of Education
had taken other steps to assist with transitional
problems. The commissioner used the prestige of
his position and office to establish in each pros-
pective borough a committee of school people to
meet and consider ways to effect a smooth transition.

Robert Isaac, assistant to the commissioner,
a long-time employee of the Department, well-
versed in school law and regulations, was made
available to advise the new borough school boards
and borough assemblies. The director of the Local
Affairs Agency also was available to advise assemblies. However, there were early indications of
differing interpretations by the representatives
of the two agencies.

In the Anchorage area the transition in education was remarkably smooth. [13] Among the major
reasons for this were:

1. All members of the Anchorage Independent
School District were elected to the borough school
board. This reflected the confidence which the
public had in the old board.

2. The transition committee formed by the
Commissioner of Education took its work seriously
and involved representatives of all areas in its
discussions. This group proposed a set of recommendations for the assembly and school board which
included provision for assumption of school debt
on an areawide basis, and assumption of all school

functions by the borough on October 1, 1964. Its
recommendations were followed without exception.

3. The borough assembly membership included
persons who had a broad understanding of school
matters. The elected chairman and one assembly
member had been recent school board members.

4. The elected school board and elected assembly met prior to the incorporation, discussed and
generally agreed upon the transition committee's
recommendations and fundamentally agreed that the
"School Board should 'run the schools.'"

5. <u>The two elected bodies agreed that there
was a need to establish written procedures governing assembly-school board relationships, particularly because of the ambiguities of the old city
school district law and the history of misunderstanding and misinterpretations in its application.</u>

This latter point, without question, became
the key to the smooth transition in the Anchorage
area and the subsequent basis for continuing good
relationships between the borough assembly and the
school board. On the basis of this recognized
need, the board prepared and presented to the assembly,through its chairman,a memorandum covering proposals for setting forth procedures.[14]

After presentation to the borough assembly in
April, 1964, the assembly requested the chairman
to have the borough attorney, in cooperation with
the school administration and school attorney, prepare a resolution for adoption by the assembly.
Thus, Resolution No. 32 came to be adopted by the
Greater Anchorage Area Borough assembly.[15]

Resolution No. 32 has stood the test through
the first three years of borough organization in
Anchorage; and there is no indication that it will
soon be abrogated or revised. There have been
minor differences in budgetary matters and some in
site selections. However, there has been only one

instance of failure to ratify a school board recommendation, and this was concerning selection of an
independent auditor, a matter not covered by Resolution No. 32.

Only one change has been made in Resolution
No. 32, and that is to remove from the school
board the right and responsibility of recommending
a financial consultant for bond sale purposes.
This occurred because it was generally agreed that
the borough, as the bond-marketing authority,
should logically be completely responsible for determining the timing and methods of bond sales.

Several other borough school districts have
followed the Anchorage plan in whole or in part.
In at least one case a borough school board and
assembly were advised by the director of the Local
Affairs Agency not to adopt this pattern. Allegedly, the director noted that the resolution was of
little value and could easily be repealed or amended; that the only reason it was adopted in Anchorage was because the school administration and board
simply outmaneuvered the assembly, aided and abet-
ted by a particularly school-conscious borough
chairman. In the opinion of the writer, this seeming hostility stemmed largely from a basic difference in philosophy. The Local Affairs Agency
director apparently believed in general purpose
government with education as a subordinate department or branch.

It is interesting to note, however, that in
the largest school district in the State,where
financing needs and constant school construction
needs might really cause unpleasant relationships,
the problems have been minimal. On the other hand,
in Juneau, the State capital, where the school district theoretically has readily available the best
possible advice on matters of education and borough
affairs, the problems have been intense.

To this writer, who has been at legislative
hearings where State, borough, and local school

officials have testified on school-borough matters,
it is evident that the Juneau borough chairman,
who has referred to himself openly as a "regional
governor," and his legal and fiscal advisors see
the school board as subservient to the borough
chairman and assembly. It is equally evident that
this opinion was consistently reinforced by Dr.
Ronald C. Cease when he was director of the Local
Affairs Agency.

The writer, as a professional educator, simply
cannot accept this position. In the first place,
it is my opinion that under the Alaska Constitution,
which specifically provides that education is a
State function, this function cannot be cast off
to the whims of local government. The State cannot
abdicate its responsibility! Secondly, there is
no logical reason for supplanting the system of
local school board control (which has served America
so well) by enmeshing it in the snarls of municipal
government. The records of school boards, with
rare exception, are free from corruption and partisan politics. They have been remarkably responsive
to public needs and demands.

There have been pleas by school officials and
school board association members for the governor's
office (where the Local Affairs Agency is located)
to seek to bring about a measure of consistency in
interpretation of school and borough laws. A delegation from the Association of Alaska School
Boards met with the Governor in late November,
1964, to urge that he seek to remedy the situation
where conflicting interpretations were given by
the Education Department and the Local Affairs
Agency. A major area of different interpretation
revolved around budget review. Proponents of borough power contended that the borough assembly had
authority to appropriate the entire budget, while
school people held that the authority was limited
to the local tax portion. More recently, in late
1965 and again in 1966, resolutions of the Association of Alaska School Boards asked that Borough
Manual II--Schools, be revised to reflect changes

in laws and regulations and to clarify interpretations. The need for this revision is most urgent.

LEGISLATIVE CHANGES

Differences of opinion between school boards
and borough assemblies and between school superintendents and borough chairmen have revolved around
two main areas: (1) budgets and fiscal control
and (2) school construction.

In the Anchorage area, Resolution No. 32 has
satisfactorily covered construction relationships.
The use of a Joint Construction Advisory Committee,
appointed by the borough assembly and city council,
has been most helpful. This body reviews site
selections, preliminary plans, and final plans and
specifications, and makes recommendations to the
assembly.

Budget relationships in Anchorage have been
relatively good, although the borough assembly did,
in 1965, reduce the borough share of the budget by
$250,000. However, the two bodies operated on the
precedents previously established in Anchorage that
the reviewing body had authority only to act on the
amount to be raised locally, and in no case did it
have authority over line items or over State and
federal funds. It should be noted that the Anchorage school budget is a comprehensive document showing all funds from all sources, all balances, and
all expenditures. The annual audit report and
financial statement is always furnished to the
assembly. In other words, "all cards are on the
table." The district maintains its own accounting
system and the assembly has not established a central treasury. There are no compelling reasons,
however, why a central treasury system and central
accounting system cannot be mutually advantageous.

Some districts, on the other hand, have had
extreme difficulties with either budgetary control,
school construction, or both. For a period in

1964 and 1965 the press in Juneau carried blow-by-
blow accounts of the disputes, most of which revolved around differences in interpretation of the
laws coupled with what might be termed "personality
clashes." Fairbanks had several skirmishes involving construction matters and budget cuts, the latter bringing forth charges that the school board
had "squirreled away" funds.

These local problems and differences had
statewide implications which inevitably found their
way to the legislative halls, particularly in the
1965 and 1966 sessions. School people in general
sought to narrow the scope of budget control by
the borough, and to obtain a stronger vote in construction matters.

There was general belief among them, in line
with prestatehood practice, that the assembly
should have review authority over only the portion
of the budget to be raised by it. With regard to
buildings there was concern that borough authorities would be obsessed with economy to the point
where educational efficiency of buildings might
become secondary. All arguments centered around
the point that school boards and school personnel,
devoting their entire time and attention to school
programs, were better equipped to determine school
needs, both financial and physical.

Most educators felt that educational matters
should all be covered in the Education Code, AS
14, which was in process of revision, rather than
in the Borough Act, AS 7. Proponents of greater
borough control took opposite stands, and another
possibility of deepening misunderstanding arose in
Senate Bill No. 101 introduced in 1965. This bill
sought to revise the Municipal Code, AS 29, to encompass boroughs, and in some versions definitely
subjugated school boards and school personnel to
the assembly or council.

In retrospect, one could not have blamed the
legislators had they become thoroughly disgusted

with the pressures and cross-currents being exerted from both sides to the point of saying, "A
plague on both your houses!" That they did not do
so can probably be attributed to the traditional
and historic concern and respect for good education which has always characterized Alaska legislatures. This was coupled with exhibitions of leadership, statesmanship, and diplomacy by some legislators and some proponents of both causes.

A combination of legislation enacted in the
1965 and 1966 sessions has eased tensions, at
least for the present. The education section of
the Borough Act was entirely rewritten in 1965 and
further amended in 1966. This combination of legislation effected the following major changes:

1. Elimination of the reference to city
school district law and the term to which school
people had objected, "except as otherwise provided
in this title." (School people felt that this reference in borough law gave the borough chairman an
opportunity to liberally interpret his powers with
respect to schools.)

2. The borough assembly may <u>require</u> school
money to be deposited in a central treasury and
can <u>request</u> the school district to operate the
central treasury.

3. With the <u>consent</u> of the school board, the
borough may provide a centralized accounting system.

4. By specifying that the assembly's determination shall be only on the amount of funds
raised <u>from local tax sources</u>, it clarifies budget
relationships. (This removes any question as to
the borough's right to determine utilization of
State or Federal funds.)

5. Makes clear the borough assembly's right
to determine school sites.

6. Makes clear that the school board selects

the architect and has responsibility for design, both subject to assembly approval.

7.   Clarifies the school board responsibility for maintenance and operation of the plant and the assembly responsibility for construction, major repair,and rehabilitation of buildings.

8.   Makes clear that the school board operates under the education code, AS 14, and has responsibility for all school employees.

These changes have clarified matters of board elections, and otherwise "cleaned up" the Education Code.   They have tended, in my opinion, toward the narrowing of areas of disagreement and the reduction of borough-school tensions.

Some borough chairmen, however, are not happy because the amendments conspicuously gave the authority to the borough assembly rather than to the borough chairman.   In a discussion at a recent Association of Alaska School Boards conference, Mr. Claude Millsap, Jr., borough chairman of Juneau, stated that this legislation would permit an assembly to override or bypass the borough chairman. This is a questionable argument since it should be assumed that this is a communications and operations problem for the assembly and chairman to solve.   Besides, the borough chairman does have a veto power .

The borough people object to the bill as written, apparently feeling that:

1.   The borough assembly should have authority to appropriate the entire budget, not just the local amounts.

2.   All construction matters should be the absolute responsibility of the borough assembly or chairman.

3.   The education code might be changed or

further amended to weaken or abort borough authority.

Objections from the school standpoint are:

1. School districts should not be subject to
any budget review by the assembly; the assembly
should be required to raise the local funds specified by the board. (This is the old fiscal independence argument which has been waged in Alaska
for years. In the opinion of this author, who has
worked under the Alaska system and others with so-
called fiscal autonomy, the argument should be
laid to rest. There are many unpleasant ramifications in systems requiring a vote of the people
for special levies, levy extensions, budget enrich-
ments, etc., which may well pose more problems
than the Alaska system.)

2. School boards should have complete authority to select sites, architects, and develop plans,
subject only to bond fund limitations.

3. Repair and rehabilitation of buildings
should be a school board responsibility.

Thus, it appears that the remaining differences still revolve around budgets and buildings.
Arguments still persist on the "you did it"--"I
didn't either" schoolboy basis. They will no
doubt continue.

It should be noted, however, that some reasonable compromises were reached, some statutory
ambiguities removed, and some procedures specified.
It should be noted, too, that nothing in the statutes prevents school boards and assemblies from
developing written procedures in the form of resolutions and ordinances similar to those in effect
in Anchorage. Nothing would prevent the assembly,
for example, from delegating authority for major
repair and rehabilitation of buildings, and perhaps even construction, to school boards.

The author, serving as a consultant to the
Association of Alaska School Boards at its October,
1966, annual meeting, urged that school boards and
borough representatives alike refrain from seeking
further legislative changes for a few years. He
stressed the point that many differences stem from
poor communication, from stubbornly holding to personal positions and viewpoints, and from failure
on the part of school boards and assemblies to
meet jointly in an attempt to develop good working
relationships. Undoubtedly, too, some differences
arise over the simple question of "who should run
the show."

Good communications cannot be legislated, nor
can people of strong will be forced into resolving
differences or developing procedures through meeting together. However, effective leadership from
the State Department of Education and the Local
Affairs Agency could bring it about, provided that
the leaders of these agencies can first agree to
reasonable interpretations and a common purpose.
If heads must be knocked together to get this type
of leadership, the Governor himself has not only
the authority but the responsibility to do so.

GENERAL PURPOSE OR SPECIAL
PURPOSE GOVERNMENT

Other contributors to this work will no doubt
stress the desirability of general purpose government and will indicate that education forces are
seeking special purpose government. They tend to
see education as a branch of local government
which is no different or more important than roads,
sewers, police protection, etc., and which should
therefore be under the direct control of the municipality and municipal executive.

We would stress not only the traditional and
historic position and development of education in
this country, but particularly note that in the
Alaska Constitution, as in that of every other state,

education is a _State_ function and a _State_ responsibility. The State cannot abdicate its responsibility by delegating complete control of education to
local government.

American law has long held to the separation
of school functions from those of municipalities.
In 78 C.J.S.*, Schools and School Districts, Sec.
25(b), it is noted that:

> As a general rule a school district,
> the school board, or other local
> school organization is a separate
> legal entity, and is entirely separ-
> ate and distinct from a city or town,
> as well as from a township, borough,
> or county which includes or is in-
> cluded in its territory, whether or
> not the two are coterminous, and even
> though they have some officers in com-
> mon or an officer of the one is ex
> officio an officer of the other.

In the case of _Wilson_ v. _School District of
Philadelphia_, 195A90, 113 A.L.R. 1401, 1406, it is
noted that:

> The school system, or school dis-
> tricts, then are but agencies of the
> state Legislature to administer this
> constitutional duty [to maintain a
> system of public schools]. As such
> agencies, they do not possess the
> governmental attributes of munici-
> palities.

Thus, it would appear that the zeal of some
to provide unique features in Alaskan government,
particularly with regard to education, should be
critically examined. We should urge some of the
late-comers to Alaska to review the tapes and
transcripts of the Constitutional Convention,
which make it quite clear that the framers of the
Constitution did not intend that education be a

---

*Editors' Note: C.J.S. is a widely used legal
encyclopedia.

subordinate and subservient arm of local government.*

The existing statutes certainly provide for
sufficient budgetary and capital improvement controls to satisfy those who insist that the borough,
as the responsible taxing unit, must be responsible
to the electorate for school costs. A school board,
elected by and responsible to this same electorate,
should certainly be given extensive authority to
establish and maintain a good school program without being unduly fettered by budgetary or facility
limitations.

There are those who hold that education, with
its far-reaching local, state, national, and international effects, deserves independent consideration rather than being mixed in helter-skelter
with the problems of sewers, water pollution,
zoning variances, dog control, etc. True, education does not operate in a vacuum and must be at-
tuned to other needs. Yet its scope and complexity
and its importance to the future deserves the attention of a school board not fettered by impossible statutes or the vagaries of another governing
body.

In Alaska, the trend in the 1961 legislature,
and in the early leadership and advice of the
Local Affairs Agency, was definitely toward the
subordination of education. The early experiences
under the Borough Act of 1963, and the obvious and
painful clashes between opposing philosophies in
school-borough relationships brought to the attention of the legislators and the public a need for
reexamination and clarification. The early trend

----

*Editors' Note: It should be noted that this
interpretation is not unanimous. Roger W. Pegues
states: "The tapes make it pretty clear that the
convention intended that education would be an integral part of local government." Letter from
Pegues to Cease.

has been reversed, and it appears that the integrity of school boards will be respected.

There will still be clashes, but the desire of the Alaskan people for a respectable and respected educational establishment will prevail.

NOTES TO CHAPTER 6

1.   Erick L. Lindman, et al., A Foundation for Alaska's Public Schools (Los Angeles, Calif.: Ford Foundation, September, 1961).

2.   Ernest Gruening, The State of Alaska (New York: Random House, 1954), chap. 17, pp. 215-16.

3.   The distribution of school children in the several school systems of Alaska is as follows: State-operated, 21 per cent (including on-base military, 14 per cent); Bureau of Indian Affairs, 8 per cent; borough school districts, 67 per cent; private denominational, 4 per cent.

4.   It should be noted, however, that the school district was responsible for the assessment of real and personal property in the area of the district outside cities.

5.   Alaska Legislative Council and Local Affairs Agency, Preliminary Report on Borough Government (Juneau: State of Alaska, December, 1960), pp. 56-59.
     [Editors' Note: Roger W. Pegues, then Director of the Local Affairs Agency, notes: "The Convention clearly wanted unification at the local level, an elimination of all special districts separate from the borough, and an elimination of duplication in function and personnel.   The Local Affairs Agency had no desire to 'subordinate'

education to local government. It very much wanted
local educational agencies to be a formal part of
local government. It objected to--and defeated--
attempts to secure fiscal independence for local
educational agencies." Letter from Pegues to Cease.]

6. Ibid., pp. 57-58.

7. The areas outside of the organized (i.e.,
incorporated) boroughs of the State are within a
single unorganized borough.

8. A Foundation for Alaska's Public Schools,
passim.

9. Ibid., p. 62.

10. Ibid., pp. 63-68.

11. Alaska, 1963 Opinions of the Attorney
General, No. 23.

12. Alaska, Local Affairs Agency, Office of
the Governor, and Department of Education (Juneau:
State of Alaska, 1963).

13. This might well be termed a biased opinion
since the writer, as superintendent of the Anchorage schools, was a central figure in effecting the
transition. However, this judgment has been supported by borough assembly members, school board
members, the local press, and various State and
local officials.

14. See Appendix F, Greater Anchorage Area
Borough Assembly-Board of Education Operating Procedures.

15. See Appendix G, resolution establishing
borough assembly-school board relationship.

CHAPTER 7 THE JUNEAU EXPERIENCE:
THE BOROUGH AS
METROPOLITAN GOVERNMENT

by Claude Millsap, Jr.

Long before Alaska became a state and Alaska's
boroughs became a reality, political scientists in
the "Lower 48" had developed the idea of metropolitan government to consolidate governmental functions, streamline local government, and save the
taxpayers' money by eliminating overlapping taxing
jurisdictions. With this thought in mind the delegates to Alaska's Constitutional Convention adopted
a concept of metropolitan areawide government they
called the borough.

It was apparent to all that this new form of
areawide local government would be fraught with
potential conflicts, particularly as it affected
existing local jurisdictions. With the hope of
reducing conflicts and encouraging borough-city
cooperation, the delegates, in drafting the borough sections, provided for city representation on
borough assemblies from city councils. Present
law gives borough areas outside first-class cities
a majority of assembly seats, but gives the council-
assemblymen from first-class cities with a majority
of borough population a weighted vote on enumerated areawide borough functions. The use of this
weighted vote has created serious problems.

In the case of the Greater Juneau Borough,
the three assembly members from the Juneau city
council together have a weighted vote of seven on
areawide matters, allowing them to override the

240

total of six votes allotted to the remaining six
members of the assembly. Unfortunately, rather
than representing the people of the Juneau area
and their best interests, the three members from
the Juneau city council have consistently supported
the city administration in its desire to retain
power and authority--despite the authority given to
the borough by law.

This, in a nutshell, is the conflict. It is
a conflict which the Juneau city administration
says is caused by "lack of necessary clarification
of borough law." I prefer to say that the conflict
has been caused by the Juneau city administration's
refusal to accept a clear and workable law which
permits maximum local determination with a minimum
of local governmental units.

In the following I will try to show what has
happened to the borough concept in the greater
Juneau area.

EARLY ORGANIZATION OF THE BOROUGH

On September 24, 1963, the voters of the
Juneau area went to the polls on a local option
basis to approve or disapprove the incorporation
of a first-class borough--with the threat that if
they did not approve, the area would become a borough anyway on January 1, 1964, under the provisions of the Mandatory Borough Act. Under mandatory incorporation, the voters simply had the option as to borough class and type of borough executive. In the September election, the people voted
for the establishment of the proposed borough and
for the chairman form of executive. However, incorporation won by a margin of only eighty-three
votes; the heaviest support came from the Juneau
city precincts and the greatest opposition from
the precincts outside the city.[1]

As borough chairman, I called the organizational meeting of the assembly on October 7, 1963.

The assembly included four councilmen--three from
the City of Juneau and one from the City of
Douglas--and five members elected from the area
outside the two cities.

From the beginning it was apparent that the
assemblymen were much influenced by the sectional-
ism so prevalent in our community, and that my
biggest job as chairman would be to act as media-
tor in keeping open conflict from breaking out.
At its first session the assembly selected members
from outside the two cities as assembly president
and vice-president. The assembly leadership was
thus to be strongly influenced by the noncity[2]
areas of the borough. In retrospect, we can see
that the lines were drawn for the conflicts that
were to arise.

From the first, I saw that I would have to
take a strong hand in the affairs of the borough,
acting not only as the elected administrator, but als
dealing with matters of policy which normally be-
long to a legislative body. The reason I took
this strong stand was because I had followed the
Borough Act in its course through the State legislature and felt that I was more familiar with the
intent of the law than the newly elected members
of the assembly. In addition, my personal background as a business executive quite naturally
made me feel that the strong executive concept,
embodied in the Borough Act, gave me the prerogative to take strong action.

At the start, organization of the assembly
necessarily fell into the newly elected chief
executive's hands, since no one else seemed to
know what should be done to organize a legislative
body. Therefore, I recommended a committee system, which I felt to be the best form for a legislative body of this type. The assembly, following
my recommendation, did incorporate procedural
rules based on the committee system and Roberts'
Rules of Order.

The first several assembly sessions were essentially organizational and educational in nature; I
used them to help educate the assembly on borough
government. Being familiar with the Borough Act
and being a serious student of municipal government,
I believed the borough to be the best form of regional or areawide government ever devised. The
areawide provisions fitted Alaska's needs perfectly,
and I expounded them vigorously both before and
after my election. As a result, the first-class
borough came to be identified with my personality.

SOURCES OF CONFLICT

During the campaign for borough incorporation,
Mayor Lauris Parker of Juneau endorsed the first-
class borough and the chairman form of administration. However, it is my frank opinion that, although he had been a member of the Metropolitan
Study Committee,[3] he failed to understand what the
borough chairman form would mean in terms of his
own political power and security.

Until the borough chairman appeared on the
scene, the mayor of Juneau had been the major local
government administrator in the Juneau area. He
enjoyed the power of making decisions affecting not
only the residents of Juneau but the residents of
other areas as well. When officials visited town,
the mayor was the first on hand to greet them and
discuss the area with them. Then along came the
borough chairman with power over a wider territory--
a man who represented not only the rural areas but
the cities of Douglas and Juneau also, and to make
matters worse, one who had more substantive power
(at least potentially) than he did--a man with whom
officials would wish to meet as they had before met
with the mayor. In short, the mayor was now forced
to share the limelight with another local executive.

Initially, I didn't realize that the mayor
would fail to understand the political factors
which could cause conflict between the chairman

and the mayor. These political factors, in fact
realities, were that a new chief executive was
created with the formation of the borough. He and
the borough would now take over some of the programs and functions formerly exercised by the mayor
and the city. These of course included the mandatory functions given to the borough under the Borough Act. I hadn't imagined that when the mayor,
the only full-time, paid mayor in Alaska, endorsed
the first-class borough and chairman form of government he didn't know what he was endorsing. To
me it was clearly stated in the law that the borough chairman would have certain duties and functions to carry out in behalf of the borough, and
further, that these would be carried out on an
areawide basis. Little did I realize that my hopes
for initiating a progressive, regional local government for the Juneau area would be so drastically
thwarted by the mayor of Juneau's fear of relin-
quishing authority. When I took office I sincere-
ly believed that there would be real cooperation
between the governmental units.

At the beginning of my term, I sent a number
of informal working papers and administrative communications to the mayor. He would then, without
discussing these matters with me, present the com-
muniqués to the council at public session and indicate his displeasure, whereupon the suggestions
were dumped. I felt this to be a violation of
confidence between two administrators.

As chairman of the State's only first-class
borough, I was invited to address the Alaska Municipal League convention in Seward on October 26,
1963. My speech was entitled "A New Look at Local
Government." It was the most naïve speech ever
made--I ended the talk with a plea that cities act
as the "big brothers" in helping the boroughs during the formative stage. The speech was well-
received, with many city councilmen and mayors,
including Juneau's chief executive, thanking me
for my cooperative stand. It didn't occur to me
that the political power groups in the cities

would immediately feel threatened, and that instead
of acting as "big brothers," many of the mayors in
the State would jealously attack the boroughs
rather than help them.

A little more than thirty days later I was to
wonder if cooperation was to be a one-way street
in favor of the Juneau city administrators.

PROPERTY TAX ASSESSMENT
AND COLLECTION

At the initial assembly meetings in October,
1963, there were some minor skirmishes caused by
Juneau's representatives in trying to assert city
power and influence on the assembly. I requested
that the borough assume planning and zoning by
November 1, 1963, education by December 1, 1963,
and property tax assessment and collection by January 1, 1964. The city representatives immediately
threw up roadblocks, especially on assessment and
collection and planning and zoning.

A variety of reasons was given by the Juneau
council members to justify their attempts at halt-
ing the assumption of these powers. It was their
feeling, for instance, that collection of taxes
could best be handled by contracting with the city
for a year. They stuck to this line although it
was contrary to advice from the borough attorney.
One of the members of the Juneau council, referring
to the proposed borough assessment and collection
ordinance, stated he "wouldn't vote for something
that had just been presented to him," although I
pointed out that the assumption of this power had
been under discussion for several weeks. This is
typical of the negative reaction of these men whenever the borough has tried to assume a function or
power.

The mayor, meanwhile, was not idle. He took
action (in the background) to control the borough
administration through the city council members on

the assembly. When he felt that his political identity was threatened, he took the course that many elected leaders would take under the same circumstances to protect their political security: divide and conquer.

It became clear that, since the city members of the assembly appeared to be under the control of the city administration, I had the fight of my political life in order to maintain my position as an effective chairman. The city members had control over many of the programs proposed by me through their bloc use of the weighted vote. I honestly admit that I failed to see how three men could so consistently disregard what was the best for the people of the area. They represented the city administration's point of view. This was a long way from representing all of the people of the borough; a borough of which the city was a major part, but still only a part.

The borough was already in the business of collecting tax monies outside of the cities, and the addition of the areas within the cities would cause no noticeable increase in percentage cost to the borough, but would substantially cut the cost of city administration. Finally the assembly did assume the power of assessment and collection, but with the city-influenced stipulations that the city continue to collect property taxes until July 1, 1964, and that the chairman be authorized to enter into contractual agreements with the cities and special districts to permit them to continue exercising this power until that date. This unwieldy arrangement was purely an administrative block on the part of the mayor.

This was the first major conflict between the city administration and myself.

An editorial in the Juneau Alaska Empire of January 6, 1964, began:

> We think the arrangements made so
> far by the City of Juneau and the

> Greater Juneau Borough in the field
> of assessment and taxation are rea-
> sonable and proper, but we are dis-
> turbed by a feeling of the city ad-
> ministration that the city needs a
> full time tax collector and will
> always need a full time tax collec-
> tor. Why?

The editorial went on to criticize the city and
mayor, outlining the Borough Act and stating that
the city should turn to the borough for the collection of all taxes and should turn over such areawide powers to the borough as would be workable,
thus cutting the overhead of the city. In a letter
to the editor, Mayor Parker attempted to justify
his position. He pointed out that the borough
should collect "borough" taxes only, and further,
that it was necessary for the city to have a full-
time tax collector since the city was still in the
business of collecting delinquent property taxes
as well as incidental water and sewer hook-up fees.
He said that the council had also indicated through
the budget and instructions to the administration
that it wished to "go into the field auditing of
certain businesses to determine whether or not all
of the sales tax due the City of Juneau is being
paid." Mayor Parker went on to state that "during
the next few years while we are growing and expanding we must properly manage the collection and use
of our sales tax funds or our capital improvement
program will suffer," and closed by asking the
editor if he "would care to suggest some other plan
of action to meet the needs of this important part
of our city administration." When the mayor referred to the collection of delinquent property
taxes in his letter, he said, "I have been told
informally that the borough does not want this job of
collection." As of this writing the borough, although
handling the collection of all real property taxes
(except the City of Juneau's delinquent property
taxes), still cannot get from the city its delinquent
property tax records. These records are a necessity
for the borough's tax administration, yet despite

repeated demands the city has continued to collect
its delinquent property taxes.

Although the City of Douglas turned over the
administration and collection of its sales tax to
the borough, the City of Juneau has failed to take
advantage of this area of cooperation and administrative savings and has, in fact, increased its
staff. This situation requires that two sales tax
forms be sent out, bringing duplication and added
costs to the businessmen of Juneau. Ironically,
the city has the law on its side. Although the
Borough Act requires the areawide collection of
property taxes by the borough, it makes no such
provision for sales taxes. My personal opinion is
that this was an oversight on the part of the legislature.*

CITY-BOROUGH CONFLICT AND
THE WEIGHTED VOTE

In the borough assembly minutes of December 4,
1963, can be found the record of an attempt by the
Juneau administration to gain control of the borough through the city's representatives on the
assembly.

As borough chairman, I had requested the borough attorney to review the law in reference to
collection of taxes. He concluded that the borough
needed an emergency ordinance[4] to provide for the
exercise of the property tax assessment and

----

*Editors' Note: Roger W. Pegues commented:
"Ironically, the draftsmen [of the Borough Act]
left sales tax collection and enforcement with the
cities because it afforded what appeared to be an
excellent opportunity for an uncomplicated, easy
transfer of functions from city [at city option]
to borough. It seemed wise to provide local officials with a few 'easy' transfers so as to gain
experience for later more difficult transfers."
Letter from Pegues to Cease.

collection function. The attorney's review and
opinion was that, although the borough had an agreement with the city for collection of taxes by the
city, it couldn't allow collection under the city's
ordinance but would have to have its own.

It was on this matter that the weighted vote
was first employed. The episode marked the beginning of many instances when the weighted vote would
be used. In one meeting the borough attorney gave
an opinion that the collection function would have
to be discharged by someone on the borough payroll,
whereupon a Juneau council-assemblyman made the following statement: "This is not the opinion of the
City of Juneau administration." (This statement
was heard again and again as the Juneau administration consistently disagreed with legal opinions relating to the borough, including those of the State
Attorney General.) A motion was made that the borough administration perform the collection function,
but it failed on a weighted vote, even though the
majority of the members present were in favor of
passage. The weighted vote was used in this instance to protect the political power of the City
of Juneau and perhaps the interests of some city
property owners who feared that the borough would
reappraise their property. Clearly the city abused
its power.

The Weighted Vote as Veto

The weighted vote has come to be used effectively as a veto tactic to prevent such programs
as areawide sanitation and areawide recreation.
In a more subtle sense, it has been used in cutting
the borough administration's proposed budgets,
thereby curtailing programs and hindering the
natural progression of the borough in providing
both areawide and nonareawide services.

A major dispute and use of the weighted vote
centered on the sales tax ordinance introduced in
March, 1964. The borough attorney and an official
of the Local Affairs Agency pointed out that the

independent school district sales tax[5] could be expanded into an areawide borough tax.[6] After much discussion the assembly directed the attorney to investigate the old school district sales tax ordinance, as well as the sales tax ordinances of Juneau and Douglas. A new ordinance was subsequently introduced with my personal notation that it was the only one which could legally be adopted. A motion was made and seconded by Juneau's councilassemblymen that the ordinance be tabled. The motion to table carried unanimously. I believe that the unanimous vote to table the ordinance came about simply because the other assemblymen wanted to see what the Juneau councilmen had "up their sleeves."

Then the trap was sprung. The City of Juneau councilmen introduced a substitute sales tax ordinance which was nothing more than a revision of the Juneau sales tax ordinance. This was done in spite of the warning to the assembly by the attorney and me that it would be legally impossible to use the City of Juneau's sales tax ordinance because of its use tax provisions. (As a home-rule municipality, the City of Juneau can levy such a tax, but a general law borough or city cannot.) There were other questionable provisions, but the city insisted that its revised ordinance be passed. Although the ordinance was attacked by the Douglas council-assemblyman and the noncity assemblymen, it was nonetheless unanimously approved for consideration at a later meeting. This seeming inconsistency can be attributed to several factors. The assemblymen from outside the City of Juneau apparently felt that they had no alternative but to approve the ordinance for subsequent consideration. They were hamstrung by the weighted vote, and possibly thought that a serious discussion of the ordinance would change the thinking of the Juneau council-assemblymen.

The ridiculous pervaded the next assembly meeting (a special meeting) when, as a start, it took over two hours to approve the minutes of the

previous meeting. The Juneau council-assemblymen
argued that a special meeting required a special
agenda and no regular business could be considered.
The presiding officer, referring to procedures
adopted by the assembly and Roberts' Rules of Order,
ruled against the Juneau representatives. Then the
real surprise was sprung. The City of Juneau members wanted the weighted vote applied to the approval of the minutes. After a long and fiery
discussion it was determined, however, that the
weighted vote did not apply to the minutes and the
presiding officer's decision stood.

The basic controversy, however, centered
around the fact that the sales tax ordinance introduced by the borough chairman had been tabled,
and a substitute ordinance introduced. A move was
made to kill the substitute ordinance by the noncity assemblymen on the grounds that it had not
been properly introduced. After further discussion, a motion was made to withdraw the substitute
ordinance. Since the weighted vote had been used
to table both the original ordinance and the substitution of the city sales tax ordinance, the
weighted vote was allowed again, and the motion
failed 7 to 6. This was a perfect weighted vote
case, since the City of Juneau's three men (with
2-1/3 votes each) outvoted the other six members
of the assembly.[7]

The intensity of this conflict is reflected
in the resignation of the borough attorney. In a
letter to the borough chairman on April 17, he
stated:

> The borough is a general law borough,
> having not yet adopted a home rule
> charter. Consequently it has the
> powers expressly granted to it by
> the legislature, together with such
> additional powers as are necessarily
> implied from such express grants of
> power.
>   I have previously discussed

with you various aspects, as well as
the scope and application, of the
Juneau sales tax ordinance, and why
the borough cannot lawfully enact a
substantially similar ordinance.
The Juneau ordinance relies on home
rule powers to support certain of
its provisions. To the extent of
such reliance on home rule powers
the borough, as a general law municipality, may not lawfully follow.

The attorney then indicated specific provisions
of Juneau's sales tax ordinance which were not
permitted under Alaska law to general law municipalities. He concluded:

It is further apparent that the
Juneau sales tax ordinance cannot
be imposed in the borough for
school purposes, because it is a
different tax than was authorized
by the voters for school purposes
at referendum.
        Having previously pointed out
all of the foregoing to you, and
through you to the assembly, and
directly to the assembly in the
emergency ordinance prepared by
me, I could presumably ignore my
beliefs as to what constitutes lawful legislation for the borough
and prepare the ordinance as
directed. Because I cannot conscientiously do so, I accordingly
submit my resignation as borough
attorney to become effective immediately.[8]

The Juneau council-assemblymen had consistently ignored the attorney's recommendations. No one
could blame him for his resignation.

The frequent use of the weighted vote by

Juneau council-assemblymen became so disruptive
that questions as to the application of the
weighted vote had to be settled. The assembly
president ruled: "that all items of business pertaining to the assembly will carry the one vote of
each member of the assembly, providing a quorum is
present, and further, that any questions, ordinances
or subjects that deal directly with an areawide
power will carry the weighted vote."[9]

This ruling was to be questioned by the Juneau
council-assemblymen again and again in subsequent
meetings. It and other procedural items eventually
led the City of Juneau to file a civil action
against the Greater Juneau Borough.[10]

Budget Battles

The next major conflict arose over the budget
I presented for fiscal year 1964-65. Rather than
considering the staff costs necessary to carry out
the three mandatory powers of the borough by reducing the city's budget to reflect the loss of
these functions, the Juneau council-assemblymen
struck at the borough by cutting the borough budget.

I presented the budget document to the assembly on May 20, 1964. The hearing for the appropriation ordinance in connection with the budget was
set for a week later; the ordinance called for a
total appropriation of $210,500. At the hearing,
the only changes suggested by the assembly were
the addition of a $10,000 contingency fund and a
possible recreation appropriation. The hearing on
the appropriation ordinance was continued until
the following meeting, at which time the Juneau
council-assemblymen and one noncity assemblyman
took everyone by surprise when they voted against
the appropriation ordinance, and moved to amend it
by cutting the total appropriation to $160,000.
At no time prior to this surprise action had there
been any indication of dissatisfaction with my
proposed budget. I vetoed the action and cited
the assembly's irresponsibility in reducing the

budget.   This veto was overridden by the weighted
vote.[11]

ADDITIONAL CONFLICTS

In the 1965-66 budget the borough administration proposed the acquisition of areawide recreation and library responsibilities.   Instead of
investigating the merit of this idea, the city
administration through the council-assemblymen
made it clear that the proposal would be an "invasion" of the city's powers and thus unacceptable.

The mayor of Juneau stated that the city
council had, on several occasions, discussed two
functions which it felt could very well be taken
over by the borough.   These were dog control and
operation of the municipal cemetery.[12]   To date,
these are the only two powers which the city has
been willing to relinquish.   (Immediately after
the borough took over the dog control function,
the Juneau city council began to point out that
it had been handled more efficiently by the city.)

At about this time (1965), the city began a
campaign to make the borough administration appear
anticity.   The campaign seemed plausible to many
because even today it is difficult for some city
residents to realize that borough chairmen represent the citizens of cities just as mayors do.
Evidently, they felt that the borough chairman's
concern for the cities was secondary.   This, of
course, is not the case.   Cities represent the
largest tax base and the largest concentration of
voters.   Thus economic and political realities demand that the chairmen must always fully consider
the cities.   In Juneau it has never been possible
to get the city administration to recognize the
tax advantages of spreading the costs of services
over the larger tax base, thereby lowering costs
to the cities.   My efforts to bring about such
economies and efficiencies have been consistently
interpreted by the Juneau municipal government as
"anticity."

Perhaps the most intense and drawn-out conflict between borough and city developed over the borough administration's program for the re-evaluation
of properties in 1965.   Re-evaluation was badly
needed since it had not been undertaken for eleven
years, and assessments were neither uniform throughout the borough nor was property appraised at full
market value as required by the Alaska Statutes.
Equally important, the cities needed the increased
value in their tax base for future capital improvement bond issues. The borough itself had the same
need, as two elementary schools and two junior
high schools would have to be built within the
next seven years.

It can probably be stated as a general rule
of American government that re-evaluation of property is always politically disadvantageous to those
in office at the time. In this instance, the City
of Juneau chose to attack the borough for doing
what in fact it itself had failed to do for eleven
years.

The Board of Equalization held twenty-eight
meetings from May through October, 1965. Everything went smoothly until the tenth meeting, by
which time most of the property owners' protests
had been heard. Then a Juneau council-assemblyman
raised a question concerning the weighted vote and
stated that the weighted vote should apply on all
equalization matters. However, the chair ruled
all actions and motions of the board to be procedural; thus the weighted vote would not apply.
The member raising the question then voiced an
official protest to the ruling, stated that he
was "no longer present," and asked to be excused.
There were even suggestions from the non-Juneau
members that the board disband until an Attorney
General's opinion on the weighted vote could be
obtained.

Throughout the next eighteen meetings, the
weighted vote question was to be raised time and
time again, with the City of Juneau members and
one noncity assemblyman voting as a bloc.

Eventually, an Attorney General's opinion[13] holding that the weighted vote did not apply to Board of Equalization proceedings was issued. However, the undercurrent of hostility still hovered over the 1966 board and although more cooperation was extended by Juneau's representatives on the assembly, the procedure was obviously still not acceptable to the city.

BOROUGH-SCHOOL RELATIONS

The borough administration made a proposal in August, 1964, for a central treasury and an accounting system consolidating the accounting functions of the general government and the school district.* Never was more idealism and political naïveté shown by an elected chief executive. Having become chairman with intentions of using the management tools I had learned in the business world, I rushed in where angels fear to tread.

Consolidation of this type is extremely desirable, but its execution is difficult when one runs into an old and integrated organization such as a school district. Before the assembly approved the treasury and accounting proposal, the school district board and administration called upon PTA members and teachers to fight the "invasion of education." As hard as it is to believe, the school people tagged the borough and members of the assembly as antieducation. By the time the political smoke had cleared away, the assembly had adopted a resolution approving a central treasury and calling for a central accounting system. The central accounting feature was never carried out because, at the urging of school officials throughout the entire State, the State legislature intervened,

---

*Editors' Note: For further discussion of centralized treasury and accounting, see Chapter 4, written by Robert J. Dupere.

passing legislation that required the consent of a
school board to establish central accounting. I
am sorry that the school district chose to resist
centralized accounting so strongly, since, in my
opinion, it is the answer to many accounting problems.

Conflict between the borough and the school
district appears in other instances. The difficulty
of convincing the school people that education is a
part of general government manifests itself most
sharply during budget considerations. When budget
hearings are held, many of the school people appear,
begging that costs be held down by the general government, but urging approval of the school budget
with no cuts.

I must add, though, that although many battles
took place with the borough administration and
assembly on one side, and the school district on
the other, reasonable relationships were eventually
developed, and today I believe we have good cooperation and most of our basic problems have been
eliminated.

PLANNING AND ZONING

The planning and zoning power was assumed by
the Greater Juneau Borough during the early months
of 1964, when cooperation seemed to be the order
of the day. Conflict came later over a "transitional" clause designed to ensure continuation of
city planning efforts already underway. It was
known that the City of Juneau had a contract with
a consulting firm for the preparation of a comprehensive plan. Further, the borough's embryonic
planning staff had its hands full with the problems of the areas outside the cities of Juneau and
Douglas. This was the reason for the transitional
section of the borough's planning and zoning ordinance, which provided:

Sec. 49.40.010. Transition. The
comprehensive plans, building codes

regulating minimum construction,
heating, lighting and other requirements and specifications and other
building and land use regulations
adopted by ordinance in the cities
of Juneau and Douglas shall remain
in effect until superseded by ordinance of the borough. (AS 07.10.140)

A conflict soon developed because the City of
Juneau was continuing to do its own planning administration, using this transitional section as justification. The wording of the transitional clause
specifying that the cities shall continue these
functions "until superseded by ordinance of the
borough" once again raised the spectre of the
weighted vote, for we knew that the Juneau council-
assemblymen would effectively veto any such borough ordinance. This knowledge tied the hands of
the borough.

Later, the administration of the City of
Juneau announced that a city planner had been
hired. Further, the city's contract with the
Alaska State Housing Authority* included the preliminary planning for an urban renewal project.
This raised the question as to who had authority
for the final approval of the general land-use
plan for the urban renewal project. I believed
that the borough assembly's approval would be required. AS 07.15.340, Planning and Zoning, states:
"(a) The first and second class borough has the
responsibility of planning, platting, and zoning
on an areawide basis." Thus, in my opinion, the
planning aspects of the project were clearly not
subject to approval by the city council. The city
challenged this interpretation.

---

*Editors' Note: The Alaska State Housing
Authority is the public corporation responsible
for administering "701" planning, public housing,
and urban renewal programs for municipalities
throughout the State.

The Attorney General was asked for an opinion. Although his opinion[14] affirmed the borough's jurisdiction, the city administration steadfastly refuses to concede. Thus the project remains in limbo and the split between the mayor and the borough chairman has become permanent. Actually, the jurisdictional question was politically advantageous to the mayor, for substantial opposition to the urban renewal project had developed in the project area. The city administration and council could thus retreat gracefully, placing the blame squarely on the borough.

One other important conflict, bringing out again the recalcitrant attitude of the city, should be cited here. In December, 1964, without any prior consultation, the City of Juneau filed an application with the Local Affairs Agency and Local Boundary Commission for a boundary change. The plan was to annex a strip of the Gastineau Channel (covered by water) and hook up with the city-owned airport 10 miles distant from the city. This finger annexation would have subsequently made it possible to "strip annex" valuable taxable properties along the way and also block good areawide planning. In my opinion, this was a most stupid political blunder by the City of Juneau, for the power grab was clear enough for all citizens to understand.

The Juneau council-assemblymen had not made it known to the assembly that annexation was being considered. This is simply incredible, considering that the members of the assembly from outside the city would be directly affected by such a move. Also, the city administration ignored the borough administration and the borough's planning and zoning responsibilities.

Ultimately, the annexation petition was rejected by the Local Boundary Commission as an obvious gerrymander. The affair indicates, once again, the lack of cooperation so often displayed by the city and the almost malevolent attitude of the city administration toward the borough.

The effect of this abortive annexation maneuver
was to focus attention on the de facto planning being done by the city in apparent disregard of the
borough's areawide planning and zoning responsibilities.

THE BUILDING CODE

In the budget for fiscal 1965-66, the borough
administration proposed that building code enforcement be carried out on an areawide basis. The
proposal was based on the fact that building codes
and zoning are interdependent, since no building
permit can be (or should be) issued that fails to
comply with zoning. In fact, in many municipalities the zoning enforcement officer is the building inspector. The borough assembly funded this
item in the 1965-66 budget and adopted a building
code.

However, the Juneau council-assemblymen soon
made it clear that areawide building code enforcement was not acceptable. With the weighted vote
available to enforce this contention, the assembly
had to pass a nonareawide ordinance with the provision that a contractual agreement be drawn up
with the city building inspector to enforce the
borough ordinances in the areas outside the city.
This was to prove unworkable because no one person
can be responsible to two administrators with different notions of enforcement.

The borough administration again proposed
building code enforcement on an areawide basis for
fiscal 1966-67. Again, although it received consideration, the concept was opposed by the city
administration and was not adopted by the assembly.

One month later, the Attorney General issued
an opinion that building code enforcement was an
areawide function of the borough under the planning

and zoning power.[15] Realizing that financial support through the borough budget was impossible for
fiscal 1966-67 (since the appropriation had already been made on a nonareawide basis), I called
a meeting with the mayors of Juneau and Douglas.
This meeting resulted in an agreement that the
cities would continue enforcing their own building
code ordinances for 1966-67, but that before any
building permit would be issued, the city inspector
would check with the borough zoning administrator
on zoning compliance. These agreements are in
force until 1967-68, when it is expected that the
building code will be enforced on an areawide
basis. Cooperation was achieved in this case, but
only through the leverage of an Attorney General's
opinion.

ADDITIONAL PROBLEMS

In the three years of its operation, the borough administration has made areawide proposals
and recommendations in the following fields: dog
control (now assumed), library services (the
City of Juneau has the only functioning library
which is used by all borough citizens), police,
public health, airport, and wharfs and docks (all
of which the city presently retains).

A signal lack of cooperation was the refusal
of the City of Juneau to support the borough administration's application for a water and sewer
facility grant in an outlying area which had been
approved by the assembly. The proposal was to
plan for that specific system and at the same
time plan for a larger total areawide system as
required by the Department of Housing and Urban
Development under P.L. 89-117. Despite the fact
that this was a thirty-year plan and the city, by
not cooperating, would cut its own percentage of
Federal funding from 50 per cent to 30 per cent
on the city's sewage treatment plant, the city administration held up passage of a required cooperative resolution. Because delay would have lost

the borough these Federal funds, the borough was
forced to capitulate and agree that the city engineering department would have final approval
over the engineering plans for the system. No one
could convince the city's administration and council that the immediate and specific program would
not obligate the city's credit.

Another recent conflict has been over the
hospital. The Sisters of St. Ann notified the
City of Juneau that the Order could not maintain
the one existing hospital for longer than a two-
year period. Consequently, the mayor appointed a
committee composed of interested citizens of Juneau
and three members of the council to study the problem. The committee quickly recommended that the
hospital (and the hospital power) be turned over
to the borough and the costs spread areawide. The
City of Juneau administration has since been anything but helpful, even though the city council
approved the transfer of the hospital power to the
borough.

After investigation, the borough administration concluded that a community hospital should
include a community public health facility. The
city administration expressed opposition immediately. Why? Perhaps to protect the city's own community public health center, which is housed in
inadequate quarters.

Rather than taking a realistic and logical
approach--spreading the cost of this facility over
the entire community--the city chose to continue
to provide sole support for it. This position is
absurd, as it commits the city taxpayers to full
support of a facility which has areawide use. The
City of Douglas passed a requested ordinance transferring the health power, but the City of Juneau
continued to hold its position for over two months
and finally won a questionable victory. The borough assembly was forced to accept the transfer
without the addition of the health power. Thus
the borough will be building a $4.9 million

facility without a community public health center.

This illustrates a crucial defect in the Borough Act. The only way a first-class borough may
acquire additional areawide powers is with the con-
currence of the cities within its boundaries. A
second-class borough, however, may acquire both
additional areawide and nonareawide responsibilities by vote of the people. Thus a first-class
borough must depend on the willingness of cities
to transfer functions to it. This, as we have
seen, does not happen when a city chooses to jealously guard its political position. At least a
second-class borough may go to the people for a
decision.

CONCLUSIONS

In conclusion, it can be seen that the city
will never willingly relinquish its powers, functions, and services to the borough, even though it
is obviously to the city's advantage to spread the
rising costs of city services over the larger tax
base of the borough. The city administration apparently feels that what has worked for the city
for forty years is still good enough.

Some progress may be forthcoming, as a committee has been appointed to study the entire complex question of city-borough merger and/or consolidation. My hope is that this committee will
arrive at the answer and present to the assembly
and city councils a workable and equitable solution.

I believe that in the end this borough will,
perhaps through the work of this committee, become
a home-rule borough, with the cities becoming service areas under one administration.

NOTES TO CHAPTER 7

1. In the space of only three years, there has been a dramatic shift in this pattern of support. In an opinion poll placed on the October 4, 1966, ballot, the rural areas gave heaviest support to the concept of the borough as the sole unit of areawide government, with the Juneau city precincts showing a marked reduction in their earlier support. Voters in these precincts indicated support for an areawide city.

2. Though both the cities of Juneau and Douglas are within the borough, the reference to "noncity" areas applies only to the City of Juneau because the City of Douglas has usually voted with the assemblymen from outside the City of Juneau.

3. The Metropolitan Study Committee was a citizens' study group created around 1960 to consider ways to unify the greater Juneau area.

4. Emergency ordinances are effective immediately.

5. A 1 per cent sales tax levied within the school district, but outside the city limits. AS 07.10.140(d) provides that "Each borough assembly shall determine the future use of any sales tax levied by an independent school district. It may make all or any part of the sales tax an areawide sales tax for areawide functions and all or any part of the sales tax a tax limited to the area outside cities only for functions limited to the area outside cities."

6. The old independent school district sales tax was subsequently expanded into an areawide sales tax.

7. Finally, it took a compromise ordinance, which was nothing more than a version of the old school district sales tax ordinance, to settle the issue. The ordinance was finally adopted on October 28, 1964.

8.   Letter from F. O. Eastaugh, borough attorney, to Claude Millsap, Jr., borough chairman, Juneau, Alaska, April 17, 1964.

9.   Greater Juneau Borough Assembly Minutes, April 22, 1964, p. 4, par. 12.

10.   City of Juneau v. Greater Juneau Borough, Civil Action No. 65-317, Superior Court, First Judicial District, Alaska.

11.   To override a veto requires a two-thirds vote. The city thus needed help from a noncity assemblyman. One particular noncity assemblyman, on record as opposing the borough, has consistently voted with the City of Juneau council-assemblymen.

12.   The borough administration is not interested in taking over the cemetery function. But, it is worth noting that a number of borough assemblymen have indicated a willingness to assume an additional areawide power or two as a device to establish a precedent for assumption of other powers at a later date, even if they are expensive or difficult to administer.

13.   1965 Opinions of the Attorney General, No. 7.

14.   Letter to T. E. Elliott, Executive Director, Alaska State Housing Authority, from Warren C. Colver, Attorney General, Juneau, Alaska, October 6, 1964.

15.   1966 Opinions of the Attorney General, No. 5.

CHAPTER **8** THE JUNEAU EXPERIENCE:
THE CITY AS
METROPOLITAN GOVERNMENT

by Joseph R. Henri

At the outset, it is important to distinguish
between things as they are and things as they ought
to be in the sphere of Alaskan local government.
At the time of this writing, we have boroughs and
we have cities. There are nine boroughs in all,
covering only a small portion of the land surface
of the State. Within all but one of the boroughs,
there is at least one first-class city. In many
boroughs there is more than one such city, and
some of those cities have home-rule charters. The
major boroughs contain a central core city, unincorporated urbanized and urbanizing satellite de-
velopments, and a great deal of rural, sparsely
settled,or even uninhabited land.

This capsule description applies to the
Greater Juneau Borough, of which the City of Juneau
is the core and a part. Within the Juneau borough
there is one other first-class city, Douglas, whose
boundaries on two sides are coterminous with the
City of Juneau's. Both are home-rule cities.
"Things as they are" in the Greater Juneau Borough
means two contiguous home-rule cities, suburban
areas more or less adjacent to the cities, and,
toward the outer limits of the borough, uninhabited
forest preserve.

The discussion that follows will center on
cooperation and conflict in the present setting--
with reference to things as they are. Whether

anyone is satisfied with things as they are is a
different, but closely related,matter. Whenever
conflict arises between the city and the borough,
the question of things as they ought to be is as
important as the problem causing the conflict in
the here and now. Hence, no one concerned with
Alaskan local government is ever very far from
questions of change in relationships between various municipal corporations. In the context of conflict, and even of cooperation, local officials
are always looking for a better way, a better
statutory ordering of local government affairs.
There is no doubt that a more satisfactory solution can be found, but there is strong disagreement as to what it is.

One from outside Alaska may well wonder why
we do so much thinking about "what ought to be."
He may question our practicality: whether we are
concerned with solving the immediate problems of
our constituents, or whether we would rather dream
than work.

Alaska has been a sovereign State only
since 1959. During its later Territorial days,
the sole municipal corporation known to it was
the city.[1]

Borough governments, with the exception of
the Bristol Bay Borough, did not come into being
as municipal corporations until the fifth year of
statehood. Borough government is thus barely over
three years old.* The 1961 legislature presented
Alaskans with the original "voluntary" Borough
Act, but from 1961 through the major part of 1963,
only one area of the State had availed itself of
the privilege of creating a borough. Though more
than two years had elapsed in which a borough
could have been formed in any section of the State

---

*Editors' Note: Four boroughs were three
years old in September, 1966, and four on January
1, 1967.

through the local initiative of the people, no serious attempt was made to do so, even though the issue had been given much attention in the press and by various study groups. People were chary of any additional government. With the advent of the borough, residents outside city limits would have local government for the first time. Most of them preferred no government, stating that they had moved beyond the boundaries of cities, and had opposed annexation over the years, in order to avoid the jurisdiction of local government. In 1963 the vast majority of Alaskans still thought of the borough as a possibly useful tool for sometime in the future, but something which was not needed then. Nevertheless, the legislature of that year further implemented the constitutional provisions, and created eight "mandatory" boroughs. Citizens in the eight locales were given no choice. The law provided that by January 1, 1964, each of the eight areas would have a borough.* So the borough is a very new government in the forty-ninth State, and most Alaskans look upon it as an experiment.

The constitutional provisions in Article X, the local government section, provide only the broadest guidelines: that the State will be divided into boroughs (organized or unorganized); that the borough's legislature will be called the assembly; that first-class and home-rule cities shall be represented on the assembly by one or more members of the city council. The rest is left to the legislature.

Few if any Alaskans are content with the borough legislation as it stands. This is the explanation for the acute interest in things as they ought to be. The legislature might well be interested in statutory changes if good ones are proposed.

---

*Editors' Note: Four of these areas actually incorporated under local option. The imminent threat of mandatory incorporation, however, was a stimulus in these "voluntary" incorporations.

This paper will deal not only with cooperation and conflict between the city and the borough,
but also with needed changes, legislative and
otherwise.

Under current legislation,[2] boroughs may be
first- or second-class, depending on what a majority of the borough's voters desire. The Greater
Juneau Borough is the only first-class borough in
the State. Had it not been for the support of
Juneau city residents at the time of the local option borough incorporation election, the greater
Juneau area would have become a second-class borough under mandatory incorporation. Most people
outside the City of Juneau, knowing that by legislative edict the area must have a borough, wanted
the one with the least power over their affairs,
namely a second-class borough.

While the Greater Juneau Borough is a first-
class municipal corporation, no home-rule charter
has been adopted. The powers of this borough, as
in all others, are delegated by the State legislature. Each borough, whether first- or second-
class, must assume the areawide powers of (1) education; (2) tax collecting and assessing as to
real and personal property; and (3) planning,
platting, and zoning. The home-rule provision of
the Alaska Constitution is simple but broad: "A
home rule borough or city may exercise all legislative powers not prohibited by law or by charter."
(Art. X, sec. 11) With very few statutory limitations enacted, a local government's home-rule
power may be as extensive as the charter commission
chooses to make it. Each locale with its peculiar
problems can adjust its laws and procedures to
meet them without the necessity of going to the
State legislature.

While all boroughs may acquire additional
areawide powers, the method of doing so differs
with the class of the borough. In the case of a
first-class borough such as Juneau, areawide powers other than the three mandatory functions are

gained only by the <u>transfer</u> of particular powers
by the first-class cities to the borough.[3]

The Greater Juneau Borough, besides the three
functions set out in the Borough Act, exercises
the areawide hospital power because of a transfer
of that function from the two first-class cities
of Juneau and Douglas. Further, the borough has
assumed the areawide dog control power, as permitted by specific State legislation.[4] The borough
exercises a number of the powers of first-class
cities in areas outside the corporate limits of
Juneau and Douglas, the so-called nonareawide
powers. Hence in a locale having a total 1960
census population of 9,745,[5] there are three separate municipal corporations exercising the nonareawide powers of first-class cities. Overlaid
upon this configuration is one of these same municipal corporations (the borough) carrying out five
areawide functions in both the city and noncity
areas.

THE HISTORICAL BACKGROUND

Before pinpointing specific instances of conflict or cooperation between the local government
entitled in the Juneau area, it is helpful to
grasp the political psychology and atmosphere in
which the three municipal corporations exist. The
City of Juneau was founded in 1900, and Douglas
shortly thereafter. The Greater Juneau Borough
came into being in 1963--more than sixty years
after Juneau.

Since 1906 the City of Juneau has been the
capital of Alaska. It has enjoyed prominence over
the years not only as the major city of southeastern Alaska, but also as the capital of the Territory and of the State. Its political, business,
and social leaders have far more prestige and influence than would normally be expected from a
town so small in population. The seat of State
government lies within Juneau's city limits.

Federal activities in Alaska spread out from
Juneau and dignitaries, foreign and domestic,
having dealings with Alaska are hosted here.

Because of the concentration of government
agencies and their workers, the city's economy has
been strong and steady, giving rise to some satis-
faction if not complacency. Juneau's political
leaders, aided by the Chamber of Commerce and other
interested groups, have sought to diversify the
economic base by attracting industries which would
more fully develop the area's multitude of natural
resources.

Douglas, like Juneau, came into being because
of the discovery of large quantities of gold near-
by. In the early years of the century, Douglas
was, for a time, bigger than Juneau. Friendly
and unfriendly rivalries, intense and casual, have
existed between the sister cities since their
founding. Douglas is bounded by Juneau on two
sides, and though it has now dwindled in importance as a city, there is no serious thought among
the leaders of that city about consolidating with
Juneau. The two cities continue to stand apart,
although Juneau's political leaders have made
overtures from time to time toward uniting the two.
Douglas' chief function today is to serve as a
so-called bedroom community for Juneau. In comparison with Juneau, the tax and economic base,
as well as the population of Douglas, is small.

During the early years of statehood, study
committees in various communities including Juneau
met to discuss what borough government should be.
Article X, sec. 2, of the Constitution provides
that "all local government powers shall be vested
in boroughs and cities," and "the State may delegate taxing powers to organized boroughs and
cities only." Alaskans had had experience with
cities, but no one had ever lived in a borough
because it was a new and somewhat different
creation. During its years as a customs district
and a Territory--ninety-six in all--Alaska never

had an intermediate or county form of government.
The constitutional fathers hoped that the "borough"
would fill the void between city and State government, and would avoid some of the pitfalls of
county government as it is known in the older
states. That is why they chose a name other than
"county." But the constitutional delegates did
not say specifically what the borough should be.
This was left to the legislature. Finally, the
State legislature enacted the Voluntary Borough
Act in 1961.

The Juneau area was one of the eight locales
selected by the 1963 legislature for the creation
of a "mandatory" borough. Juneau, like the seven
other areas of the State, was told that if it did
not adopt a borough voluntarily prior to October 1,
1963, it would have borough government anyway.
Under imminent threat of the imposition of a borough by the State legislature, the people of the
greater Juneau area chose a first-class borough
in September, 1963. This borough was an unwanted
child; the people of the cities by and large
thought that they already had enough government,
and those of the noncity areas thought that any
local government was too much. To compound the
problems, there were tensions and enmities between
the urban and nonurban sectors. These are not
peculiar to Juneau, or even to Alaska, but arise
out of the same conditions which have contributed
to acrimony between core cities and outlying areas
throughout the United States. The so-called country people were content with fewer benefits in return for lower taxes; the city people considered
that they subsidized the surrounding areas by
affording them free library service, an adequate
international airport, and other municipal services. These services were rendered to everyone
in the greater Juneau area regardless of where
the individual beneficiary lived.

But the Greater Juneau Borough became a
reality and a new set of political leaders and
figures now shares the limelight with those of

the city. These politicians are making decisions
intimately affecting residents of the cities, as
well as the area which previously had no general
local government.

The City of Juneau has the so-called strong-
mayor form of government with a full-time mayor.
The mayor found himself confronted with another
local government leader, the borough chairman, who
could exercise his areawide powers inside as well
as outside the city. The borough chairman is also
the managerial as well as titular head of borough
government. The mayor of Juneau, and everyone
else in the area, was compelled to witness the development of a borough staff carrying out areawide
functions. Questions of priority and precedence
arose. Who was the local leader? The chief of
the area's largest city, or the chairman of the
borough which includes that city? Which local
government functions were whose? Whose staff
would do what? The exploration of these questions
occupies the rest of this chapter.

PLANNING AND ZONING--DIFFICULTIES

The Greater Juneau Borough has the planning
and zoning authority for the entire area under the
following provisions of the State statutes:*

---

*Editors' Note: In the following pages Mr.
Henri presents one view of planning and zoning and
the law. On the other hand, Roger W. Pegues, a
drafter of the original Borough Act and director
of the Local Affairs Agency at the time the Act
was enacted, remarks: "The intent of the Borough
Act was to absolutely prohibit cities from exercising any of the areawide powers--by contract,
transfer, or otherwise--once the borough assumed
the powers, and at any event, after two years
[from the date of incorporation]. The purpose
was, of course, to force the transfer from the
cities to the boroughs." Letter from Pegues to
Cease.

AS 07.15.340: Planning and Zoning.
(a) The first and second class borough has the responsibility of planning, platting, and zoning on an
areawide basis and shall do so in
the manner provided for first class
cities, except that the planning commission shall also be the zoning commission. Nothing in this section
prevents any city from having a planning and zoning commission in an advisory capacity. Appointment of
borough planning and zoning commission members from a first class city
shall be made from the city advisory
commission membership.
      (b) City councils continue to
function as boards of adjustment
within their boundaries. The borough assembly is the board of adjustment for the area outside
cities and for cities which do not
exercise this power.

AS 07.15.310: Scope of Areawide
Powers. First and second class boroughs shall exercise the powers
specified in Sections 310-350 of
this chapter on an areawide basis,
both within and outside cities of
any class within its boundaries.
No city of any class, whether home
rule or not, within an organized
borough, may exercise any areawide
power provided in this section or
specified in the petition approved
by the voters for incorporation
once that power is being exercised
by an organized borough.

AS 07.10.140: Transition. (a) The
powers exercised by cities, service
areas, and special districts which
are succeeded to by an organized

borough shall continue to be exercised by them until such time as
the borough assumes the powers,
which time may not exceed two years
after the date of incorporation.
Ordinances, rules, resolutions,
regulations, procedures, and orders
in effect prior to the assumption
of these powers by the organized
borough remain in effect until
superseded by the action of the
organized borough.

(b) The borough shall make
written notice of its assumption
of the powers, duties, and other
items enumerated in Section 130 of
this chapter to the city, service
area, or special district concerned
prior to the assumption. Borough
officials shall consult with the
officials of the city, service area,
or special district concerned and
arrange for an orderly transfer.

In Ordinance 64-5, adopted in February, 1964,
the borough assembly attached a transitional section at the end of its newly passed planning and
zoning ordinance:

49.40.010: TRANSITION: The comprehensive plans, building codes regulating minimum construction, heating,
lighting and other requirements and
specifications, and other building
and land use regulations adopted by
ordinance in the cities of Juneau
and Douglas shall remain in effect
until superseded by ordinances of
the borough. (AS 07.10.140)

Thus the borough ordinance on planning and zoning
specifically referred to the transition clause in
the State statute (quoted above). That statute
provided that the powers exercised by cities

should continue to be exercised until the borough "assumes the powers." Further, the borough is compelled to notify the cities in writing of its assumption of the areawide powers.

After the incorporation of the borough, the City of Juneau enacted several changes in its zoning title by rezoning certain city areas. The rezoning was approved according to the provisions of Juneau City Code 11-16-1 under the State and borough transition sections. It seemed apparent that the city retained the power to rezone, for no notification was received from the borough that it had assumed such power under AS 07.10.140(b). A memorandum from the borough attorney to the borough chairman, dated July 1, 1965, expressed the same understanding:

> The Juneau zoning ordinance in Sec. 11-16-1 provides a method by which the zoning ordinance of the City may be amended by the City Council. The provisions of the zoning ordinance has [sic] incorporated by reference the terms of the zoning ordinance of the Cities of Juneau and Douglas. In legal effect what has happened is under the Borough Zoning Ordinance the full areawide power of zoning has been assumed by the Borough with the zoning authority within the cities being delegated to the respective cities. It was anticipated that this zoning ordinance (GJB 49.25) will be superseded by a zoning ordinance for the entire Borough when the current 701 project is completed. This was adopted as a transition measure to allow the full burden on zoning administration to be phased in gradually because of the heavy immediate burden on the Borough's zoning staff.

A copy of this was sent to the Juneau city attorney.

On July 7, 1965, the Juneau city attorney
wrote to the borough attorney:

> Thanks very much for your memorandum
> of 1 July, and the accompanying copy
> of your memorandum to the Borough
> Chairman, relative to the present
> powers of the City of Juneau pertain-
> ing to zoning. I concur completely
> in your opinion that zoning within
> the cities has been delegated, for
> the time being, to the cities, and
> that there is no need for an appli-
> cant for variance or zoning change
> within the City of Juneau, at this
> time, to appear before the Borough
> Planning Commission and the Borough
> Assembly. The City of Juneau real-
> izes, of course, that the planning
> and zoning power is within the Bor-
> ough, and that the City's power de-
> rives solely from your delegation to
> us. Furthermore, the City realizes
> that eventually the Borough will
> assume the complete zoning function
> for the area. Meanwhile I think we
> have achieved an effective way of
> dealing with current problems, one
> which is of great advantage to the
> private citizen who seeks relief.
> I understand that in several cases
> in the immediate past an applicant
> for a zoning change sought relief
> from the City Planning Commission,
> the City Council, the Borough Plan-
> ning Commission and the Borough
> Assembly, concurrently. This should
> never be. I am happy that we were
> able to work this out agreeably and
> in the best interests of the public.

The borough attorney expressed his understanding that the cities retained the right to

enact zoning changes in a letter to attorney
Douglas L. Gregg of Juneau, who was representing
two medical doctors seeking a zoning change within
the City of Juneau. The borough attorney wrote:

> For your reference, this is covered
> in GJB 49.25.010(3) which provides
> in part. . . . "The zoning ordi-
> nances of the Cities of Douglas and
> Juneau are expressly recognized and
> adopted as a part of this ordinance
> until superseded by further action
> of the Greater Juneau Borough." The
> City of Juneau zoning ordinance in
> Sec. 11-16-1 provides for amendment
> procedure. No superseding action
> has been taken to date by the Bor-
> ough.[6]

Copies of this letter were sent to the Juneau city
attorney and the borough chairman. On the
strength of it, the doctors sought their zoning
change from the city; and after the requisite
steps were taken, the city council enacted the
rezoning.

From the inception of the borough until this
writing, approximately five zone changes have been enacted by the City of Juneau. Just before final enactment of the last of these changes, the city council received a letter from the borough chairman:

> We have been informed that the City
> Council is currently contemplating
> an ordinance changing the zoning of
> certain lands located within the
> boundaries of the City of Juneau.
> The only body legally competent to
> amend the zoning ordinance is the
> Borough Assembly.
>   Such an ordinance passed by the
> City Council would therefore be of
> no legal effect and no permit could
> be legally issued under such ordinance.

The net result would be that any ap-
plicant who proceeded under any permit issued pursuant to such an ordinance would be in violation of the
zoning ordinances and therefore subject to the penalties provided for
such violations.

From the point of view of the
public interest, and most particularly from the point of view of any ap-
plicant who could act in good faith
thinking he had a legal right to
proceed and who thereafter would
find himself in violation, any zone
change passed by the City Council
would have most unfortunate effects,
because under the law the Borough
must act to prevent such violations.[7]

In May, 1966, the borough attorney disaffirmed
his earlier opinion. He was now of the opinion
that if the Juneau city council rezoned land, it
would be doing so under delegation from the borough assembly, and that the assembly had no right
to delegate such a legislative function.

Between the borough attorney's first and
second opinions, nothing had changed in the legal
relationships of the city and the borough. The
same laws and ordinances were in effect in 1966 as
in 1965, but now the borough was viewing them in a
completely different way. Perhaps this was because
in 1965 the borough government was still enmeshed
in organizational problems. The pressing need at
that time was the zoning of the outlying areas of
the borough that had previously been without land
use controls. In 1966, however, the Greater
Juneau Borough appeared to be functioning more co-
hesively, and the large task of rural zoning had
been accomplished. There was more time to turn
to zoning within the cities. For whatever reasons,
the borough chairman, without saying so, disavowed
every zone change enacted by the city from the inception of the borough. Some of the applicants

who had obtained zone changes from the city council
have since applied to the borough assembly for the
identical change. This entailed new public hearings, the rehiring of an attorney or other representative, and all of the usual complications of
seeking a rezoning.

The City of Juneau did not question that zoning was a borough function; the law was clear
enough. But the city viewed the pertinent borough
ordinance provisions as leaving zoning to the city
until the borough had time to give the matter
proper attention.

But the Greater Juneau Borough, having accomplished the zoning of the noncity sector of the
borough, then sought to attend to zoning of cities
(Juneau and Douglas) as well. This was done retro-
actively, simply by declaring that rezoning by the
cities (from the founding of the borough) was null
and void. Such action was hardly in the public interest for which the borough chairman had expressed
such great concern. The cities, and zone-change
applicants, had been lulled into thinking that the
cities had the power to rezone until the borough
specifically took it away. In furtherance of that
view, the borough attorney gave his written opinion
(previously cited) in the summer of 1965 that this
was indeed the case. It was almost three years
after the borough came into being that the cities
were apprised of the new opinion that they never
did have the power to effect a zone change!

This spectacle of contrariness and about-face
on the part of the borough is one of the most
severe abrasions in the continuing borough-city
battle. It was born of personal pique rather than
regard for what was lawful. Even if the latest
opinion by the borough is correct--that no city
has the power to rezone after the establishment of
the borough, an opinion with which many students
of the law disagree--the impact on the applicants
who had obtained zoning changes from the city
could have been lessened considerably. The borough

could simply have ratified all of the zone changes
effected by the city by means of a single hearing
and a single enactment. The borough has not chosen
to do so, and most of the rezoning done by the city
is thus still in an ambiguous state.

That the borough could delegate the zoning
power to the city appears clear from Section 13
of the local government article of the State Constitution.* It provides:

> Agreements, including those for co-
> operative or joint administration of
> any functions or powers, may be made
> by any local government with any
> other local government, with the
> State, or with the United States un-
> less otherwise provided by law or
> charter.

The first section of the article provides that "A
liberal construction shall be given to the powers
of local government units." At the Constitutional
Convention, the chairman of the Local Government
Committee, John H. Rosswog, expressed his understanding of the above-quoted section: "There will
have to be times that powers can be transferred
back and forth from the boroughs to the cities and
also between the local government units."[8] In
Alaska, powers can be transferred back and forth
between local governmental units or "delegated."
The use of the word "delegation" carries with it
the burden of all the old lore against surrender-
ing legislative functions. The term is undesirable
in the Alaskan context, and serves to obscure the
intent of the constitutional fathers. "Transfer"
of powers might be more appropriate. Local government in Alaska was meant to be a more dynamic

---

*Editors' Note: See AS 07.15.310 as quoted
by Mr. Henri on p. 274 and the comment by Mr.
Pegues under Editors' Note on p. 273, above.

creation than was evident in most of the older
states. In the borough-city fray, however, we see
that supposedly different creation called the borough invoking destructive formulae to prevent a
city from exercising any part of an areawide power.

The Alaska State legislature delegates many
lawmaking functions to local governments. In fact,
except for home-rule municipalities, a local government has only those powers delegated. The
State legislature shares many of its lawmaking
powers with local governments. It is sheer per-
versity to say that under our State Constitution,
the borough assembly may not delegate any of its
lawmaking power to the city council, so that it
may enact laws for the people in the city.

THE BUILDING CODE--ENACTMENT
AND ENFORCEMENT

The Greater Juneau Borough has taken the
position that the enactment of a building code is
a part of the planning and zoning function. The
practical result is that in the borough's view
the provisions of the building code as well as
its enforcement are within the purview of the borough. On the other hand, the City of Juneau considers the building code as a part of _its_ police
power, not subject to any areawide power of the
borough. As the Colorado Supreme Court has recently said:

> The enactment of adequate measures
> by municipalities to insure safe and
> healthful living conditions through
> housing codes designed to protect
> the health and welfare of the public
> is, in our opinion, the exercise of
> the police power in its purest
> sense.[9]

Textbook writers on municipal corporation law list
the building code function as a police power

intimately connected with the maintenance of the
health, safety, and welfare of the citizen.   Closely related to the building code are such regulations
as sewer codes, plumbing codes, electrical codes,
and littering and other sanitary codes. Some cities
cover all such items by a single enactment.*

The borough nevertheless considers the building code function a part of planning and zoning
because under an early codification of the statutes
of Alaska, Section 16-1-35(24), ACLA, 1949, first-
class cities were granted the power to enact building codes in the same subchapter in which they were
given the authority to zone.   The conclusion is
thus reached that the zoning power includes the
building code power.   The Attorney General of
Alaska, in a formal opinion, has stated his agreement with this view.[10]

The City of Juneau is not persuaded by this
logic.   It is simply not reasonable to suppose
that the legislative intent in the Borough Act,
wherein zoning is made an areawide function, also
includes an intent to transfer the building code
function.   The type and quality of building construction, the safety factors, the electrical
wiring, the plumbing and sewering lie at the heart
of what kind of a city will be created.   If an
Alaskan city within a borough is to be denied its
say on such vital, fundamental concerns, the city
is nothing more than a caricature.

During the October, 1965, meeting of the
Alaska Municipal League, the League's legislative
committee indicated its displeasure with the municipal code revision drafted by the Local Affairs
Agency, and recommended changes.   One of the

---

*Editors' Note: It should be noted here
that city planning texts and many state and municipal governments also consider the zoning power
as a police power.

committee's recommendations sought to clearly indicate that cities have authority over building
codes. Although legislation to effect this recommendation was drafted and accepted by the Municipal
League as its answer to the Local Affairs Agency's
proposed revisions, the legislature did not act on
the code.

The City of Juneau (through the Municipal
League) is supporting such an amendment for the
1967 legislative session. During the 1966 meeting
of the Alaska Municipal League, the city was successful in obtaining League support for a separate
bill which would make it clear that cities have
the power to enact and enforce building codes.

IS ZONING A PROPER AREAWIDE FUNCTION?

To a significant though lesser extent than
with the building code, a city which loses control
over zoning within its borders surrenders a portion of its ability to improve itself and direct
its own development. Under the Borough Act zoning
is an areawide function. The borough can rezone
property within the City of Juneau, or it can re-
fuse to rezone even where the city deems a change
desirable. By limiting the commercial areas, by
turning large areas into recreation zones, by
keeping annexed areas in single residence classification, etc., the borough can effectively control the city's economic future and its desirability as a place to live. In short, its destiny.

Every city should be allowed to zone itself
consistent with a master plan for the entire borough. There is no question as to the desirability
of areawide planning; it is a distinct asset for
the whole region. But within that broad framework,
cities should be allowed to do their own zoning,
for it is the cities which are clothed with the
responsibility for making their jurisdictions
viable economically, esthetically, and socially.
The cities must be good, appealing places in which

to live, and zoning is an essential tool for ac-
complishing this goal. When the zoning power is
in the hands of a different local government, the
city is shorn of much of its own ability to promote itself. In the outlying areas of the Greater
Juneau Borough there are undeniably those who wish
to see the City of Juneau falter. These people
want to see more of the economic base move to the
noncity areas of the borough and wish to deny to
the City of Juneau many of the things which the
city considers essential for survival. The influence of people such as these over our zoning matters is obviously not desirable to the City of
Juneau. Under the city's interpretation of the
power to transfer or delegate functions back and
forth, the Greater Juneau Borough could allow the
cities to zone themselves, thus giving those entities more direct control over their future.

The borough has the areawide planning function, but in my opinion, the law does not adequately define the limits of this power. If borough
authorities again dip into Territorial law
(16-1-35[23], ACLA, 1949) for direction on the
meaning of the Borough Act, "planning" is apt to
be considered a very expansive and pervasive power.
Under Territorial law, city planning commissions
were "to prepare from time to time plans for the
systematic development and betterment of such
municipality as a place of residence or for business." The Territorial act went on to say:

> The said City Planning Commission may
> consider and investigate any subject
> matter tending to the development and
> betterment of such municipality, and
> make recommendations as it may deem
> advisable concerning the adoption
> thereof, to any department of the
> municipal government, and for any
> purpose, make or cause to be made,
> surveys, maps or plans, before final
> action shall be taken by any munici-
> pality or department thereof, on the

> location and design of any public
> building, dock, beach, ski ground,
> statue, memorial, park, parkway,
> boulevard, street or alley, play-
> ground, public street, alley or the
> grade thereof, such question shall
> be submitted to the City Planning
> Commission for investigation and
> report.

Thus even street grades are a part of "planning."

The City of Juneau is agreeable to the borough's adoption and continuing reassessment of a
comprehensive plan, as that term is generally understood by planners throughout the country. But
the city's status and viability as a corporate entity is drastically impaired if "planning" means
what ACLA, 1949, may imply. Here again the law
needs clarification so that limitations on borough
authority within the cities are stated, and jurisdictional disputes and duplication of effort are
avoided.

FAIR REPRESENTATION ON THE BOROUGH
ASSEMBLY--APPORTIONMENT
AND WEIGHTED VOTING

Article X, Section 4, of the Alaska Constitution states:

> The governing body of the organized
> borough shall be the assembly, and
> its composition shall be established
> by law or charter. Each city of the
> first class, and each city of any
> other class designated by law, shall
> be represented on the assembly by
> one or more members of its council.
> The other members of the assembly
> shall be elected from and by the
> qualified voters resident outside
> such cities.

Under the apportionment formula of the Borough
Act, the City of Juneau is represented on the borough assembly by three city councilmen. By the
same formula, the City of Douglas has one council-
assemblyman, and the noncity areas of the borough
have five assemblymen to represent their interests.
Even though Juneau and Douglas together comprise
approximately 65 per cent of the borough's population,* the people of the cities have one less representative than the noncity residents.

Under the State Constitution cities are a
part of the borough in which they are located.
The City of Juneau has a suit pending against the
Greater Juneau Borough in the State Superior Court
for a declaratory judgment that the apportionment
formula of the Borough Act is unconstitutional and
that the weighted voting provisions of the act are
likewise unconstitutional.[11]

The Greater Juneau Borough, as indicated earlier, exercises certain areawide powers. In addition it may exercise all the powers of a first-
class city in the noncity areas. When the assembly votes on a main motion of legislation involving one of the areawide powers, each of the Juneau
council-assemblymen has a weighted vote of 2-1/3.
If all of the Juneau council-assemblymen are present and voting, the city then has a total of seven
votes, giving it the majority. Juneau enjoys a
weighted vote because it contains within its city
limits more than half the population of the borough. The Douglas council-assemblyman does not
have the weighted vote because that city's population does not warrant it. The noncity assemblymen
never have a weighted vote.**

---

*Editors' Note: According to 1960 Census
figures.

**Editors' Note: Except that the area out-
side first-class cities has in all cases a majority of one seat on the assembly.

Are the people of Juneau fairly represented on the assembly in areawide matters when they have only three representatives? Even though each may cast 2-1/3 votes, giving the city a bare majority if all vote the same, the city does not think so. If the 1960 census figures were still accurate, 70 per cent of the people of the borough would have only seven votes on an areawide matter, while the other 30 per cent of the population would have six. There is no reasonable justification for this disparity.

Juneau's bare majority of votes on areawide issues is destroyed, of course, if one council-assemblyman is absent because of sickness or for any other reason. While Juneau loses 2-1/3 votes for each absent representative, the noncity area loses but a single vote for each absentee. Further, it is harder for Juneau to maintain a majority because if one council-assemblyman disagrees with his two colleagues, it is not one vote which is lost, but 2-1/3. Such a defection is not off-set by one noncity assemblyman voting with the Juneau representatives, as he would have only one vote, not 2-1/3. There are other defects in the weighted vote mechanism. If seven votes were the fair number of total votes accorded to Juneau be-cause of its population in relation to other dis-tricts of the borough, it is apparent that the city interest would be better served by having seven representatives rather than three. The men-tal energies and brainpower of seven could accom-plish more than three. Seven men would provide greater accessibility and availability of council-assemblymen to the people of Juneau than do three.

Based on the 1960 population, there is one assemblyman for every 2,298 Juneau citizens, as compared to one for every 381 non-City of Juneau residents. The committees of the assembly do not use weighted voting. Therefore, Juneau's strength is unfairly diluted where strength is really im-portant, for the major work of any legislative body is performed in committee.

Before leaving weighted voting and the subject of areawide powers, mention must be made of
the practice of the Greater Juneau Borough assembly whereby the City of Juneau is forbidden the
use of the weighted vote except on the main motion
of an ordinance or resolution. This is another
obvious injustice to the majority of the residents
of the borough, the people of Juneau. For the
ruling as to the application of the weighted vote
formula was made on the advice of the borough attorney to the president of the assembly. The
Juneau council-assemblymen appealed the ruling of
the chair to the assembly, but the assembly by a
nonweighted vote upheld the chair. The three
Juneau men were voted down by the six other assemblymen on a question directly and dramatically affecting the majority of borough residents. Had
the city and its people been represented by seven
men rather than three, this never could have occurred.

Hence, even on areawide questions, the City
of Juneau may exercise the weighted vote only on
the main motion, and only when that main motion
relates to the passage of an ordinance or resolution. The Juneau voting power is accordingly reduced by over half on procedural matters and substantive amendments to the main motion because the
vote is not weighted. On a motion to table, Juneau
is accorded three votes instead of seven; this is
also true on amendments or on any matter that does
not pertain to ordinances or resolutions.

These examples serve to illustrate the patent
nonsense of the assembly's restrictions on the
power of the majority of the borough's citizens.
Yet this effrontery is what the Greater Juneau Borough compels the city residents to live with until
the courts may see fit to give redress. Even then,
the redress will not be retroactive.

The Alaska Borough Act takes a peculiar view
of the nonareawide powers of the borough. It
states that if a majority of the borough's

citizens happen to live within a city, they will
not have the majority vote on nonareawide matters.
Juneau's council-assemblymen are not allowed the
weighted vote on any nonareawide matter. The State
Constitution says nothing about borough citizens
living within cities as being second-class citizens, but the Borough Act treats them as such when
the vote is on a nonareawide subject. If the city
residents are allowed some say on these subjects,
why should they not be allowed their full vote?*

    What goes on in the noncity areas of the bor-
ough is of direct concern to the people of Juneau,
for they, too, are citizens of the borough. For
example, in a noncity area the borough government
intends to install water and sewer mains. At
present, the area is served by wells and septic
tanks. The water and sewer project is estimated
to cost $3 million. Juneau assemblymen do not
have the weighted vote on this matter because it
is not considered "areawide," inasmuch as it directly affects only those areas outside the city.
There is a serious question whether the population
density of the area to be developed is sufficient
at this time to warrant such an expenditure. Even
if all three Juneau council-assemblymen were to
vote against the project, it could be passed if
all the non-Juneau assemblymen voted for it. The
borough would then issue a bond called a "limited
general obligation bond." Theoretically, only
those within the sewer service area would be liable
for the bond. However, the law is not clear as to
what debt limitation would apply to these limited
general obligation bonds. But it is obvious that
the bond market will absorb only so many bonds
from the Juneau area. If the non-Juneau area of
the borough were to float a number of these limited

---

*Editors' Note: It should be noted that resi-
dents of boroughs outside first-class cities do
not participate in the operation of city government functions.

general obligation issues, the rest of the borough,
and the city in particular, might find itself without a bond market for its public improvements sometime thereafter.

    This is not to say that the particular water
and sewer project under discussion is not needed,
nor is this to be construed as disagreement with
the concept of a limited general obligation bond.
The point here is that the borough citizens living
in the City of Juneau have a vital interest in
what happens in the non-Juneau areas of the borough, and their voting strength in such matters
should not be arbitrarily diluted by more than
half. On all borough matters, "areawide" or "nonareawide," the majority of the borough's people
should control a majority of the borough's representatives, each having a single vote.

COOPERATION AND COOPERATIVE ENDEAVORS

The Electric Rate Cases

    The history of city-borough relations is not
only that of conflict. The outstanding example of
the local governments pulling together for the ad-
vancement of the area is their mutual effort in
the electric rate proceedings which involved the
two electric utilities in the greater Juneau area.
Early in 1965, Alaska-Juneau Industries, Inc., a
wholesale generator and transmitter of electrical
energy, served notice on its sole retail distribu-
tor, the Alaska Electric Light and Power Company,
that the wholesale rates were being raised.
A.E.L.&P. reminded A-J that before any rate adjustment could be accomplished, the company seeking
the change had to file its proposed new schedule
with the Alaska Public Service Commission. A-J
consequently did so. A.E.L.&P. approached the
City of Juneau regarding the proposed new wholesale rates which would increase costs to the rate
payer. The city was invited to join A.E.L.&P. in
opposing any raise. The city chose to intervene

independently of A.E.L.&P., and was successful in
interesting Douglas and the borough in participating
in a joint effort to keep electric rates reasonable.

The three municipalities banded together as a
municipal intervenor in the A-J case; public utility consultants were hired, and the municipal attorneys and the consultants participated in the
two hearings incident to the A-J proceedings. The
case involved the first rate regulation of a private electric utility by the Alaska Public Service
Commission. The commission's eventual decision
and order hewed very closely to the recommendations
of the municipalities. The teamwork, cooperation,
and expenditure had been amply rewarded, and a
saving of approximately $130,000 was to be realized
in the wholesale rates. The municipalities insisted that A.E.L.&P. let this saving flow through
to the rate payer. A.E.L.&P. refused on the basis
that its rate of return had been insufficient under
the old wholesale rates. So another rate hearing
was necessary in order to bring the benefits of the
A-J case to the rate payer. The second case, this
time against A.E.L.&P., was initiated by the State
Public Service Commission itself.

The municipalities again entered the proceedings on the same cooperative arrangement as in the
A-J case. The outcome of the A.E.L.&P. case had
not yet been determined when this was written.

In both cases there was a noteworthy spirit
of cooperation among the three local entities,
even though in the A.E.L.&P. case the interests of
the three were not always identical. What was advantageous to the City of Juneau was not necessarily of equal advantage to the borough, and vice
versa. Nevertheless, the two cities and the borough remained completely unified. Attorneys for
both A.E.L.&P. and A-J attempted to divide the
three local governments by asking certain pointed
questions on cross-examination. But they were unsuccessful. The three governments divided the
costs of the rate proceedings on the basis of

their respective assessed valuations, with Juneau
paying approximately 62 per cent, the borough 31
per cent (outside Juneau and Douglas only), and
Douglas 7 per cent.

Cooperation in Other Areas

The Greater Juneau Borough has certain law enforcement and prosecution responsibilities both in
its areawide and nonareawide jurisdiction, but it
has neither a jail facility nor a courtroom.
Since the City of Juneau had both a jail and a
courtroom, a cooperative agreement or contract
authorized under the Constitution was entered into
by the two bodies whereby the borough may use the
Juneau facilities. Thus, needless duplication was
avoided.

In performing its function of animal control
for the area, the borough has an animal control
officer and an impound vehicle, but neither a
pound nor a dispatch desk to handle complaints regarding stray or trespassing animals. By means of
another cooperative agreement, the Juneau Police
Department provides a dispatching service for the
borough's dogcatcher, and the city also allows the
borough to use the old city dog pound until the
borough can build a more adequate structure.

Because of the divergence of view on whether
the city or the borough has the power to enact and
enforce a building code within the City of Juneau,
the two governments entered into a temporary cooperation agreement whereby the city will enforce
the code it has had on its books for a number of
years. This of course is not a final solution to
the dispute, but is certainly a reasonable temporary expedient.

Effective on July 1, 1966, the cities of
Juneau and Douglas entered into an agreement for
the Juneau Police Department to enforce the Douglas City ordinances and to provide general police
protection for that city.[12] Although many Douglas

residents protested and lamented this action, the venture has proven to be sound in every way. Douglas has adequate, full-time police protection for the first time, and at a reasonable cost. The tax-payers of Douglas are not faced with the expensive necessity of providing a separate police force. Should the Greater Juneau Borough decide to provide police protection in its noncity areas, the Juneau-Douglas precedent should point the way to an economic and satisfactory solution.

THREE LOCAL GOVERNMENTS WHERE ONE WOULD SUFFICE

The City of Juneau has a full-time mayor, an attorney, a staff of department heads, and a large number of employees. Its sister city of Douglas has a part-time mayor, a part-time attorney, and a lesser number of staff and employees. The Greater Juneau Borough has a full-time chairman, an attorney, a staff of department heads, and a growing number of employees. The municipal functions of Juneau and Douglas are similar. Certain borough functions resemble those performed by the two home-rule cities, e.g., road maintenance (in noncity areas) and sales tax collection. Because of the duplication of effort and the resultant shortage of qualified staff people, none of the three governmental entities can perform at the optimum. There are, of course, notable exceptions to this general rule wherein certain departments are doing first-rate work.

The savings that Juneau and Douglas could realize by the consolidation of their sewer, water, and engineering departments are apparent. Similar savings could be attained by consolidating the legal offices of the three entities, the sales tax collecting efforts, and the street maintenance operations. It may well be that the total number of employees would not be greatly reduced by consolidation, but there should be some savings realized from reduction of the number of high-salaried

department heads, and the over-all administrative
effectiveness could be markedly increased. One
executive officer for any single municipal operation in the Juneau area would be sufficient.

There are certain difficulties in consolidating the municipal functions of the three governments: Each has its own way of doing things, its
own ordinances, and its own legal, technical, and
administrative procedures. An analogy would be
the problems experienced for a great many years by
the three major armed services of the United States
in procuring supplies and performing operations on a
unified basis. But just as former Secretary of De-
fense Robert McNamara had great success in overcom-
ing the rivalries between the services and in putting
procurement on an efficient basis, the three municipalities could do considerably more in unifying
their approaches to the identical problems each
face. Besides resulting in a savings of money,
such coordination, cooperation, and unification
would channel the local government energies in the
common direction of improving the area and making
it a better place to live.

A dynamic solution to the problem is available. That is, to dissolve two of the units of
local government, leaving the third to provide all
of the services needed by area residents. The
cities could be dissolved in favor of a home-rule
borough; the disadvantage of this device being
that the borough would be nothing more than a
glorified city. If the State of Alaska sees fit
to allow boroughs to fulfill no different role
than cities now do, the attempt of the constitutional fathers to provide for two types of local
government, boroughs and cities, will have been of
no avail. Boroughs should be reserved to fulfill
the role of regional governments; in Alaska, with
an area of 586,000 square miles, or one fifth the
size of the United States, regional governments,
if not now a necessity, will soon become so.

For example, the interests of southeast

Alaska communities are similar. They are seacoast
towns, unconnected by roads, dependent on fishing
and lumbering, and hopeful of a further utilization
of the numerous raw materials which lie buried
adjacent to tidewater. As the area grows, it will
have more need of coordination and joint effort in
a common cause. A regional government called a
borough is the vehicle to fulfill such a need.
This is also true of the other regions of Alaska.

For thousands of years, "city" has been the
term attached to the urban areas of the world, including the satellite areas within their sphere of
influence. When we think of New York City, Washington, D.C., or Los Angeles, the concept is
broader than the jurisdiction enclosed in city
boundaries. There is no sound reason for changing
such thinking, but many good reasons for keeping
the traditional designation. The bond market un-
derstands the idea of a city as do Federal agencies. People in general understand what "city"
means. On the other hand, Alaska can benefit itself and the rest of the country by an example of
workable regional governments called boroughs.

It is unfortunate that few Alaskans have addressed themselves to exploring how dynamic and
vigorous and legally self-sufficient an Alaskan
city might be. Under the home-rule power of our
Constitution, any city may write a far-reaching
and flexible charter which would enable the area
to legislate on any local problem. Tax districts*
based on the number of municipal services rendered
can be formed in a home-rule city. The highest
tax would be levied in the municipal core, and
would lessen as the jurisdiction proceeded through

---

*Editors' Note: Equivalent to service areas
within boroughs. The State Constitution authorizes the use of borough service areas to permit
tax differentiation. It makes no reference to
service areas within cities.

the urbanizing areas surrounding the core, until
the fringes would have little or no tax based on
little or no service. Such districts were en-
visioned during the deliberations of the Constitutional Convention by at least one member of the
local government committee, the late Victor Rivers,
a prominent Anchorage engineer and vice-chairman
of the committee.[13]

To sum up, the greater Juneau area needs one
government, a dynamic urban government called the
City of Juneau, based on a charter which assures
everyone his proportionate share of the benefits
and duties of the community, unimpeded by local
rivalries, working within the context of a southeastern regional government, or borough.

CONCLUSION

After three years of borough-city government,
knowledgeable people are fairly well agreed that
the result has not been as favorable as they had
expected. These include people who had been members of local borough study groups as well as persons who were legislators at the time the Mandatory Borough Act became law. Most say that something more and something different is demanded.

The intergovernmental problems and rivalries
set forth here constitute some of the more serious
ones in the political life of the greater Juneau
area. They are, however, far from all of them.
Although these problems may be occasioned in some
small degree by the personal ambitions and personalities of various leaders and legislators, they
are primarily caused by two factors: (1) too many
local governments in an area small by both geographic and population standards, and (2) the
vagueness of the Alaska Borough Act, which, I believe, causes more problems than it solves. Areas
of responsibility, and the responsibilities themselves, are not clearly delineated. But the singular problem of apportionment and weighted voting

on the borough assembly is engendered not by lack
of clarity, but by some very definite and unconstitutional provisions in the Borough Act.

Besides clarifying the act, and providing a
proper apportionment and voting formula, Alaska
should squarely face the problem of what kind of
local government structure it will have in the
years to come. Before statehood, cities, school
districts, and public utility districts were the
only local units in existence. This was undesirable as there was a need for something more. With
the coming of statehood the legislature was empowered to create boroughs. The Borough Act was
passed, but the results are manifestly undesirable
for the larger cities of the State, which are gradually being downgraded.

New municipal legislation is required which
will make the city the urban government of the
State and the borough the regional government. If
the borough becomes the urban government, we will
have no local government tool with which to meet
the regional needs and problems which will surely
arise. The Alaska Constitution sensibly allows
only two forms of local government. Those forms
must be wisely utilized.

NOTES TO CHAPTER 8

1. The public utility district was a semi-
municipal corporation.

2. AS 7.

3. Additional areawide powers may presumably
also be acquired by means of the initiative. 1965
Opinions of the Attorney General, No. 6.

4. AS 07.15.360.

5. U.S., Bureau of the Census, United States
Census of Population: 1960. Alaska (Washington:
U.S. Government Printing Office, 1960), PC(1)3A.
While no reliable census of the Greater Juneau Borough has been taken since 1960, estimates set the
present total population at 14,200, divided as follows: Juneau, 8,000; Douglas, 1,200; noncity area,
5,000.

6. Letter from Billy G. Berrier to Douglas L.
Gregg, Juneau, Alaska, June 30, 1965.

7. Letter from Claude Millsap, Jr., to Juneau
City Council and Mayor Lauris Parker, Juneau,
Alaska, June 20, 1966.

8. Minutes, p. 2612.

9. Apple v. Denver, 390 P2d 91 (1964).

10. 1966 Opinions of the Attorney General,
No. 5.
[Editors' Note: Roger Pegues, former
director of the Local Affairs Agency, concurs with
this view. According to him, "The draftsmen (of
the Borough Act of 1961) and the legislature were
aware of the codification (ACLA), and the intent
was to adopt it in its entirety." Letter from
Pegues to Cease.]

11. City of Juneau v. Greater Juneau Borough,
Civil Action No. 65-317, Superior Court, First
Judicial District, Alaska.

12. Prior to this agreement, Douglas had
police protection by contract with the State.
However, the City of Douglas was not satisfied
with the level of services received.

13. Minutes, p. 2715.

CHAPTER THE ANCHORAGE
EXPERIENCE: GROWTH
OF THE BOROUGH

by Richard W. Fischer

During the first three years of borough government in Anchorage, the city-borough relationship
was characterized largely by disinterest. Prior to
the passage of the Mandatory Borough Act of 1963,
the city government virtually ignored the borough
concept in the apparent hope that it would go away.
In this writer's opinion, the seeds of indifference
and apathy were sown in the early planning stages
of borough formation.[1]

After the passage of the original Borough Act
of 1961, a citizens' group known as the borough
study committee was formed in Anchorage. Many of
the future leaders of the borough were members of
this committee. In many cases these leaders were
persons who previously had not taken an active role
in local government.* Thus this leadership was not
as experienced or articulate as the established
government leaders in the City of Anchorage. This

_____

*Editors' Note: One major exception was John
Asplund, chairman of both the borough study committee and the borough steering committee. He was a
well-known leader who had been a school board member and director of the Spenard Public Utility District. Mr. Asplund was elected as the first chairman of the Greater Anchorage Area Borough in 1963
and was re-elected to his post in October, 1966.

300

substantial difference has set the tone of city-
borough relations: the city with a highly professional staff and experienced legislators, in contrast to the borough with a general lack of good
professional organization and with basically inexperienced legislators.

THE BOROUGH STEERING COMMITTEE

The original Borough Act of 1961 permitted the
creation of boroughs by local initiative. The
first organized borough activity in Anchorage occurred with the organization of the Anchorage Borough Study Committee, a group of public-spirited
citizens concerned with problems of local government. Membership on the committee was drawn from
the Anchorage area, the Matanuska-Susitna Valley,
and the Kenai Peninsula.

My contact with the borough study committee,
the original group which explored borough problems
and possibilities, came toward the end of its activity. My major involvement, however, was with
the group which succeeded the study committee, the
borough steering committee.[2]

This committee was created primarily through
the individual efforts of members of the Anchorage
League of Women Voters. The League of Women Voters,
known throughout the country for its concern with
civic betterment, governmental efficiency, and governmental reform, was very active in the Anchorage
area. The women of the league were involved in a
variety of local civic organizations, and the coordination of these activities tended to make the
league much more effective than its numbers alone
would indicate.

The borough steering committee assumed importance as the only operating vehicle for public discussion and implementation of borough legislation.
A sense of excitement, and of embarking on a new
venture, often pervaded meetings of the committee.

Many of the members were conscious that they were
in some degree the potential architects of a new
form of government for the Anchorage area: one
which they hoped would solve many of the problems
created by uncontrolled development beyond the city
limits, by the difficulties of annexation and incorporation, and by the lack of a general purpose
areawide local government. The promise of a more
efficient and effective form of local self-
government was encouraging.

The committee always met publicly and welcomed
any and all participation. But the number of
people who met together was usually small. Though
it was not recognized then, the apathy and lack of
participation by the public in the deliberations
and discussions of the steering committee were
later to manifest themselves in either disinterest
or hostility toward the new form of government.

Though unable to stimulate widespread public
participation, the borough steering committee was
an effective corridor to borough leadership. If
nothing else, the steering committee served as an
educational, and perhaps inspirational device for
its members, so that when the time came there
were people with some experience and knowledge who
could present themselves to the voters as potential borough officers. (It is interesting to note
that, presently, the borough chairman, four of the
six assemblymen, and two of the five council-
assemblymen were members of that borough study
committee.)

The committee was handicapped by a number of
factors.

It had no financing. Thus it was not able to
employ secretarial help or pay for the expert advice and assistance vitally necessary to provide
guidance and staff assistance to citizen committees.
No citizens' committee, however competent or highly
motivated, can, by itself, carry out the task of

formulating the restructuring of local government.

Though the steering committee was productive
in bringing to the surface many "natural leaders,"
it was handicapped because, with one exception, it
did not have the participation of local State legislators. Thus, not only was a valuable resource
denied the steering committee, but the possibility
of building a bridge between the grass-roots and
the elected representatives was never fully
achieved.

There was little participation by the city
councilmen or city administrators. The City of
Anchorage was attempting to cope with the fact that
its population had exploded from 15,000 to 45,000
in a ten-year period. The accumulation of problems
facing the administration and the city council was
enormous. These were not merely technical problems
which were susceptible of solution by simply spending more money or hiring more personnel. A restructuring in the thinking of the whole community,
including the Anchorage city councilmen, was painfully underway. Anchorage was no longer a small
village where everyone knew everyone else and where
problems could be solved by informal discussion on
a street corner. In short, Anchorage was in passage between small town and city, with all the dis-
ruption and turmoil implied by such a transition.
It is therefore understandable that neither the
city administration nor the city council could get
very excited about a borough steering committee or
about a unit of government that no one had yet seen
and few believed they would see. At best, the borough was merely a word in the Constitution and an
unimplemented concept. The problems of the here
and now were pressing and did not leave time for
reflection about future possibilities.

The State Local Affairs Agency was too understaffed, inexperienced, and underfinanced to be of
any real assistance in advising the committee.
Moreover, with the passage of the Voluntary Borough
Act of 1961, similar study committees had been

established throughout the State. The staffing of all of these committees would have been impossible for the Local Affairs Agency.

In 1963 the State legislature passed an amendment to the existing Borough Act. This amendment, commonly known as the Mandatory Borough Act, required the formation of a number of boroughs throughout the State. It permitted a choice in the form of executive organization and in the adoption of first- or second-class status. Most of the members of the steering committee[3] supported a first-class borough. Adoption of a first-class borough in the committee's judgment would indicate confidence in the borough concept. However, the proposed first-class Captain Cook Borough was decisively defeated. In analyzing the voters' rejection, one discovers the following:

1. Press coverage was extensive but negative, allegedly because of the mandatory feature of the Borough Act. Although Alaskans had been given a two-year period by the 1961 legislature in which to voluntarily organize boroughs, it became apparent that this was not going to come about as a result of the community's free will. In the 1963 session of the legislature, the so-called Mandatory Borough Act was passed, which required incorporation by the following year. It was the "mandatory" feature which aroused the ire of many citizens' groups, individual citizens, and the mass media. It was felt that a form of government unwanted by many was being forced upon people with no choice whatsoever. Paradoxically, voter rejection of the local option proposal for a first-class borough, the form with the greatest number of governmental powers and prerogatives, may be interpreted as a revolt against compulsory borough formation. The voters appeared to feel that if a borough were to be forced on them, they wanted one with the least powers.

2. Candidates for borough office did not generate enthusiasm for this new form of government. As is usual in Alaskan local elections, most

candidates ran on an individual, name-familiarity
basis. They desired to present themselves as responsible and responsive individuals. The borough
concept was not well enough known, even to candidates, for them to discuss it fully, persuasively,
or eloquently.

3. The small turnout at the polls indicated
the lack of a "felt need" for the borough by the
citizenry.

4. There were no observable crises. To a
traveler arriving in Anchorage from another part of
the United States, there would doubtless have been
"observable crises" galore. However, the citizens
of Anchorage had long lived without any form of
general purpose local government outside of cities.
Though it cannot be said that the people of Anchorage were happy that dogs ran loose without adequate
means of control, that groundwater was in a pol-
luted or semi-polluted state, or that there was
neither fire service nor road maintenace, etc., the
long absence of such services dulled their awareness of what was lacking. Perhaps by any objective
standard there were crises indeed. However, to the
citizens at that time and that place, these crises
were not sufficient to generate enthusiasm for
their solution by the adoption of a new form of
government.

5. City residents feared a loss of identity
and services. The City of Anchorage was the most
professionally run local government unit in the
State. In spite of the problems and difficulties
brought about by an explosive period of growth, the
city had done well in dealing with these problems.
City residents themselves were relatively satisfied
and pleased at the progress that had been made by
the city. They feared that another unit of government, one which could take over certain functions
which were then performed by the city, might well
give them a lower level of service than that to
which they were accustomed. In addition, the citizens of Anchorage felt pride in the growth and

development of their community. They identified
with the community, its progress, and its efforts
to improve services. They felt that they had a
ready forum for their complaints and problems in
the city council, and had no wish to exchange a familiar set of political leaders and a known set of
political rules for an unknown and untried alternative.

6. Residents outside the City of Anchorage
feared the assumption of city debt and loss of
identity. Although the only city of any magnitude
in the Anchorage metropolitan area was the City of
Anchorage, there were also several tiny incorporated cities, the Spenard PUD, and a number of unincorporated but identifiable neighborhoods. The
residents of these areas did not wish to be assimilated by the city and lose their individual identity. Over the years, the City of Anchorage had
pursued a vigorous annexation policy which had begun to encounter serious opposition in the late
1950's. Noncity residents viewed the annexation
attempts as an effort by the city not only to absorb them into the larger political structure, but
also as a means whereby the bonded indebtedness of
the City of Anchorage could be spread over the whole
area. This was a particularly tender point; the
areas outside the city had little bonded indebtedness because they generally lacked municipal services.[4] They felt that it was not reasonable for
them to pay for the services and benefits that the
City of Anchorage enjoyed.

Traditionally, the noncity residents of Alaska had known no government, had not experienced the
benefits of governmental services and protection,
and really saw no need for them. There was a dis-
trust of government which sprang from more than a
simple desire to escape bonded indebtedness or loss
of neighborhood identity. The wellspring of much
of the hostility of noncity residents toward the
city sprang from a diffuse fear of government as
government. These residents feared coercion, com-
pulsion, and loss of the customary "liberties"
which they enjoyed.

In short, the noncity public seemed to fear
that the city, under auspices of the borough, would
extend its powers like a giant octopus. The city
residents, in contrast, feared that the city would
lose its power and that their capable, functioning
government might fall into the hands of officials
less capable and less concerned with the needs of
the city.

A SLOW BEGINNING

The first year of borough operation was relatively unproductive, and only the property tax
assessment and collection function was assumed.
Borough government suffered from a general lack of
leadership. The chairman did not assume a leadership role and the assembly president was out of the
State for four months during the year. Most of the
assemblymen had been elected on a "go slow" plat-
form. The city council experienced difficulty in
getting five of its nine members to serve on the
assembly.[5] The borough assembly averaged only two
meetings a month during the first year.

Following borough incorporation, the city
council (at the behest of individual members of the
League of Women Voters) appointed a citizens' committee to:

> . . . study the working relationship
> of the borough and city; to make rec-
> ommendations on the mechanics of tran-
> sition from the city to the borough of
> the taxing-assessing, and planning-
> zoning functions. We should know what
> costs might accrue to the city when
> these functions are transferred.
>   The committee might also consider
> if it will be in the best interest of
> the city to either transfer other ser-
> vices to the borough or, on the other
> hand, to offer the extension of cer-
> tain city services to residents of

the whole borough or part of it.

Although we feel we will be a
part of the borough, and therefore
obligated to work for it, we believe
our primary responsibility is to the
residents and taxpayers of the city
who elected us. Therefore, we should
be prepared to conduct our relationship with the borough toward that
end.[6]

The last paragraph is indicative of the fear
and concern that even the most enlightened city
councilmen and city administrators felt about the
impending borough take-over. These city officials
had labored long and hard to give Anchorage the
best possible government and felt a keen sense of
responsibility and a real personal obligation to
the people of the city. A frequent comment was,
"We simply can't turn the assets of the city over
to the borough without adequate assurances that
services will be performed efficiently and the City
of Anchorage will be protected."

THE BOROUGH ASSEMBLY

The Anchorage Borough Assembly has eleven members. Six of the eleven members are elected from
the area outside the city and the remaining five
are Anchorage city councilmen.

Although the original five council-assemblymen
approached their duties somewhat indifferently,
their interest began to quicken as they became more
involved. They seemed to become quickly aware that
the borough could be a significant form of government with tremendous potential. This is typified
by a comment of one of the councilmen who, in 1966,
said of the assembly, "That's where the action is."

During the first years of the borough, the
council-assemblymen made many of the major contributions to the borough. The members of the city

council were, for the most part, well versed in local government. In comparison, the members of the
assembly elected from outside of the city generally
had no local government experience, no contact with
the functionings of local government even as citizens, and little awareness of the magnitude of the
problems which faced the borough. The city representatives had been in office and had served with
the professional administrators who ran the City of
Anchorage. Thus, they had expectations of how an
assembly and the executive officer of the borough
should perform. When they began to actively participate in the borough assembly, it began to assume a leadership role.

The role of the council-assemblymen takes on
added importance because of the weighted vote.
Since the city has the majority of the borough's
population, the council-assemblymen are entitled to
a weighted vote on all matters pertaining to areawide functions. Each council-assemblyman has 1.4
votes on these, which gives the city a 7 to 6 majority. Therefore, if the council-assemblymen vote
as a bloc, they can control the exercise of areawide functions.

In the first three years, there were few instances of an identifiable "city line." Similarly,
there were few instances of an "outside-city line."
The tendency of the council-assemblymen to vote for
the good of the entire borough, rather than the
narrower interests of the city, indicates their
public-spirited attitude and their desire to do the
"right" thing. This was stimulated primarily by a
harmonious relationship between assembly members.
One of the advantages of living in a relatively
small community such as Anchorage is that there can
be many close personal and social relationships.
Most of us on the assembly knew each other before
we gained elective office,* and these informal

---

*Editors' Note: Mr. Fischer was elected to
the borough assembly in 1964.

relationships and personal contacts were to serve
us well. It was not uncommon for me to get together for lunch with other assemblymen to discuss
items on the agenda, to explore policy issues, and
to simply talk about government in general. The
advantage of dissecting controversial issues over
lunch or at a social event often helped to lubri-
cate the workings of the assembly.

Most elected local government officials are
involved in government only one or two nights a
week, as they all have full-time jobs and outside
interests. Thus, there has to be some mechanism
which allows citizen-representatives to get together informally and thrash out problems. Fortunately, the social setting of Anchorage makes this possible.

THE BOROUGH CHAIRMAN

The assembly has never been quite certain of
its role because of the theoretically strong position of the elected borough chairman. Primarily,
this is because the council-assemblymen have not
been accustomed to a strong elected executive in
the city. The chairman is allowed to participate
in assembly meetings, and while he is not allowed
to vote, he does have the veto power. The chairman
was deliberately given wide policy prerogatives by
borough law.

The degree of borough vitality is, therefore,
closely dependent upon the leadership of the chairman. For the past three years the Anchorage borough chairman has exhibited a tendency to follow
rather than to lead. Although the assembly has
substantially eroded the chairman's powers, there
have been few open conflicts between the present
chairman and the assembly. Several actions taken
by the assembly, which in most cases came about at
the chairman's request, illustrate this erosion:

1. An assembly resolution delegating admin-
    istrative functions to the school board;

2.   A purchasing ordinance that has substan-
     tially limited the chairman's prerogatives;

3.   A personnel ordinance that has limited the
     flexibility given to the chairman by State
     statute.

The present borough chairman is a person who
has been active for many years in local government
and civic affairs in Anchorage. He accurately reflects the conservative nature of the citizenry.

The chairman has also displayed a reluctance
to attract sufficient professional staff members
because he has recommended salaries below the going
rate. Moreover, he does not appear to be able to
properly use the talents of those whom he has been
able to retain. Perhaps both these deficiencies
are a result of an inability to appreciate the value and necessity of strong, efficient staff assistance. The chairman is a sincere "economy-in-
government" advocate, who appears to apply this
principle across the board. This has been exhibited by the low salary for the administrative assistant, who lacks the skills needed for such a
sensitive position. Accordingly, we see a highly
paid and competent borough attorney actually functioning as an executive assistant. The practical
result has been that the chairman is unable or unwilling to provide the assembly with the factual
data and policy alternatives necessary for decision-
making.

Everyone connected with government in Anchorage agrees that the borough will grow and expand.
It is, therefore, necessary that capable qualified
staff members be hired even before their talents
can be put to immediate use. One of the primary
requirements of a growing entity is that a professional structure be established that will allow for
proper planning.

Legislative bodies may function ill or well
depending upon the quality of their membership, the

professionalism of the staff advice available to
them, and the clarity with which policy alternatives and factual information are presented. At
best, a legislative body in our system of government is designed to react to proposals and situations. It is neither structurally nor functionally
set up to effectively initiate and sustain action
over a period of time. "The executive proposes and
the legislature disposes." When the executive, in
this case the borough chairman, fails to propose,
the other gears of the system function haltingly at
best.

MAJOR AREAWIDE FUNCTIONS

Property Tax Collection and Assessment

The Borough Act requires that the mandatory
areawide functions of education, planning and zoning, and property tax assessment and collection be
assumed by the borough within two years of incorporation. In the Anchorage area the city exercised
a leadership role in the transfers of these functions and thereby gained substantial advantages.

In general, the functions were transferred
with a minimum of planning and cooperation. The
primary role was assumed by the city, and only that
which was required by law was accomplished. These
transfers took place without rancor or emotional
involvement on the part of most city officials, except the city attorney, but also without enthusiasm
or energy. The city assumed a "what will be, will
be" attitude simply because the city administration
was a professional organization, and took the view
that life must go on.

A major factor in the smooth if unenthusiastic
transfer of powers from the city to the borough was
the orientation of the city council members who
served on the borough assembly. These men better
understood the borough law than the other members
of the city council. Their practical experience on

the borough assembly showed them that the borough
was not an ogre which would devour the city, but
merely a fledgling governmental unit trying to get
its feet on the ground.

Prior to the establishment of the borough, the
city and the school district had maintained separate assessing departments. The Spenard PUD contracted with the Anchorage Independent School District to perform its assessing services. Interestingly, however, collection services were performed
separately by each of the three units of government.

In the transfer of the city property tax assessment and collection function to the borough,
leadership was assumed by the aggressive city attorney. This is particularly significant because
the city attorney apparently felt that the Mandatory Borough Act was an immoral plot designed to
strip the city of its home-rule charter powers. To
him the home-rule charter was the embodiment of all
that good government could and should be, and any
weakening of the powers granted the city by its
home-rule charter was to be contested vigorously.
As a practical matter, he did not wish to see powers
pass from the effective and established city government to a government which he perceived was run
by amateurs.

Rather than talk in terms of a power struggle,
the attorney usually used the legal pretext of dis-
crepancies between the old Municipal Code, the new
Borough Act, and the State Constitution.

The tax assessing and collecting function
could simply have been transferred by letter of notification, as provided by law. Instead, the attorney recognized an opportunity to limit the power
of the borough and prepared a cooperation agreement
entitled "Agreement for Joint Administration of the
City and Borough Tax Assessing and Tax Collection."
The agreement began: "Whereas, Article X, Section
12 of the Alaska Constitution and Chapter IX, Section 9 of the Anchorage Municipal Charter permit

local governments [to enter into an] agreement for
the joint administration of common functions" and
went on to provide among other conditions that either party could cancel it upon sixty days notice.
It also provided that the city would foreclose on
tax-delinquent property inside the city.

Although this agreement substantially compro-
mised the borough's power, the chairman recommended
its approval. The assembly would not accept the
agreement. It recognized the strangulatory effect
it could have on the ability of the borough to exercise this function as required by law.

Most of the provisions objectionable to the
borough were removed by a negotiating committee
which contained members of the city council and the
borough assembly. While the final agreement still
contains the cancellation and foreclosure provisions, it was the best that could be done to sal-
vage the powers granted to the borough. The property which the city can acquire through tax foreclosure is frequently more valuable than the tax
lien against it, and the city knew this.

Because the city assumed a leadership role, it
strengthened its position and established a pattern
for future dealings with the borough.

Planning and Zoning

The city was the only governmental unit in the
area with a planning department prior to borough
incorporation. The city planning director was
hired by the borough as borough planning coordinator early in 1965, six months before the anticipated borough assumption of the planning and zoning
function, to provide a basis for an orderly transition.* The borough planning coordinator was a

---

*Editors' Note: The assistant director was
named the new director of the city planning

professional planner, trained in the techniques and tools of that profession, and it was hoped that he would set up the administration of a planning department and draft the ordinances and resolutions necessary for the exercise of the planning and zoning function. Thus, when the July, 1965, take-over date arrived, the borough would be prepared to receive and effectively operate this function. The impetus for this very sensible procedure came from the borough planning commission itself, not the borough chairman.

At the time, the citizenry generally suspected that planners were visionaries out of touch with practical exigencies. The borough chairman typified the attitude. He spoke glowingly of the growth of the Spenard area (hardly a model of exemplary urban development) without the intrusion of planning and zoning. Within the city, the planning department had frequently seemed inarticulate and insecure, and the new borough planning coordinator seemed to bring this diffidence with him.

The officials of the City of Anchorage did not customarily have a very high regard, except in the abstract, for planning and zoning. The general concern in the Anchorage area was for development and growth without restriction. City councilmen reflected the attitudes of most of the residents in their desire for continued growth. Restrictions of any sort, however beneficial, were generally viewed as unreasonable, arbitrary, and unnecessary. Therefore, I viewed with alarm the prospect that this might also become the case outside the city, where there had never been any substantial restriction or regulation of land development.[7]

---

department. He supported the transfer of the planning function intact--urged, without success, that the city relinquish the board of adjustment function, and questioned the need for a city advisory commission.

The city attorney, on his own initiative, again prepared a cooperative agreement. This was entitled "Agreement for Joint Administration of the City and Borough Planning and Zoning Function." This agreement retained the city planning commission as an advisory body to both the city council and the borough planning commission.[8] Evidently the city attorney hoped that the advisory commission would act as had the old city planning commission. However, the city planning advisory commission was not given any specific powers and has never functioned. The members of the city planning advisory commission generally felt that they would be duplicating the efforts of the borough planning commission and never managed to come up with a quorum on the infrequent occasions they were called upon for an opinion. A number of the members from the old city planning commission had been appointed to the borough planning commission, thus giving the city full and adequate representation to protect its interests. Understandably, the city advisory commission members did not feature themselves attending meetings of two commissions, each performing the same function. The advisory commission was not viewed as a terribly important instrument of city control by the city council, even though the city manager did foresee some usefulness to be gained from it. It was mainly an unsuccessful attempt by the city attorney to retain the planning and zoning power within the city.

Another stipulation of the agreement was that the city council would retain its power to sit as the zoning board of adjustment within the city limits. This function is generally considered to be an integral part of the planning and zoning power, but could, under the statute, be either retained by the city or transferred to the borough.* The city

---

*Editors' Note: AS 07.15.340(b) provides that the "City councils continue to function as boards of adjustment within their boundaries. The borough

kept it. The fact that this function could, by
law, be retained was not the only justification for
the city keeping it. There was also a clear real-
ization by the city manager and some members of the
city council that the board of adjustment function
was a valuable and powerful tool in directing the
future course of development of the city. Zoning
is the tool by which land use plans are implemented
and those who control the zoning of an area will
control its development. The city council has subsequently sat as a board of adjustment several
times involving controversial cases. The lack of
coordination between the borough and city has become obvious in these cases. With the planning
power residing in one governmental jurisdiction and
the board of adjustment power in another, there is
a discernible gap between the guidelines for development and the administration of these guidelines.

Though there was no overt conflict over the
transfer of the planning and zoning function to the
borough, the city attorney actively opposed the
transfer, the city manager did not indicate that he
was inspired by the prospect of shedding this power,
and the city council was merely somewhat confused
and perhaps resigned. The borough chairman and
even the borough planning coordinator were not en-
thusiastically pushing the assumption of this power.
It is a tribute to the law-abiding nature of the
citizens and their representatives that the planning and zoning function transferred at all; and it
is even more surprising that it transferred relatively intact. Perhaps the impetus created by the
simple existence of the Borough Act was sufficient
to carry the day.

---

assembly is the board of adjustment for the area
outside the cities and for cities which do not exercise this power." It is noted that in Alaska,
local legislative bodies act as boards of adjustment.

Education

Before the borough came into being, the school
district was a smoothly operating independent areawide authority.[9] The school superintendent was a
popular administrator with a deservedly excellent
reputation who had been hired by the school board
when the present borough chairman was a member of
it. He had worked closely with the borough study
committee and was not only well versed on the provisions of the Borough Act but also recognized the
formative and groping nature of the borough.

The school board and administration had a well-
defined goal while the borough did not. Like the
city, the school district had a record of achieve-
ment and success. Rather than discuss its desire
to maintain complete control, the school administration talked about "professionalism" and "keeping
schools out of politics."

The school superintendent presented a resolution[10] which delegated all legislative and administrative responsibility for schools to the school
board. The borough chairman was reluctant to assume the school responsibility;[11] it was his recommendation that the borough assembly agree to the
resolution. Under it, the assembly retained only
the power to ratify school board action. There is
some question whether or not the assembly is permitted under the law to so broadly delegate its responsibility, but nevertheless it did so. It is
not now likely that the borough assembly will demand that the education function be more closely
tied to the general borough government, and even
less likely that the chairman will initiate a
change. However, the longer the borough delays in
assuming its school responsibility the more difficult it will be. The State legislature is con-
stantly under pressure from school administrators
to dilute the borough's school power in order to
strengthen theirs. In Anchorage, the situation desired by the school people has already been accomplished by the failure of the borough to exercise

one of its most important functions and responsibilities.

Additional Areawide Functions

The areawide health function which the borough
acquired in October, 1964, by referendum was actually performed on an areawide basis before borough
incorporation. This was a State function that received contributions from the city and the Spenard
PUD, and little change in either operation or relationships was necessary.

The borough got off to a late start in performing its dog control function.[12] The public has
not been satisfied with the borough's performance
in this area, any more than it was when Anchorage
and the Spenard PUD were responsible for dog control.

AREAS OF COOPERATION

There have been areas of cooperation between
the Greater Anchorage Area Borough and the City of
Anchorage involving relatively minor items. The
two units have signed contracts or agreements authorizing:

1. The borough to use city data processing
    equipment;

2. The use of the city dispatcher for fire
    calls in an outlying area of the borough;

3. The city to provide fire protection ser-
    vice in the borough's Spenard service area;

4. The borough to lease space in a new govern-
    ment office complex to be constructed by
    the city;

5. The city to administer the borough's dog
    control program inside the city limits.

The contract authorizing the city to furnish
fire protection in the Spenard area is particularly
significant, for Spenard has long had an anti-
Anchorage bias. Prior to the contract, fire protection in the area was provided by the Spenard
Volunteer Fire Department, a small but vocal group,
which was active in local politics and which zeal-
ously guarded its independence. The contractual
arrangement has many advantages, including the providing of professional fire protection by the city
and a reduction in fire insurance rates. The borough chairman recommended the contract and the assembly approved it, in spite of heavy opposition
from the citizens of Spenard, including the Spenard
Volunteer Fire Department.

ATTEMPTS TO STRENGTHEN THE BOROUGH

The acquisition of areawide functions by the
borough is the basis for a stronger borough government. It is, conversely, the basis for a weaker
city government. Achieving one areawide government
for the Anchorage area rests with the ability of
the borough to acquire additional areawide functions.

Although the voters rejected a first-class
borough in 1963, many of us still pursued the goal
of first-class status. I campaigned on this issue
when I ran for and was elected to the borough assembly. I felt that the borough, as a second-class
entity, was hampered and restricted by the scant
powers at its disposal. Although first- and second-
class boroughs have the same mandatory areawide
powers, the second-class borough is seriously handicapped in the area outside cities.

I was instrumental in getting the question of
a first-class borough again placed on the ballot
(October, 1965). Unfortunately, the reclassifica-
tion was decisively defeated by the voters.

Voter rejection of first-class borough status

reflects a mistrust of government and a failure to recognize the need for general local government. It may also reflect a basic lack of faith in the competence of local government officials. However, the voters seem willing enough to approve the acquisition of powers on a piecemeal basis. The growth of borough government in the Anchorage area thus appears dependent upon this approach.

In addition to my support for a first-class borough, I have from time to time asked the assembly to place a number of proposed areawide powers before the voters. Many of these proposals have failed to receive majority support on the assembly. As an example, in early 1966, I proposed that a number of additional areawide powers, such as sewer, water, fire, and parks and recreation be presented to the voters. This proposal was rejected by the assembly. The opposition came principally from the council-assemblymen, who appear reluctant to allow the borough to acquire additional areawide powers.

In one particular case, that of the areawide sewer power, the opposition was perhaps justified. Sufficient negotiations had not taken place between the city and borough administrations for the assembly to intelligently determine the disposition of city assets and liabilities connected with this function. There was also considerable concern whether the borough administration was sufficiently staffed to administer such a responsibility.

Nonetheless, following some months of discussion and argument, the proposed areawide sewer power was approved by the assembly for inclusion on the October, 1966, ballot.[13] The voters approved it by an overwhelming majority. I believe that the voters hoped that approval would curb a tendency for two governments, each providing the same functions, to grow side by side.

The mechanics of transferring the sewer power to the borough will be the first true test of borough-city cooperation. Before this, the

functions transferred were either mandatory or involved essentially areawide functions in which the
city only participated (with the State). No substantial assets or liabilities were involved in
these transfers.[14] The assumption of the sewer
power not only involves the transfer of substantial
assets, but also entails significant operational
responsibilities. It is too early to predict how
effectively the borough will handle this new responsibility and how well it will master the challenge of providing sewer services effectively and
economically. It is even too early to judge how
smooth the actual transfer from city to borough
operation will be.

                      THE FUTURE

    With the acquisition of the sewer power, the
comparatively harmonious relationship between the
borough and city has shown definite signs of dete-
rioration for several months preceding this writing.

    Recently, elected assemblymen from outside the
city, who are viewed as anticity, have created
tensions in the relationships with the council-
assemblymen. These tensions have in turn caused
the council-assemblymen to begin to form a "city
line."

    The apathy that existed in the beginning
stages of the borough seems to no longer exist.
Whether or not this will be replaced by vigorous
cooperation or animosity remains a subject for con-
jecture.

    After three years of borough operation, the
only major areas of borough-city cooperation had
come about because of the mandatory features of the
Borough Act. Although there has been no hositility,
it is reasonable to assume that left to their own
devices, the borough and city would not have
achieved areas of meaningful cooperation, unless
forced by crises or strong leadership.

The Alaska State Constitution and State law have furnished a framework for modern local government. But whether the government can effectively approach problems on a coordinated basis depends on its leadership. It will depend upon the ability of the leaders to visualize, articulate, and implement long-range goals.

NOTES TO CHAPTER 9

1.   Small segments of the Anchorage population became interested in boroughs after the Constitutional Convention. The convention was held in 1955-56 at the University of Alaska, where I was an observer. In fact, attendance at the convention gave me my first exposure to borough government.

2.   This organization, formed in early 1963, came into prominence after the borough study committee went into decline. Essentially, the borough study committee was a phenomenon of the optional borough period, 1961-63. The borough steering committee came into being after the passage of the Mandatory Borough Act and was composed only of Anchorage area residents. Though the borough steering committee contained a few former members of the study committee, in general its membership was different. The borough steering committee supported the same goals as the study committee, in particular a "large" borough which would include Anchorage, the Kenai Peninsula, and the Matanuska-Susitna Valley. But after the defeat of this concept at the polls in September, 1963, it shifted support to a "small" borough containing only the Anchorage metropolitan area.

3.   It was at this juncture that the steering committee came into prominence and the study committee completely faded away.

4.   The only bonded indebtedness had been incurred by the school district and the Spenard

Public Utility District. The Spenard PUD encompassed ten square miles adjacent to the city and contained a population of approximately 20,000. It was responsible for its own library, roads, fire protection, and health services. Its assets, liabilities, and functions were later absorbed by the borough.

5. In contrast, following the 1966 elections, seven of the nine councilmen asked to serve on the assembly.

6. Letter from Anchorage Mayor George Sharrock to all proposed committee members, Anchorage, Alaska, November 8, 1963.

7. Except for the Greater Anchorage Area Platting Board, which exercised its prerogatives somewhat haltingly and ineffectively.

8. The planning and zoning section of the Borough Act (AS 07.15.340) provides that "nothing in this section prevents any city from having a planning and zoning commission in an advisory capacity."

9. The Anchorage Independent School District encompassed all of the borough area with the exception of approximately 4,500 people, who lived in the Chugiak-Eagle River and Girdwood areas.

10. Greater Anchorage Area Borough, Alaska, Resolution No. 32, establishing borough assembly-school board relationship. See Appendix G for text of this resolution.

11. This responsibility included site selection, selection of architects, school construction, bonding, and budget approval. [Editors' Note: The chairman's power over the selection of architects for school buildings was reduced by amendments to AS 07.15.330 in 1965 and 1966.]

12. The areawide dog control function was acquired by referendum in October, 1965.

13.   Initially, a $20 million bond issue to
fund the areawide sewer program was also approved
by the assembly for placement on the ballot.   Subsequently, the assembly reversed itself and removed
this item from the ballot because neither adequate
fiscal policies had been established nor adequate
fiscal information provided.

14.   The old Anchorage Independent School District was, of course, absorbed in toto by the borough.

CHAPTER **10** THE ANCHORAGE
EXPERIENCE: THE
CITY IN DECLINE

by Karl Walter

The Alaska Constitution specifies that "all
local government powers shall be vested in boroughs
and cities." (Art. X, sec. 2) The creation of the
borough was an attempt to achieve an intermediate,
flexible form of local government between the
cities and the State different in function and purpose from the typical county. An examination of
the Constitutional Convention minutes on local government reveals the desire to avoid a rigid form
and concept of the borough while endorsing the
principle that a new form of government was necessary to resolve and provide local government in
fairly large geographical areas. Unfortunately,
the Constitution did not set forth specific guidelines as to the functioning of borough government
and did not indicate the lines of power and authority between cities and boroughs. Today, the problem remains as to what ends are to be attained by
the borough and how these ends are to harmonize
with the existence of cities within boroughs. This
chapter pursues the problem by reviewing the relationships between the City of Anchorage and the
Greater Anchorage Area Borough.

THE CITY OF ANCHORAGE

Under the provisions of the Constitution,
statute, and its own charter, the City of Anchorage
is classified as a first-class home-rule city.[1]

Under the Constitution, the city is a part of the
Greater Anchorage Area Borough.[2]   The Greater Anchorage Area Borough is classified by law as a
second-class borough.[3]   The practical difference
between these classifications is that as a first-
class home-rule charter city, the City of Anchorage
may exercise all legislative powers not prohibited
by law or by charter,[4] but the borough is limited
to the exercise of powers specifically delegated by
statute or acquired by referendum or transfer from
the city.[5]

The City of Anchorage is the largest city in
Alaska and in 1966 had an estimated population of
53,000. The population of the borough is approximately 105,000. Although the borough occupies some
1,500 square miles, only a small triangular portion
or approximately 200 square miles is suited for human habitation because the remaining area consists
of surrounding mountains and Cook Inlet waters.[6]
The city constitutes the core area of the borough
and comprises within its official limits 15 square
miles, of which approximately 10 square miles are
habitable.

The territory available for urban expansion in
Anchorage and its environs is therefore limited and
would naturally force the population to remain in a
small geographic area. The size of the useful area
of the borough creates a situation in which the
aims of both city and borough governments are urban-
oriented. A view of the borough as a unit covering
a cohesive metropolitan area may assist in understanding the emphasis on cooperation between the
city and borough.[7]

THE GREATER ANCHORAGE AREA BOROUGH

The Greater Anchorage Area Borough exercises
both areawide and nonareawide powers.[8] An areawide
power is a power which is solely exercised by the
borough throughout the entire borough and cannot
be exercised by any cities within the borough.[9]

Initially, the areawide borough powers were property tax assessment and collection, education, and
planning and zoning.[10] Areawide health, animal
control, and sewer powers were subsequently added
by referendum. The borough also exercises limited
powers in the areas outside the city. To spell out
borough-city jurisdictional authority in certain
powers and functions, the borough and the city have
entered into written agreements.

COOPERATIVE AGREEMENTS

In the first two years of the borough's existence, the city and the borough negotiated written
agreements concerning platting, planning, zoning,
property taxation, park and school use, dog control, sewage disposal, engineering, street cleaning,
and fire protection. At the time of this writing
agreements concerning sewers, engineering, and joint
purchasing are being considered. In addition, officials of the borough and the city administrations
have met to discuss mutual problems, and many solutions have been reached without recourse to written
agreements. For example, at such a meeting, the
borough and city formulated a program for the sale
of their various authorized but unsold bond issues
in an adverse bond market created in part by the
1965-66 tight money situation.

The Alaska Constitution allows a local government to enter into agreements, including those for
cooperative or joint administration of any function
or powers with any local government, the State, or
the United States. (Art. X, sec. 13) This provision exemplifies the Constitution's rather unique
way of promoting flexibility in government.

But the legal catalyst is not the sole or main
reason for borough-city agreements. It is fair to
state that the city and borough administrations and
governing bodies have attempted to resolve problems
harmoniously without the conflict that apparently
exists in other areas. The 1965-66 city council

and borough assembly unanimously voted for city-
borough consolidation.[11] Both the borough chairman
and the city manager adopted an approach based on
agreement and consensus. Without the spirit of cooperation in the leadership, both in the respective
administrations and governing bodies, such consensus and compromise would not be possible.[12]

Taxation Agreement[13]

The first agreement between the city and borough concerned property assessment and the collection and foreclosure of taxes. Although the borough
by law possessed the areawide power to assess and
collect taxes, this power had to be implemented. A
city staff member became the borough assessor and
the city staff became the borough assessing staff.
Experience and similarity of law and function fa-
cilitated the administrative transfer. However,
the city retained one prerogative: foreclosed un-
redeemed properties within the city were to be
deeded to the city rather than kept by the borough.
Moreover, the collection of city special assessments was retained by the city on the ground that
assessments are not actually taxes.

The tax agreement helped satisfy criticism
that the city was being denied participation in a
major municipal function.[14] It may be viewed mainly as a gathering of loose ends.[15]

Platting, Zoning, and Planning[16]

Like the taxation agreement, the platting,
zoning, and planning agreement sought to implement
an areawide power already given by law to the borough. The agreement was unique in that the city
zoning ordinance was continued in force within the
city until superseded by a borough zoning ordinance.[17] The borough, recognizing the existence of
an available functioning city building department
staff (which had previously enforced the city zoning ordinance), contracted for the city to enforce
the zoning ordinance with the costs to be paid by

the borough. In addition, the agreement provided
that the borough planning commission would undertake and conduct studies for the city, and that the
city would have the right to approve all long-range
land use plans for lands within the city. The
agreement was silent on the problem of whether borough approval was necessary for the type, feasibility, or sites of city structures.

The agreement was adopted without controversy
although the then city attorney asked the council
(without success) to commence legal proceedings to
test the validity of the borough's right to assume
and exercise the zoning power. In final analysis
the agreement was more an expression of a policy of
cooperation than a resolution of details. It did,
however, recognize the practical problem of not
creating another zoning enforcement staff.

Dog Control[18]

This agreement implemented the borough areawide dog control power. Under it the city, among
other things, enforces the borough dog control ordinance within the city limits in the name of the
borough, and the borough pays for the animal control officers, trucks, and animal shelter which are
provided by the city. The agreement is more detailed than most because the subject is more susceptible to delineation of the way in which the
services are to be provided by the city. Little
difficulty was encountered in negotiating the
agreement.

Joint Park-School Use[19]

This agreement provided for the joint use of
city parks and recreational facilities and borough
school facilities. As one example, the school district uses the city baseball stadium for high
school football games and the city uses school
property for a ski rope tow. The agreement was
noteworthy because it was an easy administrative
solution to the problem of promoting full and

varied use of many facilities to mutual advantage.
No transfer of power or function was contemplated,
but recognition was given to the concept that recreational facilities and areas should receive maximum use.

Fire Protection[20]

The first truly politically significant agreement was the city-borough fire protection agreement
for the Spenard area.* This concerned a service
which the borough needed and which the city could
furnish with a distinct advantage to the city.

The city did not want to construct a new fire
station within the city limits which would duplicate the already existing fire department of the
Spenard area adjacent to the city. By necessity,
however, the city had to upgrade its service in the
Turnagain area (a neighborhood abutting Spenard but
inside the city) to maintain its fire rating. The
city had to build either a new station to serve
Turnagain or use the Spenard station. An agreement
was reached between the borough and the city for
the city to assume and operate the Spenard Fire Department.

At first, the Spenard residents, who have long
been "antiannexation" and suspicious of the city's
motives, were against such an agreement, but this
sentiment has practically disappeared in the face
of the fait accompli. Suspicions were also allayed
by the city's promise that the Spenard firemen
would not be involuntarily transferred to other areas when they became city employees. The city had
to covenant that it would not use the agreement as
grounds for any attempt at annexation. The areas
within Spenard with adequate city water did later
obtain the forecasted lower fire rating.

----

*Editors' Note: The Spenard area is a borough
service area. It was previously a PUD.

Sewer Treatment Agreement

The city, to meet Federal financial aid requirements for an areawide sewer program, agreed with the borough not to construct any sewer treatment facilities within five years of the agreement and to contract with the borough to use the borough treatment facilities when constructed.[21] In other states such an agreement would either be impossible or could be accomplished only with specific detailed statutory authorization.

THE BOROUGH IN PRACTICE

The following matters illustrate some of the successes and problems in the relationships of the city with the borough. As a whole, the relationship has been rather harmonious and city department heads appear unanimous in stating that they have always had fine working relationships with their borough counterparts. However, it is the view of some council and assembly members that conflicts will increase in the future when the borough is more fully staffed and expands its activities.

Planning

When the borough assumed the planning function, most of the city planning staff, including the planning director, became members of the borough staff without loss of continuity. The city had to create a new position of planning coordinator to assist it in coordinating planning matters with the borough, State, and Federal governments. The planning coordinator handles all Federal funding and capital improvements problems.

By statute, city members of the planning commission must be members of the city advisory planning commission.[22] However, the city members have been involved with the borough planning commission to the point that the city planning advisory commission no longer functions, primarily because it is considered a duplicative body without any special purpose.

To some city personnel, it is somewhat frustrating that the city must now appear before the borough planning commission as an interested party without the special standing and attention that the city received when the city planning commission dealt with the city's interests.

To date, city capital improvements and planning and location of city buildings have not been presented to the borough planning commission and the question whether borough planning approval is or should be necessary remains unanswered.[23]

The liaison between the city and the borough over planning commission matters has been good; however, at first the city was not advised of planning matters within the city limits which were brought before the borough planning commission. Having the planning department in the borough creates a situation under which the city does not always know what the borough planning commission is doing on a day-by-day basis. The creation of an areawide borough planning coordinator whose salary would be paid by both the borough and the city has been suggested. This person would be responsible for coordinating all city, borough, State, and Federal programs on an areawide basis in order to obtain the maximum benefits. Inherent in this suggestion appears to be the notion that a person other than the planning commission is necessary as a liaison to expedite planning activities.[24]

Zoning

The areawide zoning power has created several interesting situations. A legal problem arose because the borough, upon assumption of the areawide zoning power, failed to enact a zoning ordinance to replace the city zoning ordinance, which became of no force and effect upon the borough's exercise of the zoning power,[25] although the planning, zoning,

and platting agreement stated that the city zoning
ordinance would continue in force until superseded
by the borough. Nearly three months elapsed before
the borough assembly adopted its own zoning ordinance for the city.* Several interesting questions
were raised as to the continuity of the zoning ordinance, the status of existing nonconforming uses,
and the creation of new nonconforming uses and
structures. The borough assembly should not have
assumed the areawide power until it had a zoning
ordinance to substitute for the city zoning ordi-
nace. This hiatus may create future difficulties
in city zoning.

The city council may sit as a board of adjustment to hear appeals from the planning commission
(and on matters within the city as a board of ex-
aminers and appeals).[26] In one case, the city
council sitting as a board of adjustment granted to
a church a variance which was appealed to the court
by adjacent property owners, with the borough later
intervening against the city. It is not unusual
for a municipality to seek an appeal from an adverse decision. However, in this instance, the
borough had to become an advocate under a procedure
which enables a nonlegislative body, the court, to
adjudicate unpopular zoning decisions on appeals.

The city has faced some difficulties in revising or maintaining the zoning ordinance. Problems
involving ordinance definitions, signs, and other
matters have been transmitted to the borough as
proposed amendments. To date, these amendments
have not even been processed through the planning
commission. In addition, on one occasion the borough assembly rezoned a portion of the city even
though the city council had made a recommendation
to the borough that the area not be rezoned.

---

*Editors' Note: The borough adopted the sub-
stance of the city's existing ordinance by reference.

Under the existing statutory scheme, boroughs do not have the authority to promulgate and enforce building and safety codes on an areawide basis. This conclusion remains the firm opinion of the writer, despite a contrary Attorney General's opinion (and the practice in the Sitka Borough). The contrary interpretation must infer from the planning and zoning power the authority to adopt building codes, which have been legally and historically viewed as separate powers.*

The city administration has been against any extension of this power on an areawide basis because building and safety codes are a matter of strictly local concern. For there is no possibility of a uniform code including all disparate contingencies within the borough. However, the separation of the building code power from the zoning power may create some theoretical if not practical problems. For example, the city has a trailer court ordinance[27] which regulates spacing, wiring, sanitary facilities, and lean-tos and includes other regulations which analytically constitute an admixture of many powers. The spacing and setback requirements for trailers appear to fall under the zoning power which is not permitted the city, but wiring and lean-tos fall under the building code power.[28] Although such a regulation may have a legal basis in what are loosely defined as police powers, some agility in legal theory may be necessary when many of the police and other powers are split between the city and the borough.

Another interesting facet of the separation of powers concerns the Anchorage watershed area. Because of encroachment, both the city and the borough

---

*Editors' Note: For the Attorney General's reasons that the building code enforcement is part of the planning and zoning power, see Chapter 3, written by Theodore E. Fleischer. See also Chapter 8, written by Joseph R. Henri.

found it necessary to declare the same territory a
watershed area against such encroachments and im-
proper uses. The borough ordinance necessarily was
based upon its zoning power because the borough has
no water or police powers per se. The city watershed regulations were based upon a license and permit concept, rather than on a use principle. Thus,
both the city and the borough had to join together
in a lawsuit concerning the watershed because of
this problem of split authority.

The borough enforces the zoning ordinance by
contract with the city by which the city provides
one employee known as the zoning officer to enforce
the zoning provisions. During the first year of
this operation, the borough paid only for the salary of this one person, but the city found that
other city personnel, including the building department head, were also frequently consulted by
borough staff members.[29] Otherwise, the transition
from the city to the borough of the city zoning
power was accomplished rather easily, and this
spirit of cooperation still exists.

A critique of the borough zoning power should
end with the observation that the borough has not
enacted a zoning ordinance for any area outside the
city limits. At the present time, it appears that
neither the borough assembly (nor the administration) has plans to provide zoning in any other area
of the borough unless the people in the area petition the assembly for zoning. This attitude of "if
the people want it they will ask for it" may be de-
batable in a metropolitan borough. Zoning, for
example, is necessary in order to forecast population densities which must be utilized when the borough makes plans for over-all sewer and water systems, highways, parks, and subdivision control in
rapidly growing suburban areas. In addition, the
absence of zoning and building codes had led more
than one developer to locate outside the city limits in order to avoid such land and building control existing in the city. This abdication of responsibility for zoning appears to be one of the
present shortcomings of the borough.

Platting

Initially gaps in communication between the borough and city developed when the borough neglected to inform the city of platting matters affecting city property and interests.   Fortunately, most of these communication problems have been resolved.

Taxation

In the area of property tax assessment and collection, the city and borough have operated under their agreement without many major problems. (The borough succeeded to the city records.)   However, in 1966, the city council was critical of the manner in which the borough assessor was reevaluating and reassessing properties because a higher percentage of city properties were reassessed than of properties outside the city.[30]

The borough assessor's office is doing a good job in assessing properties, although, at first, collections of personal property taxes appeared to be less than when the city handled the function.

Finally, it should be remarked that the city has had excellent coordination and working relations with the borough in matters of taxation and finance, and as this is being written the city and borough are working on an agreement for the joint use of a computer.

Representation

By statute five council members are presently members of the eleven-member borough assembly.[31] The commendable concept that city council representation on the borough assembly would enable the borough and city to better coordinate their activities and in general to know "what is going on" overlooks an important practical consideration.   In serving on two bodies, a city council member must devote an unreasonable time to public service.   The

city council in 1965 and 1966 averaged almost one
lengthy meeting a week without counting numerous
work and budget sessions. In addition to the assembly meetings, the council member on the assembly
must devote many hours to equalization matters and
to "informal" work sessions and budget sessions.
Capable public servants may be difficult to find
under these circumstances. A further consequence
of this work load is that, normally, the new and
sometimes inexperienced council members are appointed to the borough assembly, although the city at
the present time does have seasoned council members
on the assembly. Several council members have
questioned whether one person can adequately serve
two masters, and many instances have occurred where
a council-assemblyman has voted differently on the
same question at the city council and borough assembly meetings. No attempt has been made by the
city council to hold a caucus to instruct council-
assemblymen how to vote, or to present a united
city front on the borough assembly, a future possibility which may create further difficulties.

The weighted vote concept, which has been contested in court by the City of Juneau, creates in-
equalities too complicated for discussion here.*

Financing

The city, borough, and borough school bonds
have generally been treated by the city and the
borough as separate and distinct items in the past,
but the present bond market situation has compelled
greater cooperation. The city and the borough had
to arrive at a common plan in order to sell their
1965 bond authorizations. The city by far has the
greater bonding capacity[32] and any borough bond

---

*Editors' Note: For a discussion of the
weighted vote, see Chapter 7, written by Claude
Millsap, Jr., and Chapter 8, written by Joseph R.
Henri.

issue merely subtracts from the city's bargaining
position on the bond market.

In the field of financing each unit must of
necessity duplicate some of the work of the other.
Thus, despite planned agreements concerning com-
puters, data processing, and other financing matters, the borough must develop its own fiscal
staff.[33]

Health

When the borough assumed the areawide health
power, the city staff became the borough staff.
Many city ordinances require health inspections for
licenses. The lack of a city health department
thus causes some problems, particularly in situations concerning city licensing and inspections. A
serious difficulty arose in 1966 when the borough
health department refused to give its approval to
already established trailer courts within the city,
because the trailer courts did not comply with
State regulations--which had never been enforced by
the State and which were contrary to the city ordinances.[34]

The city has also on occasion been asked by
the borough health department to enforce certain
health ordinances because the city was better
equipped to handle violations. Although the city
was willing to assist, such assistance does represent time and costs to the city.

Fire Protection

The borough has no areawide fire protection
power, but the borough did succeed to several fire
departments when it incorporated. These fire departments were primarily local, volunteer departments.

At the October 4, 1966, general election, the
residents of the Muldoon and Wonder Park areas in
the borough voted for fire protection to be financed

by a two-mill tax levied only on the residents of those areas. The question for the assembly was whether the borough should furnish the fire protection itself or contract with the city for this service at the mill levy rate. Public sentiment in these areas, stimulated by Rural 30 and other anti-annexation elements, was against city take-over of the fire department, even though it would probably mean lower fire insurance rates. Despite this emotional opposition, the borough assembly voted to have the city supply the necessary fire service under contract at a cost equal to the mill levy, a recognition of the value in using an operating, experienced fire department.

Sewer

At the October 4, 1966, election the borough was granted the areawide sewer power. The city council did not oppose the borough assumption of such power nor make a recommendation for the assumption. The council decided simply to stand mute on the question.

Prior to the election the city and borough had entered into a sewage treatment agreement to enable the borough to apply for Federal matching funds in order to construct a long-range extensive collection and sewage treatment system for the city and a large portion of the borough. Although the area-wide sewer power will facilitate the borough plans, it needs to be stated that the necessary Federal approval and funds could have been obtained with city assistance and agreement without the necessity of adding the areawide power.

At first, the borough proposed to exercise the areawide power on January 1, 1967, with the city to pay for the costs of the maintenance of city sewers until the end of the borough fiscal year in June, 1967.* However, certain problems arose. Could the

---

*Editors' Note: The city operates on a calendar year.

city after January 1, 1967, still sell sewer bonds
to discharge previously issued bond anticipation
notes maturing in 1967?   Other questions were
whether the borough succeeded to the ownership of
the sewerage system and whether it assumed the
sewer indebtedness[35] of the city for past improvements to the sewer system.

A meeting between the city, borough, and bond
attorneys concluded that the best course would be
to request the State legislature to pass city and
borough drafted legislation specifying what would
be assumed by the borough, the disposition of indebtedness, the transfer of the assets, etc.   In
the interim, the borough would pass a resolution
stating that it would not assume the areawide sewer
power, but would enter into a contract with the
city for the borough to furnish the maintenance of
the city sewer system for a six-month period.   If
all goes well, the borough and city will have a
maintenance agreement until June 30, 1967; the legislature will pass a statute which will avoid the
problems caused by the assumption; the city will
sell its bonds to repay the bond anticipation notes;
and the borough will finally assume the sewer power
on July 1, 1967, hopefully with all of the transitional problems resolved.*

Borough assumption of the sewer power also affects city subdivision agreement practices.   The

----

*Editors' Note: The transitional problems
have not been subsequently resolved.   The proposed
maintenance agreement was much discussed but never
implemented; the proposed State legislation was
withdrawn at the request of the city and borough,
because the two entities believed that they could
work things out themselves.   Finally, the borough
did not formally notify the city of the sewer take-
over, although in October, 1967, the borough presented a $20 million sewer authorization question to
the voters which was narrowly approved.

city normally requires the subdivider to enter into
a subdivision agreement to ensure that all improvements and utilities are put in by the subdivider
without the city having to provide at a future time
the necessary improvements and utilities on a
piecemeal basis by special assessment districts.
The exclusion of sewers from the package subdivision agreement lessens the city's bargaining power
with developers. Whether the borough will continue
the city policy of furnishing storm sewers from the
general fund without the levy of assessments may
also affect subdivision costs in the city.

Miscellaneous

Water

The borough established a watershed ordinance
to protect the area which the city had previously
established as a watershed. At present, the borough has no over-all water plan,[36] and development
of a plan is complicated because of private ownership of water facilities in the outlying areas.
An increasingly serious pollution problem of water
wells and percolating water in recharge areas may
require an areawide water power, in addition to
the areawide health power, for proper enforcement.
The city water division encounters no difficulty
with the borough concerning water problems, and
is not adverse to an areawide water power in the
borough.

Municipal Building

The borough has consistently advocated the
development of a city center and joint-use municipal building with the city and has assisted in the
preparation of a study. However, no action has
been taken by the city on the study despite several
presentations to the council. The city's unwillingness to move is due to the fact that the project
would cost several million dollars.

Staffs

Under its city manager form of government, Anchorage has long had an experienced and capable staff, while the borough has had to develop an entirely new staff and administrative procedures. The assumption of additional areawide powers and functions by the borough may result in more city employees becoming borough employees. Assimilating these persons, however, may create personnel problems, since city employees usually have earned certain seniority and longevity benefits which could be lost upon becoming borough employees. In most personnel arrangements the city and borough have tried to protect the employee's position as much as possible. The borough administration, without much apparent success, is seeking to adopt personnel regulations, rules, and procedures similar to those of the city.

Junk Vehicles

The borough maintains an excellent campaign to dispose of junk vehicles outside the city limits. The effectiveness of the campaign shows that the borough can on occasion bring about some remedial enforcement--unfortunately, an infrequent occurrence in this borough at its present stage of development.

CRITIQUE OF THE BOROUGH

The experience with local government since the incorporation of the borough indicates that difficulties between the borough and the city cannot be finally or feasibly resolved until the theory or concept of borough government is more fully developed and determined. The basic problem with the borough concept is in the failure of the Constitutional Convention and the legislature to answer the question: What is the aim of borough government? The answer to this question is extremely important in establishing the role of the city as a local

government within another unit of local government,
the borough. A predetermined understanding of this
role is vital to city administration, planning, and
financing. For example, whether a city is to be
gradually assimilated into the borough or whether
the borough is to prepare noncity areas for gradual annexation to the city should be known before
two administrative staffs are developed or long-
range capital improvement programs planned.

The present discussion is limited to the present constitutional scheme of local government and
does not consider local government problems in
philosophical terms. A perusal of the minutes of
the Constitutional Convention affords little en-
lightenment as to the meaning of the Constitution's
local government article. The Convention's Local
Government Committee operated too much on the basis
of consensus. Consequently, the Constitution merely provides for a new approach in local government
and leaves to the legislature the problem of defining the concept and of determining the jurisdictional relationships between cities and boroughs.

The Constitutional Convention's decision directing the legislature to perform the task of establishing local government with only a few constitutional guidelines as assistance was unfortunate.
As a matter of fact, the legislative and executive
branches have practically abandoned or disregarded
these few guidelines. In effect, the legislature
has made the borough into simply another city.

Present legislation provides little, if any,
insight into the problem of evaluating or determining the ultimate end of cities and boroughs. An
example of the legislature's unwillingness to cope
with the Constitution is its avoidance of amplify-
ing or requiring implementation by statute of the
constitutional provision limiting the establishment
of "service areas" by the borough.[37] The legislature could have provided standards or requirements
in the statutes consistent with the premise that
services which could be provided by a city would

be provided by the city instead of the borough.

The only statutory provision somewhat consistent with the constitutional limitation on the establishment of service areas states that before a first- or second-class borough may exercise any of its powers in an area outside cities it must first seek to have transferred from cities or jointly exercise with cities, those powers.[38] Furthermore, it does not appear that the Local Affairs Agency and the Local Boundary Commission have ever recommended against the addition of any power by a borough.

An indication of the legislature's proborough and anticity attitude appeared in the proposed municipal code[39] which was drafted by the State Local Affairs Agency[40] and revised by the Senate Local Government Committee after review of a compromise proposal advanced by the Alaska Municipal League in conjunction with borough officials.[41] Although the code failed to pass, much significance can be attached to a legislative attitude implied in the code that boroughs are the preferred form of local government. This attitude is evident in the provisions favoring the borough in situations in which either the borough or city could operate, and especially in the section listing prohibitions on the exercise of city home-rule powers. As the major cities in Alaska are home rule, the prohibition on their home-rule powers in favor of the borough indicates a legislative intent to foster boroughs at the expense of cities. (Moreover, the executive branch has done little to attempt a reappraisal of local government law in the light of experience or to seek the cities' attitudes.)

The most noteworthy example of the legislative attitude is 1966 legislation emasculating to some extent the annexation policy of the Constitution by requiring that annexation recommendations of the Local Boundary Commission are not effective until approved by a majority vote in the respective areas to be annexed.[42] The provision for a majority vote

is a step back from the constitutional removal of
the voting requirement barrier decried for years
by local governments and even by the Alaska courts.
In abandoning the concept that the city is the
"core" to which developing areas are added when
services can reasonably be supplied, the legislature instead intensified the conflict between
cities and boroughs and between cities and areas
outside cities.[43]

The creation of another city (the borough)
outside the city limits prohibits or at least
greatly curtails any meaningful annexation to
cities, and provides cities (such as Anchorage) in
a metropolitan borough with only an historical reason for continued existence. The downgrading of
the Anchorage city government results in the loss
of an extremely valuable resource, an already developed local government with its instituted services and its experienced and expert administration, and the development of a duplicating form of
government.[44] It is too early to determine if
another more intangible resource--the spirit of
community identification and pride--has also been
lost.

A growing problem in the Anchorage area is the
legislative sanction of the inside and outside city
concept. Such a division obfuscates ready solutions to areawide problems.[45]

The legislature has fostered this inside-
outside dichotomy by the creation of the weighted
vote[46] and the inadequate and inequitable representation of the city on the assembly.[47] The problem
in representation, however, may be resolved by a
pending State court action,[48] which should prove
invidious discrimination and a lack of true representation as required by the United States Supreme
Court.[49] The inside-outside dichotomy is further
stimulated by the legislative policy of limiting
cities to their present boundaries through the
removal of the incentive to annex, created by the
existence and development of the competing form

of local government and through the 1966 anti-
annexation legislation.

The borough appears to be adopting a piecemeal
policy of creating "service areas" within certain
unrelated areas in order to provide services for
which only the residents in the respective areas
are assessed a tax.[50] Although, for example, the
Sand Lake Fire District may be a service area wisely created because the city probably cannot furnish
the service to so distant an area, other service
areas capable of being served by the city are being
established and supported solely by taxation from
the residents within the respective areas. The
question may be asked whether the existence in one
borough of many different service areas with dif-
ferential taxation is any different than the existence in one area of many local governments with
powers to tax. In other words, the borough appears
to be creating a problem plaguing many metropolitan
areas, i.e., the existence of numerous independent
taxing jurisdictions.* The borough, of course,
levies and collects the taxes for service areas,
but, although it technically furnishes the services,
it has been delegating quite a bit of authority to
service area boards.[51]

The Greater Anchorage Area Borough has, in
fact, acquiesced in a trend to create additional
boards. The borough is now considering the formation of a health board with the same status as the
school board and in many respects the planning commission. These board are being delegated many
self-governing powers within guidelines established
by the borough assembly. The State legislature
similarly appears to be delegating greater independence to the school boards.[52]

_____

*Editors' Note: Service areas cannot be cre-
ated without the authorization of the borough assembly.

The over-all developing decentralization in
the borough is in strange contrast to the downgrading of the city and the support for assimilating
the city into the borough. And the diffusion of
legislative control in the borough is in opposition
to the city system of tight administrative control
under an experienced city manager with council inquiry and direction.[53]

In view of the development of heterogeneous
service areas and of diffusion of control (and in
light of the local government article of the Alaska
Constitution), it must be asked whether the aim of
borough government should not be basically to establish certain areawide planning guidelines, and
obectives, with services to be furnished and implemented by the expanding core city or cities. In
this way the borough would act as an overseer to
determine that an areawide approach is being made
to highway, utility, and other problems concerning
an area greater than the cities. Under this approach, the borough could also perform certain
functions, such as property tax assessment and collection, which are more efficiently and cheaply
performed under a central administration.[54] The
absence of any zoning, for example, in the area
outside the City of Anchorage indicates a mixture
of submission to rural pressures, a recognition of
the concept that a borough cannot in some respects
be just another city, and a philosophical indeci-
sion as to the appropriate route to take in the absence of legislative direction.

In the Anchorage area the only practical solution to the borough-city problem appears to be a
consolidation of the borough and the cities within
the borough. This action would gradually eliminate
boundary line animosities, and concentrate borough-
city efforts toward the resolution of local government problems and the furnishing to the area of all
necessary services on a feasible and practical basis.[55] The consolidated borough would be more able
to plan and finance services rather than the separate city and borough governments with their

disparate or duplicate aims and services. Without
a sweeping re-examination of the borough and city
relationship the pattern appears to be set that
the city will gradually dissolve itself into the
borough with considerably more expense and difficulty than if cities were to develop as contemplated by the Constitution. The goals of local
self-government, understandable taxation, nonpolit-
ical annexation, and governmental cooperation for
the benefit of the city and borough citizens somehow appear to be lost in the quest to establish a
borough and not a borough-city form of local government.

NOTES TO CHAPTER 10

1. The city was incorporated on November 23,
1920, and adopted its charter on October 6, 1959.

2. "Cities . . . shall be a part of the borough in which they are located." (Art. X, sec. 7)

3. The borough was incorporated on January 1,
1964.

4. According to Article X, Section 11, of the
Alaska Constitution.

5. AS 07.15.350, 720-800, and 910. [Editors'
Note: See Chapter 1, written by Ronald C. Cease
and Jerome R. Saroff.]

6. This does not consider the Girdwood area,
which is 40 miles southeast of Anchorage and whose
economy is based on skiing.

7. Outside of the two military installations,
the Alaska Methodist University, the Alaska Psychi-
atric Institute, and the Providence Hospital area,
few places of employment or activity exist which
would create a nucleus for the development of a
distinct city outside Anchorage. The Chugiak and

Eagle River communities exist because of their proximity to Anchorage and the two military installations.

8. AS 07.15.310 and 720.

9. AS 07.15.310.

10. AS 07.15.320, 330, and 340.

11. With one exception, city and borough legislators and administrators in 1966 testified before a State legislative hearing in favor of House Bill No. 409, which provided for city-borough consolidation.

12. Two civil actions between the city and borough concerning water rates inside and outside the city and a sewer interconnect were later dismissed; the city lowered the water rates outside the city in one case and eliminated the basis for the other action by entering into an interconnect agreement with the private utility concerned. The mayor and several council members, for example, viewed the borough as being actually supreme. The cooperative attitude of the legal staffs was also of considerable importance.

13. Section 18-5 of the city code, July 1, 1965.

14. Objections were raised in the borough assembly as to the inclusion by the then city attorney of certain "whereas" clauses which implied that the city still possessed taxing powers and was executing a joint agreement. The problem was solved by deleting these clauses.

15. During the 1966 city budget hearings one council member could not get a satisfactory explanation of why the finance department staff did not decrease in proportion to the tasks relinquished to the borough, even though the borough had long since assumed the tax assessment and collection function.

16.   Agreement dated July 1, 1965.

17.   The borough zoning ordinance for the city, Ordinance No. 32, became effective on October 1, 1965.   To date, the borough has not enacted a zoning ordinance for the area outside the city.

18.   Agreement dated June 16, 1966.   Dog control may seem a peculiar power to be assumed so early but the tendency of dogs to collect in packs or to run loose is a distinct hazard in Alaska.

19.   Supplemental agreement dated August 5, 1966.

20.   Spenard Agreement dated February 1, 1965. The Muldoon Agreement was executed in 1967.

21.   With the borough exercise of its areawide sewer power this agreement will be unnecessary.

22.   AS 07.15.340(a).

23.   Robert H. Oldland, city manager from 1962-66, was of the opinion that borough planning approval was not necessary or appropriate.

24.   An argument for borough-city consolidation is the increasing amount of liaison time now spent between the two entities.

25.   AS 07.15.310 states that the city cannot exercise any areawide power when that power is exercised by the borough.

26.   An administrative organization set up under the Home Rule Charter of the City of Anchorage to hear and decide variances, etc.

27.   Anchorage Code of Ordinances, chap. 20.

28.   The borough also has a trailer court ordinance covering building code matters.

29. As the city attorney's office is across
the hall from the City Department of Building Inspection, much free legal advice has been given the
borough. In more than one instance, the borough
has received services for which payment would be
made if an exact cost accounting was had, including
rent-free use of city space by the borough planning
department during its first several months of operation, use, and sometimes donation of certain types
of office equipment, etc., not to mention free access to city professional staff for advice and assistance.

30. A taxpayer's suit is now pending as to
this reassessment.

[Editors' Note: Borough officials indicate that the reassessment involved an unusually
large number of city properties because of in-
creases in the value of city properties which had
not been reassessed for a number of years.]

31. AS 07.10.040.

32. Compared with the area of the borough
outside cities.

33. The school district staff also devotes
considerable time to this highly sophisticated area.

34. The city solved the problem by issuing
the licenses where the only justification for refusal was due to the enforcement of the State regulations for the first time.

35. These questions arose because the statutes were silent as to what occurs when a borough
assumes a power (from other than a special district) involving tangible assets, such as land,
buildings, etc.

36. The efficacy of areawide planning without
concomitant areawide power is questionable and perhaps theoretically unsound.

37.   "A new service area shall not be established if, consistent with the purposes of this
article, the new service can be provided by an existing service area, by incorporation as a city, or
by annexation to a city." (Art. X, sec. 5)

38.   AS 07.15.710-720.   This requirement has
been ignored in practice by the Greater Anchorage
Borough.   [Editors' Note: AS 07.15.710-720 relates
only to nonareawide borough powers.]

39.   The code was first introduced in 1965 as
Senate Bill No. 101.   The final version was 2nd
Committee Substitute for Senate Bill No. 101.

40.   The attitude of this agency during the
formative period of the borough was almost entirely
proborough.   At an Anchorage city council meeting
with Governor William A. Egan in December, 1965,
the Governor asked, off the record, if the council
really thought the agency was proborough.   The
Governor received an emphatic affirmative reply by
one council member without disagreement by the other council members.
        Senate Bill No. 101 was primarily pre-
pared and drafted by a layman fresh from college
without any municipal government experience.   Significantly, cities were not invited nor their comments solicited prior to the bill's preparation or
before its initial introduction in the Senate.

41.   The compromise proposal was viewed by
most city members of the legislative committee of
the League solely as an effort to recoup at least
some sovereignty for cities taken away by the bill.
Most city members of the League were in fact opposed to the compromise because in their opinion it
was not a real compromise but the fruit of despera-
tion.
        A pun at the 1965 Municipal League Con-
vention was that "cities were living on boroughed
time."
        An influential member of the legislature,
who was responsible for the bill's failure to pass

in 1966, acknowledged that the legislation failed
to recognize that "there are such things as cities
and that people live in them."

42. SLA, 1966, chap. 161. The Annexation Act
of 1957 may also be viewed as inconsistent with the
Constitution's philosophy of annexation without
referendum. Its constitutionality is also questionable.

[Editors' Note: It is noted that the
statute in question (SLA, 1966, chap. 161) concerns
commission step-annexation recommendations only and
not recommendations for immediate and total annexation.]

43. The ubiquitous "nationalism" created by a
local boundary line cannot be minimized, only lamented. The development of an extremely active association calling itself "Rural 30," which was
first created in early 1966 to fight against a per-
missive city-borough merger or consolidation bill,
is a manifestation of this anticity attitude. Rural 30 can be credited with the election of at
least two of the borough assemblymen from areas
outside the city.

44. The existence of a number of built-up
areas adjacent to cities indicates that the Local
Boundary Commission has been inactive and has not
pursued its annexation function as intended by the
Constitution.

45. Forgotten appears to be the fact that
cities exist only to provide services to their inhabitants. The logic why a borough without staff,
facilities, and long-gained experience and expertise should now provide the city services in areas
adjacent to cities may perhaps be found in ancient
philosophical discussions of "human nature" rather
than in rational solutions to local government
services rendered at the smallest possible level.

46. AS 07.20.070(d).

47. AS 07.10.040(b).

48. City of Juneau v. Greater Juneau Borough,
Civil Action No. 65-317, Superior Court, First Judicial District, Alaska.

49. The U.S. Supreme Court has accepted such
a situation in local government for review.

50. Such taxes are permitted by Article X,
Section 5, of the Alaska Constitution. The explanation and definition of a "service area" seems an
uncomplicated and easy solution to the provision of
governmental services in different areas. But having many service areas in a metropolitan area
raises the question of where service areas end and
cities begin.

51. The distinction between service areas,
special assessment districts, local improvement
districts, and just plain cities diminishes with
refinement. A rather difficult question is whether
there should be many overlapping service areas providing different services, or whether once a service area is created it should be used to provide
new services.

52. AS 07.15.330, as amended.

53. This remark is not intended to belittle
the commendable efforts of the borough chairman who
has been a strong advocate of city-borough cooperation and areawide solutions to problems.

54. A possible solution is: Rather than the
borough initiating legislation for the city in
areawide matters, the city could enact such legislation subject to veto by the borough, which would
determine whether the over-all plans of the borough
were met. For example, the city appears to be an
appropriate service area for zoning, and it should
be permitted to enact its own zoning ordinance so
long as it is not in conflict with borough plans
and desires.

55. A city-borough study committee jointly
appointed by the borough and city in 1966 to determine the merits of consolidation or merger of the
city and borough has concluded that unification is
desirable.

CHAPTER **11** TOWARD ONE
UNIT OF LOCAL
GOVERNMENT

By Jerome R. Saroff
and
Ronald C. Cease

During the Constitutional Convention when
Alaskans were considering the structure and organization of local government, the Committee on Local
Government pondered several alternatives. One of
these was "Abolition of cities and their reconsti-
tution as special urban tax districts within the
larger units [i.e., the borough]."[1]

Though the committee seriously considered the
possibility of a single unit of local government
for urban areas, it rejected the idea as an immediate goal, for

> . . . it was the opinion of the Com-
> mittee that while . . . [the aboli-
> tion of cities] had very definite
> advantages of one completely unified
> government . . . it was too drastic
> a step to take at one point . . . to
> abolish these units altogether.[2]

As a practical solution, the committee proposed a dual system of local government--borough
and city. Significantly, however, it "viewed the
long-term relationships between the borough and
the city as a gradual evolution to unified government."[3] The committee hoped that there would be
cooperation between the two units, and that "where
functions overlapped, they would be integrated."[4]
It intended that those functions of government that

could best be performed on an areawide basis would
be handled by the larger unit, the borough. However, the relationship between boroughs and cities
has been characterized more by conflict than by cooperation.

Conflict, in fact, has so often been the hall-
mark of the relationship that many people in the
more urbanized parts of the State have begun to
agitate for the unification of the two units. Accordingly, there is a recent interest in legislation which would bring about borough-city integration, without waiting for the slow, gradual, and
perhaps painful absorption of city functions by
boroughs.

Late in 1965, the mayor of the City of Anchorage, who felt that the existence of two units of
local government was wasteful and productive of
needless conflict, discussed with various local
leaders, including the Anchorage borough chairman,
the desirability of merging or consolidating the
city and borough.[5] The reception was favorable.

A prominent member of the House of Representatives, Ted Stevens of Anchorage, working closely
with city and borough officials, provided a draft
of a bill designed to permit unification of city
and borough. Before formally introducing the bill,
he brought it to the House Local Government Committee for review and suggested changes. After some
discussion and study, the bill was redrafted and
introduced as House Bill No. 409. Mr. Stevens introduced the bill, which was cosponsored by John L.
Rader (the original sponsor of the Mandatory Borough Act), the chairman of the House Local Government Committee from Kodiak, and a Juneau area legislator. The sponsorship indicated support from
several major areas of the State. The news media
gave House Bill No. 409 wide coverage. Editorial
comment was almost uniformly favorable:

> We believe local officials have taken
> a bold step in advancing the idea of

> a new form of local government. It
> demonstrates awareness of a problem
> too often ignored--the problem of
> conflicting boundaries, overlapping
> services and expensive conflicts of
> jurisdiction. . . . The proposal as
> it has been sketched could represent
> a pioneering form of local government
> that avoids mistakes made elsewhere.[6]

At the request of the mayor of Anchorage, a
joint meeting of the House and Senate Local Government Committees was called to hear the testimony of
Anchorage city and borough officials. The witnesses indicated their general support for creating
a single unit of government, but were vague on details.

House Bill No. 409 was intended to facilitate
the formation of consolidated boroughs:

> In order to promote local autonomy,
> eliminate duplication of local gov-
> ernmental units within a borough and
> foster more efficient services with
> lessened local tax burdens, an orga-
> nized borough and first class and
> home rule cities within the borough
> may upon approval by public referen-
> dum form a consolidated borough to
> provide a single unit of local gov-
> ernment. Formation of a consolidated
> borough must be in accordance with
> the provisions of this chapter and
> vests the borough with home rule
> status as provided in this chapter
> pursuant to the Legislature's au-
> thority under Article X, Section 10
> of the State Constitution.

At the same time, a group of noncity residents
of the Anchorage borough formed an organization
known as Rural 30, whose avowed purpose was to oppose any form of borough merger or consolidation.

Its members believed that their individual neighborhood needs, their opportunity for contact with
local government, and indeed some of their basic
liberties would be lost by such a move. They
quickly called a convention. At it they drew up a
number of resolutions indicating the scope and direction of their opposition:

> WHEREAS, it is not known whether the
> majority of the residents either with-
> in the city or in the outlying areas
> are in favor of a consolidated, en-
> larged form of local government at
> this time; and . . .
>
>   . . . . .
>
> WHEREAS, a First Class, City-Borough
> "Metro" merger would have a direct
> impact on both City and Rural resi-
> dents through loss of their present-
> ly self-determined choice of a First
> Class City and a Second Class Borough
> and any opportunity for further self-
> determination; and . . .
>
>   . . . . .
>
> WHEREAS, there seems to be undue
> haste, lack of understanding, and
> lack of information concerning the
> consequences of such a merger;
> and . . .
>
>   . . . . .
>
> WHEREAS, the past and present record
> of borough and city officials is not
> always worthy of either public trust
> or the salaries they draw from tax
> funds; . . .
>
>   . . . . .
>
> WHEREAS, citizens of the outlying
> areas are apprehensive of a plan
> which would grant sweeping powers,
> both economical and political, to a
> single political body for the nebu-
> lous reason of more efficient, co-
> ordinated self-government; and . . .
>
>   . . . . .

> WHEREAS, the people still wish to re-
> tain control over their local govern-
> ment and the industry of their own
> labor over the years before local gov-
> ernment: the city people of the city
> they built, and the rural people of
> the freedom of area and minimum ser-
> vices; and
>
>   . . . . .
>
> WHEREAS, a consolidated borough and
> city administration with its imper-
> sonal, professional, supposedly more
> economical, efficient and co-ordinated
> improvement of government may or may
> not reflect the wishes of the majority
> of the borough residents, either with-
> in the cities or in areas outside the
> cities; . . .
>
>   . . . . .
>
> NOW THEREFORE BE IT RESOLVED, that
> House Bill 409 be returned to the
> people for public hearings and study
> group action before further consid-
> eration in the Alaska State Legisla-
> ture.[7]

Spokesmen for Rural 30 requested that they be
allowed to appear before a joint meeting of the
Senate and House Local Government Committees. The
request was granted. At the meeting, Rural 30's
representatives spoke out vigorously against the
concept of merger as a general proposition and
against House Bill No. 409 specifically. This was
the first overt political opposition to the bill.[8]

Members of the Senate and House Local Government Committees began to realize that there were
a number of questions not answered or completely
covered in House Bill No. 409, and that further
study of the question of merger or consolidation
was essential. If, for example, a city were
"merged" into a borough, what would happen to city
assets and liabilities? What would happen to a

home-rule city if it dissolved and became part of a
first-class borough? Could second-class boroughs
absorb a first-class home-rule city, or would the
borough have to first become first-class itself?
When these questions began to percolate to the surface, the move for merger legislation lost impetus.

House Bill No. 409 never reached the calendar
for a vote on the House floor. However, the House
of Representatives did pass a resolution requesting
the Legislative Council to conduct hearings on the
problem of borough-city unification and report its
findings to the next legislative session.

MERGER STUDY GROUPS

A characteristic Alaskan response to a new
governmental challenge has often been the creation
of citizen study groups. The formation of borough
study groups had been fostered and encouraged by
the Local Affairs Agency, which saw them as useful
vehicles for citizen participation. They were to
perform an invaluable service in educating the general public and in building support for the borough
form of government. The questions and the controversy generated by the borough merger concept, particularly after hearings on House Bill No. 409,
triggered the formation of two borough merger
groups.

Soon after the legislature adjourned, the
Borough-City Study Committee was formed in Anchorage to study problems of merging the borough and
city, and the Juneau Borough-City Study Committee
was formed several months later. To date, these
are the only two committees organized, although the
unification concept has generated diffuse interest
throughout the State. In some respects, it is
rather surprising that the Juneau and Anchorage
areas, where intergovernmental relationships have
been dissimilar, should be the focus of borough
merger efforts. In Anchorage, relative harmony has
prevailed between the city and the borough, whereas

in Juneau, hostilities commenced between the borough
and city almost immediately and these skirmishes
continue to this day. The reason for the strength
of borough merger movements in two areas with such
different experiences lies perhaps in the feeling
of governmental leaders and other "influentials"
that one unit of local government is "simply a good
idea." The traditional reasons given by governmental reformers, such as efficiency and economy of
governmental operation, are in themselves a major
rationale for pursuing the goal of one government.

The Anchorage Borough-City
Study Committee

The Borough-City Study Committee in Anchorage
has been most active and vigorous. Members of the
committee were selected by the borough and by the
City of Anchorage to represent their respective
areas. The borough assembly and city council in
creating the Committee requested it to:

> . . . investigate apparent overlapping
> authority, lack of clear-cut respon-
> sibility, and gaps between the pub-
> lic need and the government's author-
> ity to perform.
>   The purpose of this committee
> will be to study the facts, to define
> the issues, and to recommend alter-
> native solutions to the problems con-
> nected with and inherent to the present
> local governments.
>   The committee will hear presenta-
> tions by government agencies and in-
> terested citizens' groups, will hold
> public hearings on proposed committee
> recommendations, and will submit a
> final report jointly to the borough
> and the city with suggested appro-
> priate action.[9]

Soon after its creation, the Borough-City Study
Committee began to hold hearings. These hearings

are significant for what they reveal about leaders'
perceptions of the existing situation vis-à-vis
cities and boroughs and the anticipated good (or
evil) to be derived from the creation of one and
only one unit of local government in the Anchorage
area.

A major witness at one of the hearings of the
Borough-City Study Committee was the mayor of Anchorage. He eloquently sketched the problems of
two units of government:

> I feel that the emphasis should be
> placed on the area concept. . . .
> I personally feel that the govern-
> ment of the borough with its divi-
> sion between the city and so-called
> borough powers was founded without
> adequate consideration of the chang-
> ing considerations taking place.
> I believe that the borough con-
> cept represents a composite of two
> ideas which are not necessarily com-
> patible in the best sense of the
> word. I think that the borough con-
> cept embodied an idea that certain
> power was given to it by the legis-
> lature--education, taxation, and
> planning and zoning; these are very
> easy powers to give on this basis,
> especially planning and zoning.
> It certainly makes sense to have a
> very broad concept of how we are going
> to plan and zone. Those of us that
> have been in the firing line of bor-
> ough assemblies and city council know
> the problems are usually around the
> [variances] . . . and exceptions.
> That is at the present time partly
> with the city and partly with the
> [borough] assembly. You tell one
> citizen to go through this door to
> the assembly or the borough planning
> commission, and having gone through

> that, you go back to the city. It is
> confusing to the citizens involved and
> does not mean that you are getting the
> best answer. It is confusing.[10] [sic]

The mayor had touched upon a serious problem
in the Borough Act itself, a problem created because a bifurcation of power existed between planning and its administration. The boroughs have
responsibility for general planning but the cities
may retain--and have indeed retained--the board of
adjustment function.

The mayor's comments were broad-gauged and
ranged over a number of other problem areas: "Personally, I feel that the idea of weighted voting
should be completely scratched in any approach to
this consolidation. Areawide voting is undemocratic."[11] The conclusion of the mayor's statement was
summarized in the minutes:

> . . . the mayor referred to majority
> votes outside the city and stated
> that we need a new broad approach and
> that we have ways to do it. You can
> have it go into the city but it is a
> very difficult procedure to follow.
> The present situation is intolerable.
> The easy way is to have an areawide
> type of government in which you have
> different services given to the peo-
> ple in which they pay proportionate-
> ly. . . . We have gone . . . [beyond]
> the time when you can make city-borough
> government work in this kind of make-
> shift [fashion]. The mayor further
> stated that "we have no personality
> problem between the borough and the
> city."[12]

The testimony of city representatives contained many references to existing duplication of
services and facilities in contrast to the elimination of conflict and the efficiency that one unit
of government could hopefully provide.

Mr. Groh then spoke of costs of duplication of city and borough management. He stated that the longer we
wait before we consolidate the more
administrative hierarchies we are going to have and the more difficulties
we are going to have. He advised that
legislation is necessary. . . .
Mr. Groh touched upon the subject
of the increasing of the staffs of the
borough and the city and the cost to
local taxpayers and emphasized the
point that the city and borough should
be under one government as it would
not work any other way. . . . Mr. Groh
also recommended that the borough-city
consolidation, if voted upon favorably,
would be better off with professional
management rather than a part-time
chairman. . . . Mr. Groh recommended
again one form of government for both
areas and the need to eliminate the
city.[13]

Coupled with idealistic descriptions of the
possibilities and potential of one unit of government in the Anchorage area, however, were discussions and queries on the practical means and approaches, both legal and fiscal, necessary to accomplish such a goal.

Sentiment in favor of one unit of government
was by no means unanimous. The opposition was vocal, persistent, and though inclined to be somewhat
emotional, occasionally persuasive. Dissolution of
either the borough or the city was not merely a
technical matter of shuffling assets back and forth,
but involved also a complex political equation.

There exists a long-term hostility of noncity
residents to the City of Anchorage. The noncity
residents which Rural 30 represented were part of
this tradition, and they were not prepared to look
on silently while plans to unite the borough and

city were pondered. Accordingly, Rural 30 made a
presentation before the Borough-City Study Committee. The presentation attempted to describe
comprehensively the attitudes and feelings of residents living outside the City of Anchorage concerning one unit of government and the thinking of
Rural 30 concerning possible alternatives to the
status quo. It ended with five points which Rural
30 felt should be included in any merger legislation. The opening remarks framed the problem:

> The City of Anchorage is responsible
> for the accelerated growth of the
> area outside the city limits. By
> their [sic] actions and political
> maneuvers of the past, which the rec-
> ords are full of, people simply moved
> out. And this includes business as
> well as home owners. Somehow, gov-
> ernment officials (especially local
> and State) feel today that the gov-
> ernment is their private piece of
> property, and that they should be
> able to employ its power without
> accounting to the public for their
> actions.
>   Hitler was totally enthusiastic
> about his form of government too!
>   Political and civic power is
> always exercised in the favor of
> some element of society to the harm
> of others. This is why it is vital-
> ly important that the participation
> and the concern of as many people as
> possible be involved in political
> decisions.
>   . . . . .
>   Because the city bit off more
> than it can chew without wisdom or
> financial control, to my way of
> thinking, it is not a rural problem
> and should not be.
>   The bonding companies are be-
> ginning to shy away from, and charging

> penalty interests on the bond drives
> of the city. In order to overcome
> this difficulty . . . , the City and
> its Mayor are pushing us in the rural
> areas to come in and share their ir-
> responsibility!
>
> It is not difficult to envision
> the impossibility of the merger plan.
> What single borough administration
> could ever treat the detailed con-
> cerns of the widely spread communi-
> ties on the basis of each need of
> every community. Each community has
> the right to sponsor itself in its
> own way, and steer its own course of
> destiny. To do otherwise amounts to
> surrender of freedom, absolutely and
> totally.[14]

Thus in the Anchorage area two impulses contend: one toward unification of government, professionalism in government, and cost effectiveness;
the other emphasizing the virtues of traditional
small town local government close to the people,
operating on a first-name and face-to-face basis,
and bending the uses of government to fulfill the
needs of the electorate directly and immediately.
The impulse articulated by Rural 30 spokesmen for
small "personalized" local government, or perhaps
no government, is not entirely removed from the
main currents of Alaskan thinking, for many Alaskans claim that they live in the "last frontier"
precisely to escape the bigness, impersonality, and
government regulation that exists in other states.
The ebb and flow of such attitudes usually depends
on the specific issue. The mandatory incorporation
of boroughs and the proposed merger apparently both
have the ability to trigger such responses.

Though the Anchorage Borough-City Study Committee was established without fuss and began operations soon thereafter, the appointment of a similar committee in the Juneau area became a focal
point for some rather involved maneuvering and some
not-quite-covert conflict.

The borough chairman worked up a list of
Juneau-area residents, representing both city and
noncity areas, and presented the list to the Chamber of Commerce for suggestions and recommendations.
The list was also given to the mayor of Juneau.
The by-play between the president of the Chamber of
Commerce, the mayor of Juneau, and the borough
chairman over the names on the list, and over who,
in fact, would appoint those on the list, is not of
particular concern except as a symptom of the continuing skirmish between the city and the borough.
After almost a summer's delay, the borough chairman
unilaterally appointed a merger committee composed
of the names he had originally proposed. It had
its first meeting soon thereafter, but has only
fitfully operated since that time.

The League of Women Voters has plunged into
the merger issue with its characteristic zeal. The
Juneau League held a general meeting on the subject
and other leagues throughout the State have discussed it at unit meetings.

UNIFICATION UNDER EXISTING LAW

The brouhaha over borough and city unification
has tended to obscure the fact that several methods
are presently available which would accomplish the
goal of one government. The Borough Act provides
that "a borough is dissolved whenever its entire
territory becomes included within a city or cities."[15] In such an instance "all property and
debts owing to the borough become the property of
the government succeeding it."[16] It is possible
for any area to actually have one unit of government by simply annexing to the city.[17] Thus a remedy under the law already exists. This, in fact,
was the way in which the cities of Anchorage and
Fairbanks grew during the period of explosive population growth in the fifties and early sixties.
However, it is unlikely at this time that the Local
Boundary Commission would take the required initiative, as the matter is so highly charged politically.

Unification may also be accomplished under present law by city dissolution, though the conditions for dissolution are rather restrictive.[18] Perhaps more accessible and feasible as a tool of "near unification" is the spin-off of functions which can be accomplished by the acquisition of areawide borough powers either by petition and vote or by the voluntary transfer of a city's powers to the borough. (The assembly must approve the transfer and the city may later revoke it by majority vote of its council.[19]) Unfortunately, the voluntary transfer of city functions has been rarely used and does not appear to be a practical approach for the future. On the other hand, the acquisition of areawide powers by petition and voter approval has been successfully and widely used and will continue to be used. However, this approach tends to heighten the conflict between boroughs and cities. Moreover, the law does not permit its use in first-class boroughs (Greater Juneau Borough).

Thus despite legal provisions, unification of boroughs and cities under existing law is still somewhat problematical.

BOROUGH AND CITY ATTITUDES
TOWARD UNIFICATION

The concept of unification, whether through merger or consolidation, has taken on the aura of a crusade, if a somewhat well-modulated one. As a "motherhood" issue, the lofty goal of one unit of government is not subject to attack by local political leaders. Nor do they wish to attack it. Both city and borough officials support and agree with the agitation for one unit of government. They merely do not agree on which unit it should be, the city or the borough, nor do they entirely agree on specifics.

The Alaska Municipal League is made up primarily of the cities of Alaska, and though several boroughs do maintain membership, the League is the

main organ and spokesman for cities. The Municipal
League is solidly behind the formation of a merged
or consolidated city or borough, and so went on
record at the 1966 convention in Fairbanks, Alaska,
when the delegates unanimously accepted by voice-
vote, on October 28, 1966, a bill prepared by the
Municipal League's legislative committee: ". . .
authorizing a borough and first class and home rule
cities within the borough to form a single unit of
local government upon approval by public referendum; . . ."20

     To the cities, the major points of special in-
terest in the draft bill were the voting provisions
and the provisions for dissolution of either a borough or city. After a charter commission has been
elected and produces a proposed charter, the charter is submitted for approval at a special election.
"If a majority of the qualified voters voting on
the question of approval or rejection of the proposed charter vote to approve the charter, it is
ratified."21 The wording is significant because at
present the preponderance of population in Alaskan
urban areas is within cities. If merely a majority
of the total qualified voters in the entire area
were required to carry the issue, it is possible
that the population within cities could force unwilling and reluctant noncity areas into its em-
brace.22 The apparent immediate advantage to the
cities in such a procedure is plain. However, such
a move might well guarantee continued strife and
friction. The alternative to such a proposal would
be the requirement of concurrent majorities in both
city and noncity areas. But such is not provided
for in the Municipal League's draft.

     The draft bill also contains the injunction
that: "The charter shall include among its provisions: (1) A plan for dissolution of each first-
class or home rule city within the borough or the
dissolution of the borough."23 [Emphasis added.]
Merger or consolidation is thus seen as a two-way
street, with either the city dissolving into the
borough or the borough into the city. Coupled with

the voting provisions requiring a majority from the
whole area regardless of whether inside or outside
the city, this could give considerable impetus to
the city succeeding to the role of metropolitan government which the borough now exercises in urban
areas.

Shortly before the Municipal League convention,
the borough chairmen held a conference in Anchorage
to exchange views and experiences and to discuss
strategy relating to common problems. Though no
formal vote was taken on the question of merger or
consolidation, the general atmosphere indicated re-
ceptivity to the concept of one unit of government
by chairmen from the larger and more urbanized boroughs.[24] The borough chairmen also voted favorably
on the Municipal League's draft legislation providing for merger or consolidation.

It is relatively easy for both cities and boroughs to support the idea of one unit of government,
because each believes that it will be the unit
which absorbs the other. Evidently each side believes it has the advantage and only when the contest is actually joined will an answer be forthcoming.

THE FUTURE OF ONE UNIT OF GOVERNMENT

Widespread though diffuse support in favor of
one unit of local government exists throughout the
State. But no specific organizational support, except for that by the interested boroughs and cities
themselves, is apparent, nor is any organized campaign for merger or consolidation being run.

Though the Legislative Affairs Agency[25] was
not able to conduct formal hearings on the question
of merger and consolidation in 1966, as requested
by the House of Representatives, it did contact
borough and city officials to elicit their opinions
and preferences. The proposition of one government
was received with cautious favor.[26] Thus this

small but significant group is well-placed to exert
the influence and leadership necessary to promote
the move toward one unit of government. It appears
that the public regards the idea of one unit of
local government as an unalloyed good, and the sooner it is achieved the better.

The distinguishing characteristic of existing
legal approaches is that the move toward one unit
of government would be gradual. Merger or consolidation by one decisive act of the people is seemingly simpler and more direct. At the root of merger
and consolidation impulses lies a desire to reduce
conflict at the local governmental level, if not to
altogether eliminate it. Ironically, the "power
struggle" between boroughs and cities provides the
immediate impulse toward one unit of government.
Perhaps the larger wish is simply for government
without friction.

Some may doubt that intractable political problems can be easily solved via legislation which
changes the rules of the game. However that may be,
there are no signs that the general support in
favor of one unit of local government will soon
abate, or that Alaskans will no longer seek new
forms of local government to conform to the style
of operation they prefer.

NOTES TO CHAPTER 11

1. Minutes of the Committee on Local Government, No. 19.

2. John H. Rosswog, in Minutes, p. 2612.

3. Final Report on Borough Government, p. 17.

4. Minutes, p. 2625.

5. In this chapter "merger" and "consolidation" are used as they are colloquially, i.e.,

simply as catch-alls for unification. Actually,
the two terms are not the same. "Merger" means dissolution of a municipality and its absorption by
another municipality. "Consolidation" means dissolution of two or more municipalities and their incorporation as a new municipality.

6. "What About the Merger?" Anchorage Daily
News, February 14, 1966.

7. Approved unanimously by the delegates at
the Rural 30 convention, February 27, 1966.

8. Some of the cities were not entirely satisfied with House Bill No. 409 because it provided
only for dissolution of cities into a borough and
not for the dissolution of boroughs with the city
as the surviving unit of government.

9. "Statement of Purpose," Minutes of the
Borough-City Study Committee, Anchorage, June 2,
1966, p. 5.

10. Comments by Elmer Rasmuson, mayor, City of
Anchorage, as quoted in Minutes of the Borough-City
Study Committee, Anchorage, May 12, 1966, pp. 2-3.

11. Ibid.

12. Ibid.

13. Ibid., pp. 3-4. Councilman Clifford J.
Groh had also served as a city council representative on the Greater Anchorage Area Borough Assembly.

14. Art Ashley, chairman, Section 4, Rural 30,
presentation before the Borough-City Study Committee,
June 16, 1966, Exhibit No. 2, pp. 1-2.

15. AS 07.35.510.

16. AS 07.35.520.

17. AS 29.70.

18. AS 29.10.543-549 and AS 29.80.010-050.

19. AS 07.15.910.

20. Legislative Committee, Alaska Municipal
League, Draft Bill, October, 1966, p. 1. Hereafter
cited as Draft Bill.

21. Ibid., p. 7.

22. House Bill No. 409, like the Municipal
League draft bill, requires only a simple borough-
wide majority to approve a proposed charter. Significantly, the Anchorage Borough-City Study Committee draft bill requires concurrent majorities
both inside and outside city limits. It will be
interesting to see which approach the legislature
takes.

23. Draft Bill, p. 5.

24. Private communication from Claude Millsap,
Jr., Chairman, Greater Juneau Borough, January 11,
1967.

25. An act of the 1966 legislature changed
the name of the staff of the Legislative Council
to Legislative Affairs Agency.

26. The number of responses was actually
rather small. However, the authors have contacted
a number of borough and city officials and found
them uniformly in favor, in principle, of borough-
city unification.

APPENDIX A

SHORT INTRODUCTION TO ALASKA'S

GEOGRAPHY, POPULATION, AND ECONOMY

APPENDIX A

SHORT INTRODUCTION TO ALASKA'S
GEOGRAPHY, POPULATION, AND ECONOMY

The size of Alaska and its geographical setting have a crucial influence on the political,
social, and economic development of the State.

The vast size of the State is often discussed
but rarely comprehended. Alaska has an area of
586,400 square miles, making it one fifth the
size of the continental United States--as large as
France, Spain, England, and East and West Germany
combined, or more than twice the size of Texas.

Although Alaska is seen by many as one large
icebox, the State has a variety of climates. The
northern and western regions are arctic and sub-
arctic in character and are sparsely populated,
largely by Eskimos. The southcentral area is much
more moderate; it is here that the majority of
Alaska's population lives and where the largest
city, Anchorage, is located. Southeastern Alaska,
the panhandle, is humorously referred to by Alaskans as the "banana belt" because its climate is
more similar to the coastal areas of the Pacific
Northwest than to the other parts of Alaska.

The population of Alaska has almost quadrupled
in twenty-five years, increasing from 72,524 in
1940[1] to 265,192 in 1965,[2] though it is still the
least populous state in the Union. The largest
part of this growth occurred in the decade 1950-60,
when the economy was spurred on by the construction of several major Army and Air Force installations. These installations are mainly located in

379

the Fairbanks and Anchorage areas, stimulating the
growth of both parts of the State so that presently over half the population is clustered in these
areas.

In spite of the size of Alaska and the dis-
persed settlement pattern of its Eskimo and Indian
populations, the State is highly urbanized.   Approximately three quarters of the population is
clustered in the major cities and their environs.

Perhaps 20 per cent of the population of the
State is of Eskimo, Indian, or Aleut descent.[3]
These groups are only now in the process of absorption into the economy and culture of mid-twentieth
century America. Naturally, their needs and demands often differ sharply from those of other inhabitants. In 1960 Alaska's population was the
most youthful of any state, and with the continuing
high rate of natural increase, particularly among
Eskimos and Indians, it continues to have an extremely young population.

The initial stimulus to population growth in
Alaska was the gold rush at the turn of the century. However, after gold mining went into decline, the salmon industry became the leader in
the Alaskan economy. Presently, Federal employment, both civilian and military, accounts for almost 45 per cent of the total wages and salaries
paid, although military spending and the number
of military personnel have declined since the mid-
1950's. The emergence of a resource-based (and
distributive industry) economy has been marked
from that time.

Dependence on Federal expenditures varies
from one region of the State to another. Southeastern Alaska has long had a natural resource
economy based on timber and pulp, fishing, and
tourism. The Anchorage area is the administrative
and service center for Alaska by virtue of the
city's position as terminus on the Alaska Rail-
road, its nearness to the oil fields in the Cook
Inlet area, and the presence of two large military

bases which provide almost 20 per cent of the area's population.

Since the mid-1950's a change in the factors of population growth has occurred. Natural increase has become more important than migration, a trend accompanying the change from an unstable population dominated by single men to one of young families. Alaska's population, however, is still more mobile than the national average and is characterized by a high degree of transiency.

Thus, Alaska is a developing State with a variety of climatic regions, a diversity of groups in its population, and different levels of economic development.

NOTES TO APPENDIX A

1. U.S., Bureau of the Census, Sixteenth Census of the United States: 1940. Population-- Alaska, Second Series, "Characteristics of the Population," p. 1.

2. Alaska, Alaska Department of Labor, Employment Security Division, Research and Analysis Section, Current Population Estimates--Alaska--By Election District, July 1, 1965.

3. The Eskimo population is located mainly along the coasts of western and northern Alaska. The Indian population is found in interior and southeastern Alaska; Athabascans predominate in the former region and Tlingit, Haida, and Tsimshian in the latter. The Aleuts, primarily residents of the Aleutian Chain, are numerically the smallest of the indigenous groups.

APPENDIX B

GREATER JUNEAU BOROUGH GENERAL

TREASURY MANAGEMENT PLAN AND

CENTRAL ACCOUNTING OFFICE

APPENDIX B

GREATER JUNEAU BOROUGH

RESOLUTION NO. 23

CREATING A GENERAL TREASURY MANAGEMENT
PLAN AND A CENTRAL ACCOUNTING OFFICE
FOR ALL OF THE GREATER JUNEAU BOROUGH
OPERATIONS INCLUDING OPERATIONS OF THE
GENERAL GOVERNMENT AND OF THE SCHOOL
SYSTEM.

WHEREAS, it is necessary for the efficient
operation of the Borough Government of the Greater
Juneau Borough, that financial operations and accounting procedures be consolidated and

WHEREAS, one official of the Borough should
be charged with the responsibilities of the investment program of the total resources of the entire
Borough in order to centralize responsibility for
investments, and

WHEREAS, a general treasury reduces the need
for total operating balances to be kept on hand
and thus frees moneys that would otherwise be used
for operating balance for investment from which
income can be realized:

NOW THEREFORE, BE IT RESOLVED:
1.   That a general treasury management plan
be adopted as set out in this section.
        (a) Appropriation.
            All monetary resources of the Borough
    shall be allocated by appropriation made by
    the Borough Assembly.

385

(b) <u>Responsibility for Treasury Management</u>.
The Borough Chairman shall be responsible for treasury management, including investment and reinvestment of all revenues of the general government, the School District and of any other agencies or districts subsequently created or incorporated into the Borough.

(c) <u>School Board Treasurer as Borough Treasurer</u>.
The School Board treasurer shall be ex officio Borough treasurer. Should the School Board treasurer decline his responsibilities under this section, the Borough Assembly of the Greater Juneau Borough shall designate a borough treasurer.

(d) <u>Borough Treasurer as Financial Agent</u>.
The Borough treasurer shall be the financial agent for the general government of the Borough, the School District and of any other agencies or districts subsequently created or incorporated into the Borough, and shall receive and disburse all revenues from whatever source received.

(e) <u>Disbursement Procedure</u>.
The Borough treasurer shall pay out money held for the account of the School District on vouchers approved and signed by the president, clerk and treasurer of the School District and shall pay out money held for the account of the general government on vouchers approved and signed by the Borough Chairman. Should any other agencies or districts be subsequently created or incorporated into the Borough, the Greater Juneau Borough Assembly shall by resolution designate the official or officials to approve and sign vouchers. No such vouchers shall be approved unless drawn against appropriations previously made by the Borough Assembly. All treasury funds shall be invested and reinvested at the order of the Borough Chairman given directly to the depository at which the treasury account is maintained. An information copy of such order shall be sent to the Borough treasurer

and to the Chairman of the review and audit
committee of the Borough Assembly.
    (f) <u>Permissible Investments</u>.
      The Borough Chairman shall invest
money only in the following types of investments:
      1. Bonds, notes or other obligations
of the United States.
      2. Bonds or other evidences of in-
debtedness of the State of Alaska.
      3. Bonds or other evidences of in-
debtedness of any municipal or political
subdivision of the State of Alaska.
      4. Savings accounts or certificates
of deposit or any bank authorized to do
business in the State of Alaska.
      5. Certificates of deposit of any
nationally chartered bank, provided that
the total certificate of deposit of any
such bank shall not exceed the paid up
capital of such bank exclusive of revenues
and surplus.

      2. That a central accounting office to handle
accounting functions for the general government,
the School District and any other agencies be hereby created. The central accounting office shall
be under the direction of the School District Business Manager or such other official as the Borough
Chairman shall designate and shall not be responsible for detailed tax accounting. The costs of
operation of the central accounting office shall
be borne jointly by the general government and the
School District in proportion to the amount of
work required for each. Should any agency or district be subsequently incorporated into the Borough, such agency or district shall bear its pro-
portional share of the costs of operation of the
Central Accounting Office in the same manner.

      3. That a review and audit committee of the
Borough Assembly be hereby created. The number of
members shall be determined by the Borough Assembly President. The Borough Assembly President

shall appoint the members of the committee who
shall serve at his pleasure. The review and audit
committee shall review the investment program of
the Borough Chairman at least monthly and shall
give a full report to the Borough Assembly of the
amounts available for investment, the amount invested and the type of investments made at least
quarterly. The committee may require an audit of
the investment program at such times as it deems
necessary.

Adopted October 7, 1964.

APPENDIX C

GREATER ANCHORAGE AREA BOROUGH ORDINANCE

ESTABLISHING TAXATION STRUCTURE AND

PROCEDURE FOR ASSESSMENT AND

LEVYING AND COLLECTING TAXES

APPENDIX C

GREATER ANCHORAGE AREA BOROUGH, ALASKA

ORDINANCE NO. 5

ORDINANCE ESTABLISHING TAXATION STRUCTURE
AND PROCEDURE FOR ASSESSMENT AND LEVYING
AND COLLECTING TAXES

THE GREATER ANCHORAGE AREA BOROUGH ORDAINS:

SECTION 1. PROPERTY SUBJECT TO TAXATION.
    a. All property not exempt under the Constitution or laws of the State of Alaska or the ordinances of the borough is subject to taxation.
    b. When any real property exempt from taxation is leased, loaned or otherwise made available to and used by a private person, such person's interest therein shall be taxable. Taxes shall be assessed to such person and collected in the same manner as taxes assessed to owners of real property, except that taxes assessed under this subsection shall be a lien only on the interest of such person in the property. When due, taxes so assessed shall constitute a debt due from such person to the borough, and shall be recoverable by an action against such person, this remedy being available as an alternative to or in addition to the remedy of foreclosure of the interest of the person in the property.

SECTION 2. EXEMPTIONS.
    a. The household furniture and effects of a head of family or householder as well as the personal effects of any taxpayer, not exceeding $200.00 in aggregate value, shall be exempt from

391

taxation. Only one exemption shall be allowed a husband and wife under this subsection on either a separate or joint return.

b. A modification or addition to an existing structure, or a new structure, designed to provide shelter from radioactive fallout, bombs, or like disaster, shall be exempt from taxation to the extent of the increase in valuation attributable to such construction, not exceeding $5,000.00. Such exemption shall be granted by the assessor upon submission to him of an application therefore accompanied by satisfactory proof that such shelter has been approved by the local office of civil defense and by all building officials having jurisdiction. This exemption shall not reduce the valuation of the main premises if the shelter is built as a part thereof, but shall only reduce any higher valuation of the premises resulting directly from the construction of the shelter.

SECTION 3.   ASSESSMENT.

a. The assessor shall annually compile a list of all property in the borough, in the name of the persons by whom it was owned on the first day of the tax year for which the list is made.

b. Personal property returns shall be filed on or before February 15 of each year. Upon written request and a showing of good cause the assessor may grant an additional period for filing not exceeding thirty (30) days. Failure to file a timely return adds penalty to the tax on the property which should be listed in such return, as in the case of delinquent taxes.

c. Property returns shall be confidential, and shall be inspected only by officers authorized to administer the tax laws and law enforcement officers of the United States, State of Alaska, borough, and municipalities within the borough, or in response to a valid subpoena. Any employee violating this restriction by communicating information obtained from property returns not required to be shown on the assessment roll, or allowing any person not legally entitled to access to such returns to have access to them, shall immediately

be discharged from borough employment, and shall
be guilty of a misdemeanor punishable under this
ordinance.

SECTION 4.   ASSESSMENT NOTICE.
        Assessment notices shall state that an appeal
may be taken to the board of equalization only by
filing written notice of appeal specifying the
grounds for the appeal with the board of equalization within thirty (30) days after notice of
assessment is mailed.

SECTION 5.   PAYMENT IN INSTALLMENTS; DELINQUENT
             DATES; PENALTY AND INTEREST.
        a.   Any taxpayer may pay the property tax for
a tax year in two (2) installments of equal amount.
The first installment shall become delinquent on
June 1, and the second installment shall become
delinquent on September 1 if the first installment
was paid before June 1. The foregoing delinquent
dates apply to property listed on the original
assessment roll and on supplementary rolls.
        b.   If the first installment is not paid be-
fore the delinquent date, the entire tax becomes
delinquent, and penalty and interest accrue as
follows:
        1.   A penalty of eight per cent shall be
added to all taxes delinquent until the delinquent
date for the second installment, and interest at
the rate of eight per cent a year shall be charged
on the whole of the unpaid taxes, not including
penalty, from the delinquent date until paid in
full.
        2.   On and after the delinquent date for
the second installment, a total penalty of ten per
cent shall be added to all delinquent taxes, and
interest at the rate of eight per cent a year
shall accrue upon all unpaid taxes, not including
penalties, from the delinquent date until paid in
full.

SECTION 6.   PRORATION OF TAXES.
        The assessor shall delete from the assessment
roll the portion of the taxes otherwise due for

the second half of the tax year which are attributable to improvements on real property, upon written application within the tax year, and satisfactory evidence that said improvements were demolished
or abated during the first half of the tax year pursuant to an agreement between the borough or any
city thereof and the taxpayer that said improvements constituted a public nuisance, or pursuant
to a valid final determination by the assembly or
an administrative body or court that said improvements constituted a public nuisance and should be
demolished.

SECTION 7.   PERSONAL PROPERTY TAXES; DELINQUENCY;
              REMEDY.
     Owners of personal property assessed shall be
personally liable for the taxes assessed against
such property together with penalty and interest.
The borough may after such taxes become delinquent
bring suit against such owners to collect the taxes,
penalty, and interest.

SECTION 8.   SEVERABILITY.
     If any provision of this ordinance, or its
application to any person or circumstance, is held
invalid, the remainder of the ordinance and its application to other persons or circumstances shall
not be affected.

SECTION 9.   PENALTY FOR VIOLATION.
     Unless another penalty is expressly provided
by the laws of the State of Alaska or by borough
ordinance, every person convicted of a violation
of this ordinance shall be punishable by a fine
not exceeding $300.00, by imprisonment for not
more than thirty (30) days, or by both such fine
and imprisonment.

SECTION 10.   DEFINITIONS.
     In this ordinance, unless the context other-
wise requires,
     a.   "board of equalization" means the assem-
           bly sitting as a board of equalization;
     b.   "borough" means Greater Anchorage Area
           Borough;

    c.   "person" includes an individual, a partner-
ship, a corporation, an association, an
organization, a fiduciary, and any other
entity;

    d.   "personal property" includes any property
other than real property;

    e.   "property" includes real property and per-
sonal property;

    f.   "real property" includes land, whether
laid out in lots or otherwise, all buildings, structures, improvements, and fixtures of any kind thereon, and all posses-
sory rights and privileges belonging or
pertaining thereto;

    g.   "tract" includes all lands and pieces or
parcels of land which may be separately
assessed, together with fixtures and improvements thereon.

SECTION 11.   TRANSITIONAL MEASURES.

    a.   The purpose of this section is to effect
an orderly transition from the present taxation
structure within the borough to assumption of taxing functions by the borough pursuant to the laws
of the State of Alaska.   Transitional measures are
needed because the City of Anchorage tax year commences on January 1 and ends on December 31, while
the Anchorage Independent School District tax year
commences on July 1 and ends on June 30, and the
borough must assume taxing functions of both entities, and because the limited time before taxes
for the area outside of the City of Anchorage will
be delinquent for borough tax year 1964 requires a
temporary change in the delinquency date for such
taxes.

    b.   The borough shall assume the taxing func-
tions of the Anchorage Independent School District
in regard to property not in the City of Anchorage
on the effective date of this ordinance, and shall
assess, levy and collect taxes on such property
for school purposes for borough tax year 1964.
The taxes for school purposes collected and to be
collected by the City of Anchorage for the second
half of its tax year 1964 will by agreement between

the City of Anchorage and the borough be paid to
the borough during its tax year 1964. The borough
shall assume its taxing functions in the City of
Anchorage on January 1, 1965.

c. For borough tax year 1964 only, property
returns shall be filed only for property not in
the City of Anchorage, and shall be filed on or
before July 15, 1964, and the assessor shall grant
no extensions for filing property returns. For
borough tax year 1964 only, the entire tax levied
on property not in the City of Anchorage shall become delinquent on October 30, 1964, and shall be
paid in one installment.

APPENDIX D

FAIRBANKS NORTH STAR BOROUGH

FISCAL MANAGEMENT PROCEDURES ORDINANCE

APPENDIX D

ORDINANCE NO. 65-18

FISCAL MANAGEMENT PROCEDURES

AN ORDINANCE PROVIDING FOR A FISCAL YEAR
FOR THE NORTH STAR BOROUGH; PREPARATION
AND SUBMISSION OF BUDGETS AND CAPITAL
PROGRAMS AND ASSEMBLY ACTIONS ON THE
BUDGETS; CREATING A GENERAL TREASURY
MANAGEMENT PLAN; CREATING A CENTRAL
ACCOUNTING OFFICE; PROVIDING FOR POST
AUDIT PROCEDURES; AND PROVIDING FOR
REVIEW BY A COMMITTEE OF THE BOROUGH
ASSEMBLY.

BE IT ORDAINED by the Assembly of the North
Star Borough:

Section 1. Fiscal Year. The fiscal year of
the borough shall begin on the first day of July
and end on the last day of June.

Section 2. Budget and Capital Program.
(a) Submission of a Comprehensive Budget and
Budget Message. On or before the 15th day of
March each year, the Borough Chairman shall submit
a comprehensive budget to the Borough Assembly
with an accompanying message and the proposed appropriation and tax levy ordinance.
To assist the borough chairman in the
preparation of this budget, the school administration shall submit through the chairman to the
borough assembly, a budget for that department's
operations for the ensuing year with suggested in-
clusions for the budget message. This school

budget shall be a part of the comprehensive borough budget.

(b) Budget Message: Contents. The budget
message shall explain the budget both in fiscal
terms and in terms of work programs. It shall outline the proposed financial policies for the ensuing fiscal year and summarize the debt position
and include such other material as the submitting
authority deems desirable.

(c) Budget Contents. The budget shall provide
a complete financial plan of all borough funds and
activities for the ensuing fiscal year and shall
be in such form as the chairman deems desirable or
the assembly may require. It shall show in detail
all estimated income, indicate the proposed property tax levy; and show in detail all proposed expenditures, including debt service for the ensuing
fiscal year; and shall be so arranged as to show
comparative figures for income and expenditures
for the current fiscal year and estimated income
and expenditures for next succeeding fiscal year.
The total of proposed expenditures shall not exceed the total of estimated income and available
fund balances from the prior year.

(d) School System Budget: Contents. The contents of the school system budget shall be the
same as that provided in Section 2. The school
system shall provide the chairman with estimated
income figures for the items of support from
federal, state, and other sources.

(e) Capital Program. The chairman shall, after receiving the proposed Capital Improvements
Program from the Planning Commission, review, supplement and submit the Capital Improvements Program
to the Assembly prior to December 15th of each
year. The Program shall include:

(1) A clear general summary of its contents.
(2) A list of all capital improvements
which are proposed to be undertaken during the
five fiscal years next ensuing after the
budgeted year, with appropriate supporting information as to the necessity for such improvement.
(3) Costs estimates, methods of financing

and recommended time schedules for each improvement.

(4) The estimated annual cost of operating and maintaining the facilities to be constructed or acquired. The above information
may be revised and extended each year with regard to capital improvements still pending or
in process of construction or acquisition.

(f) Assembly Action on the Budget. The assembly shall publish a general summary of the budgets
and the capital program. The public hearing on
the budgets and capital program shall follow the
required publication by at least one week, and it
may be held separately or in connection with a
regular or special assembly meeting and may be
adjourned from time to time. After public hearing,
the assembly may adopt with or without amendment,
the proposed annual budget and the proposed capital program by passage of the annual appropriation
tax levy ordinance. No payment may be authorized
or made and no obligation incurred against the
borough except in accordance with appropriations
duly made. Nothing contained in this section or
in other sections of this ordinance is intended to
prevent the authorizing of payments or making of
contracts for capital improvements to be financed
wholly or partly by the issuance of bonds nor is
it intended to prevent the making, when permitted
by law, of any contract or any lease providing for
the payment of funds at a time beyond the end of
the fiscal year in which the contract or lease is
made. But any contract, lease, or other obligation requiring the payment of funds from the appropriation of a later fiscal year, or more than
one fiscal year, shall be made or approved by
ordinances.

(g) The assembly shall adopt the budget by
the first day of May of the fiscal year currently
ending. If it fails to adopt the budget by this
date, the budget submitted by the chairman is considered adopted. Adoption of the budget shall
constitute appropriations to the general government and school system in the total amounts specified therein for each, as expenditures, from the

funds indicated and shall constitute a levy of the
property tax therein proposed.

(h) A Bond Election Ordinance will be introduced by the chairman based on his recommended
capital improvement program which will outline all
the propositions to be placed before the voters at
the next general election. The Bond Election Ordinance as finally approved by the Assembly shall
contain those projects outlined in the approved
Capital Improvement Program. Subsequent additions
of projects to be financed by bonds must be scheduled for inclusion in the following year's Capital
Improvement Program.

Section 3. Transfer of Appropriations. No
transfer from one appropriation level to another
appropriation level may be made except by ordinance.
Within the appropriation levels, the chairman may
transfer part or all of any unencumbered appropriation balance among activities.

Section 4. Lapse of Appropriation. Every
appropriation, except an appropriation for a capital expenditure, shall lapse at the close of the
fiscal year to the extent that it has not been expended by the receipt of goods and services by
June 30th. An appropriation for a capital expenditure shall continue in force until the purpose for
which it was made has been accomplished or abandoned; the purpose of any such appropriation shall
be deemed abandoned if three years pass without
any disbursement from or encumbrance of the appropriation.

Section 5. General Treasury Management Plan.
The borough chairman shall be responsible for
treasury management and shall be authorized to invest and reinvest all revenues of the general government, the school district and or any other agencies or districts subsequently created or incorporated into the borough, the proceeds of bond or
note issues and moneys deposited in special funds
created by the borough in connection with the issuance of bonds or notes.

(a) <u>Permissible Investments</u>. The borough chairman shall invest money only in the following types of investments:

(1) Bonds, notes or other obligations of the United States.

(2) Bonds or other evidences of indebtedness of the State of Alaska.

(3) Bonds or other evidences of indebtedness of any municipal or political subdivision of the State of Alaska.

(4) Savings accounts or certificates of deposit or time open account of any bank authorized to do business in the State of Alaska.

(5) Certificates of deposit of any nationally chartered bank of saving accounts or time open accounts, provided that the total deposit in any such bank shall not exceed the paid up capital of such bank exclusive of revenues and surplus.

(6) Federally insured savings and loan associations to the extent that the investment is insured by Federal Deposit Insurance Corporation.

<u>Section 6. Central Accounting</u>. All accounting functions, the school system and any other agencies of the borough shall be performed by the central accounting office. The central accounting office shall be under the direction of such persons as the borough chairman shall designate.

<u>Section 7. Post Audit</u>. The assembly shall provide for an annual independent audit of the accounts and other evidences of financial transactions of the borough and of every borough department. The audit shall be made by an accountant, designated by the assembly, who has no personal interest, direct or indirect, in the fiscal affairs of the borough or of any of its departments. The designated accountant shall be a certified public accountant.

<u>Section 8. Review Committee</u>. That a review committee of the Borough Assembly is hereby

created. The number of members shall be determined by the Borough Assembly Presiding Officer.
The Borough Assembly Presiding Officer shall appoint the members of the committee who shall serve
at his pleasure. The review committee shall review the investment program of the borough chairman quarterly and shall give a full report of the
amount invested and the type of investments made,
to the Borough Assembly. The committee may recommend an audit of the investment program at such
times as it deems necessary.

    Section 10. Severability Clause. Any or-
dinance or resolution inconsistent with the provisions of this ordinance is hereby repealed.

    PASSED this 3rd day of June, 1965.

APPENDIX E

SAMPLE POST-AUDIT CONTRACT

CONTRACT AND AGREEMENT

This agreement, entered into this _____ day
of _____, 19___, by and between
_____,
hereinafter referred to as the municipality, and
_____,
hereinafter referred to as the auditors.

WHEREAS, the municipality requires a complete
financial report on the total functions and activities of the municipality not later than 2 1/2
months after the end of the fiscal year; and

WHEREAS, it is desirable that only one financial report covering the same fiscal period be
prepared; and

WHEREAS, it is desirable to standardize the
reporting form so as to contain the financial
statement illustrated through Part Two of the
Municipal Accounting and Auditing publication by
the Municipal Finance Officers Association of the
United States and Canada which is also described
as Publication No. 14 of the National Committee on
Governmental Accounting; and

WHEREAS, it is desirable to standardize the
statistical tables to the form illustrated and described in Section I-III of Part Two of the above
publication, these tables will not be considered
part of the opinion;

NOW, THEREFORE, the parties hereto do mutually agree as follows:

1. Scope of Services. The auditor shall complete
    an audit in accordance with the generally ac-
    cepted auditing standards prescribed by the
    American Institute of Certified Public Ac-
    countants recognizing the recommendations of
    the National Committee on Governmental Ac-
    counting.
    a. The audit shall be within the definitions
        of a Limited General Audit as described in
        the Municipal Accounting and Auditing pub-
        lication of the National Committee on Gov-
        ernmental Accounting.
    b. The audit report shall be transmitted to
        the municipality's legislative body within
        two and one-half months after the end of
        the fiscal year.
    c. The report shall cover all functions and
        activities of the municipality and shall
        be on the modified accrual basis as de-
        fined by the National Committee on Govern-
        mental Accounting.
    d. The report shall be in the form outlined
        in Part Three, Section III, The Audit Re-
        port, Municipal Accounting and Auditing,
        containing a letter of transmittal, a finan-
        cial section, and a statistical section.
    e. Completion and submission of the Report of
        Expenditures required by the State Depart-
        ment of Education.

2. Compensation. The fee is based upon the
    amount of time necessary to perform the audit.
    However, the auditor, after being notified of
    his selection, has surveyed the fiscal records
    and identified the principal problems, esti-
    mated the cost of the services to be $_____,
    which is not likely to be exceeded unless he
    encounters unforeseen problems. Payment is
    to be made upon receipt of the reports and an
    invoice for said services.

3. Consulting Services Arising Out of Audit
    Recommendations. The auditor in being awarded
    this contract is fully aware that the munici-
    pality shall not engage the auditor for future

work to implement any of the changes in the
"general accounting procedures and suggestions
made during the course of the audit." In
addition, the firm shall not be considered for
other management or any feasibility study designed to improve accounting, organizational
or management procedures of the municipality.

APPENDIX F

GREATER ANCHORAGE AREA BOROUGH

ASSEMBLY-BOARD OF EDUCATION

OPERATING PROCEDURES

APPENDIX F

ANCHORAGE INDEPENDENT SCHOOL DISTRICT
Anchorage, Alaska

DATE: March 24, 1964

FROM: Frank M. Reed, President, Board of
            Education

TO: Mr. John M. Asplund, Borough Chairman

SUBJECT: Borough Assembly-Board of Education
            Operating Procedures

     I.   Buildings
          1. Planning, Designing
          2. Construction

    II. Sites
          1. Location
          2. Acquisition

   III. Financing
          1. Bond Authorizations
          2. Bond Sales

    IV. Contracts--General

     V. School District Elections

The Boards of Education, both the Greater
Anchorage Area and Anchorage Independent School
District as presently constituted, recognize the
need for well established operating procedures at
the time when all education functions have been
amalgamated into a single borough school district.

We are certain that you as Borough Chairman and
the Borough Assembly are equally cognizant of that
need.

Accordingly, we have, based upon our combined
years of experience in school matters, prepared
for your consideration some suggested procedures
to be followed in the listed five areas of physical services. If you agree with the proposals, we
urge you to recommend them to the Borough Assembly
for early consideration.

> Each organized borough constitutes a
> borough school district and the first
> and second class borough shall estab-
> lish, maintain, and operate a system
> of public schools on an areawide
> basis, and shall do so in the manner
> provided by law for city school dis-
> tricts, except as provided otherwise
> by this title. (AS 07.15.330 [a])

The above cited statute becomes the basis for
the responsibility which the borough has in the
function of education, a responsibility which the
Board of Education of Anchorage Independent School
District currently has. The "law for city school
districts" requires the Council (in the case of
the borough, the assembly) to "provide the school
district with suitable schoolhouses, and the necessary funds to maintain public schools." (AS 14.15.
240). It follows, of course, that the providing
of schoolhouses involves site acquisition, equipping the buildings, and bonding or otherwise providing for the payment thereof in addition to the
construction.

I. Buildings--As you, from your own experience, are well aware the planning, designing, and
constructing of a school facility involves much
work and skill beyond the technical drawing of
plans, drafting specifications and actual building of structures. We believe the Board of Education and its administrative staff has and always

will have the facts and necessary skills to assist
you and the Borough Assembly by assuming, subject
to your approvals, these functions.

1.   Planning, designing--The need for
school facilities arises from pupil enrollments as
indicated on the projection charts of the school
district. Or, in the case of a non-instruction
facility, the need arises from operating program
requirements.

It will, under the law, be our responsibility
to operate program and maintain plant. Consequently all records will be kept by the Board of Education, all pupil data upon which the need for facilities is based is our responsibility to process
and maintain. Instruction and operation program
planning will be the sole responsibility of our
Board. We believe that the proper method of planning and designing facilities is by those charged
with the use and care of those facilities. We believe that we can serve you and the Borough Assembly best by assuming for you this detailed function and in so doing avoid a duplication of effort
and thereby effect some considerable economy.

2.   Construction--In our experience during the past 10-12 years we have found that structures which have been planned and designed by us
were most economically and efficiently constructed
under our supervision. The continuous supervision
of construction and co-ordination of construction
with planning and design has, we feel, produced
the best quality and economy in facilities. We
would propose to use, subject to Assembly approval,
the Clerk-of-the-Works program which we as a Board
currently use in the Anchorage Independent School
District. This technician is in the direct employ
of the School District and would, if approved, be
in the direct employ of the Borough, but under the
coordinating responsibility of the Board of Education.

The Board would like at your pleasure and

that of the Assembly the opportunity to analyze
construction bids received and recommend to the
Assembly the final contract award.

Finally we would be pleased to have the responsibility on behalf of the Borough to follow
through on the enforcement of construction contracts, including the warranty periods following
completion of facilities.

PROPOSAL NO. 1. The Board of Education proposes that you recommend to the Borough Assembly
the following:

   a.   The Borough Assembly by proper resolution
        charge the Board of Education with prepar-
        ing and maintaining the Master Building
        and Financing Plan of the Borough School
        District, subject to formal approval by
        the Assembly.

   b.   The Borough Assembly by formal resolution
        require the Board of Education to assume
        the responsibility for recommending to
        the Assembly the choice of architects
        and/or engineers for the designing of
        capital improvements for education.
        That such resolution further requires the
        Board of Education to coordinate the work
        of the architects and/or engineers repre-
        senting the Borough in these functions,
        submitting plans and specifications and
        other contract documents to the Assembly
        for final approval only.

   c.   That the Borough Assembly by resolution
        establishes jointly with the City of
        Anchorage the Construction Advisory Com-
        mittee to assist the Board of Education
        in its work of planning and designing
        capital improvements for education.

   d.   That the Borough Assembly by resolution
        require the Board of Education to

supervise construction of facilities after the Assembly has awarded the contracts
therefor.

e. That the Borough Assembly by resolution
    require the Board of Education to plan
    proper equipment for new and present
    facilities, submitting equipment plans to
    the Assembly for final approval.

f. The Borough Assembly by resolution require
    the Board of Education to obtain and main-
    tain proper casualty and liability insur-
    ance, subject to final Assembly approval.

II.   Sites--One of our most difficult tasks
as a Board of Education has been the choice of
sites for placing schools. The entire community
is affected by the location of a school facility
and the effect is one with which the community
must live for many years.

As in the case of planning and designing
the actual structure, most of the influencing data
is in files maintained in the operation of schools.
In addition to pupil enrollment records there is
also required close scrutiny of economic information, planning and zoning regulations, public improvements planned and constructed by other agencies, and health and safety regulations.

We believe again that we can serve the
Borough best by assuming at the direction of the
Assembly the function of determining all factors
relating to the proper location of education
facilities and recommending their designation and
acquisition.

PROPOSAL NO. 2. The Board of Education proposes that you recommend to the Borough Assembly
the following:

a. The Borough Assembly by resolution charge
    the Board of Education with preparing

recommendations to the Assembly for the
location of sites for placing education
facilities, coordinating such locations
with plans of other public agencies
charged with the planning and developing
public facilities.

b. The Borough Assembly by resolution dele-
    gate to the Board of Education the re-
    sponsibility of negotiations with property
    owners for the purchase of sites, making
    final recommendations to the Assembly for
    purchase thereof.

c. That the Borough Assembly charge the
    Board of Education with all negotiations
    for on-site and off-site utilities, sub-
    ject to final approval by the Assembly.

III. Financing--Inherent in statutes estab-
lising Borough responsibility for providing "suitable schoolhouses" is the responsibility to provide the funds for these facilities. The need now
and in the foreseeable future is so great that
general obligation bonding is the only available
source of funds sufficient to accomplish our task.

At the present time (June 30, 1963)
Anchorage Independent School District has outstanding bonded indebtedness in the amount of $21,111,000
to which debt the Borough will succeed upon assuming the function of education. (AS 07.10.130)

In addition, the District has unissued
voter authorization to sell bonds in the amount of
$7,500,000 (from the October 1, 1963, Special Bond
Election).

Several legal questions remain to be
answered with respect to the use to which the
authorized $7,500,000 may be expended. The School
District General Legal Counsel as well as the Fiscal Legal Counsel are currently working on the research in this matter. Their report and opinion,

upon its receipt, will be communicated to you immediately.

   1.   Bond Authorizations--It is our opinion
that we as the Borough Board of Education can be of
great service to you and the Assembly by continuing
with the preliminary fact finding in preparation
for bond authorization elections, recommending to
the Assembly the necessary amounts and suggesting
amortization schedules. We believe we can be of
further assistance to the Borough in its bond election campaign by being available to interpret to
the voting public our understanding of the need
for proposed bond issues.

   2.   Bond Sales--We believe that our experience since 1950 in the sale of general obligation bonds may prove valuable to the Borough. We
will have on our administrative staff people
skilled and experienced in bond sales. If you and
the Assembly agree with us and direct us accordingly, it would avoid the necessity for the Borough
to have in its direct employ the personnel to carry
out such ministerial functions unless they are
needed in other areas of Borough service.

   PROPOSAL NO. 3. The Board of Education proposes that you recommend to the Borough Assembly
the following:

   a.   The Borough Assembly by resolution charge
        the Board of Education with the prepara-
        tion of recommendations for general obli-
        gation bond authorization elections.
        That such resolutions also charge the
        Board of Education with the responsibil-
        ity, after Assembly approval, of prepar-
        ing supporting information for public
        dissemination.

   b.   The Borough Assembly by resolution direct
        the Board of Education to recommend to
        the Assembly the schedules of sale of
        bonds.

That this resolution further direct the
Board of Education to act for the Borough
in preparing the basic resolutions, prospectus and other supporting documents required in the sale of bonds.

IV.   <u>Contracts--General</u>--You have already
recommended and the Assembly has approved the delegation to the Board of Education contracting authority during this transitional period. Both the Borough Board of Education and that of the Anchorage
Independent School District are proceeding under
the guidelines established by Assembly action.

Upon the amalgamation of the entire area
of the Borough into a single education unit, it
will not be necessary to establish such a procedure
as the statutes already clearly set out the responsibility of the Board of Education to manage
the fiscal affairs of the school district once the
Assembly has provided the funds for education purposes by approval of the annual budget (<u>AS</u> 14.15.300,
<u>AS</u> 14.15.310, <u>AS</u> 14.15.330, <u>AS</u> 14.15.350). The
funds so obligated by the contracting activities of
the Board of Education do not, of course, include
those for construction and equipping of schoolhouses
and the acquisition of sites. Our proposals affecting that area of operation are provided elsewhere
in this communication.

V.   <u>School District Elections</u>--At the present
time little or no attention, to our knowledge, has
been given to this area of operation. It is assumed, however, that the Borough does assume the
legal responsibility for this function of government.

Your attention is directed to this at
this time because only six (6) months remain until
the Borough will hold its election, including the
choosing of members for the Board of Education.
Subtracting advertising time for the election
leaves less than five (5) months in which to consolidate voting records of the Anchorage Independent

School District, of the Girdwood City School District and establishing new voter records for eligible voters in the previously unorganized area.

The problem you face, we believe, is one in which you will want our suggestions on detail and possibly other assistance. The present Anchorage Independent School District, as you know, requires pre-registration of voters; the eligible voters in the previously unorganized area were not so required. It would seem to us that uniformity on a borough-wide basis would be your recommendation and the decision of the Assembly.

We do not with this document present a formal proposal. We do, however, stand ready and willing to counsel with you, utilizing the knowledge gained through experience of our administrative staff.

APPENDIX G

GREATER ANCHORAGE AREA BOROUGH RESOLUTION

NO. 32 ESTABLISHING BOROUGH ASSEMBLY-

SCHOOL BOARD RELATIONSHIP

APPENDIX G

GREATER ANCHORAGE AREA BOROUGH, ALASKA

RESOLUTION NO. 32

A RESOLUTION OF THE ASSEMBLY OF THE GREATER ANCHOR-
AGE AREA BOROUGH FIXING THE OVERALL RESPONSIBILITY
OF THE BOARD OF EDUCATION OF THE GREATER ANCHORAGE
AREA BOROUGH SCHOOL DISTRICT IN CONNECTION WITH
SCHOOL FACILITY SITE SELECTION, SCHOOL CONSTRUCTION,
AND BOND AUTHORIZATION IN THE DISTRICT AND SPECIFY-
ING THE SEVERAL AREAS IN WHICH THAT RESPONSIBILITY
SHALL BE EXERCISED AND SPECIFICALLY CHARGING THE
BOARD OF EDUCATION WITH THE ADOPTION OF PROCEDURES
FOR THE PERFORMANCE OF DUTIES IN THE FOLLOWING
OPERATIONAL AREAS: (1) THE SELECTION OF SITES FOR
LOCATION OF SCHOOL FACILITIES, INCLUDING THE HAND-
LING OF NEGOTIATIONS LEADING TO THE ACQUISITION OF
SUCH SITES, AND PROVIDING FOR ALL ON-SITE AND OFF-
SITE UTILITIES; (2) THE OPERATION AND MAINTENANCE
OF THE BOROUGH SCHOOL DISTRICT MASTER BUILDING AND
FINANCE PLAN; THE SELECTION OF ARCHITECTS AND EN-
GINEERS; THE SUPERVISION OF CONSTRUCTION OF SCHOOL
FACILITIES; THE APPOINTMENT OF CITIZENS' ADVISORY
CONSTRUCTION COMMITTEES WHEN DEEMED ADVISABLE; TO
SERVE AS THE AGENTS OF THE ASSEMBLY IN THE ACQUISI-
TION OF CAPITAL EQUIPMENT FOR NEW OR REMODELED
SCHOOL FACILITIES; PROVIDE INSURANCE COVERAGE FOR
SUCH FACILITIES; (3) TO RECOMMEND AS THE NEED EX-
ISTS TO THE ASSEMBLY, GENERAL OBLIGATION BOND
AUTHORIZATION ELECTIONS, AND IN CONNECTION WITH
THAT NEED, TO PREPARE SUPPORTING INFORMATION FOR
PUBLIC DISSEMINATION; RECOMMENDATION OF BOND SALES;
PREPARATION OF BASIC RESOLUTIONS, PROSPECTI, AND
OTHER SUPPORTING BOND SALE DOCUMENTS.

SECTION 1.   School Facility Locations

(a) The Borough Board of Education is hereby
charged with the responsibility of developing and
maintaining records and formulating plans for the
location of needed school facilities.

(1) Such records shall include basic data
indicating the residence location of school pupils,
the economic nature of the immediate neighborhood
where a facility may be needed, planning and zoning
regulations, public improvements planned and/or
constructed by other agencies, and health and safety regulations.

(b) The Borough Assembly hereby charges the
Board of Education with the responsibility to
negotiate with property owners for the purchase
of school facility sites, requiring the Board to
submit recommendations for final purchase approval
by the Assembly.

(1) The Board is authorized to adopt appropriate acquisition procedures, including employment of technical advice which may include, but is
not limited to land appraisals, surveys and sub-
soil tests.

(c) The Borough Assembly hereby designates
the Board of Education its Agent to negotiate with
suppliers for providing all on-site and off-site
utilities to serve school facilities, reserving to
the Assembly final contract approval.

SECTION 2.   Master Building and Financing Plan

(a) The Board of Education is hereby charged
with preparing and maintaining a Master Building
and Financing Plan of School District facilities,
amending and extending such plan at least annually.

(1) The plan shall contain such basic
school facility data as pupil enrollments and pro-
jections, current inventory of school facilities,
projected school facility needs, estimated costs
of projected school facilities, schedules of acquisition or construction of needed school facilities and proposed financing programs to provide
school facilities.

SECTION 3. School Facility Architects and/or
                Engineers
         (a) The Board of Education is hereby charged
with the selection of architects and/or engineers
for designing school facilities and coordinating
the work of such architects and/or engineers.
         (1) The Assembly reserves to itself the
final approval of school facility architectural
and/or engineering contracts including the fee
basis to be paid.
         (2) The Board will act as agent for the
Borough Assembly in coordinating the work of architects and engineers of school facilities approving
final plans, specifications and other contract
documents, submitting such documents in each case
with appropriate analysis and recommendation to
the Assembly for final approval.

SECTION 4. Joint Construction Advisory Committee
         (a) The Board of Education is authorized to
create by appointment, a citizens' advisory construction committee and if deemed advisable to
join with the City of Anchorage in establishing a
City of Anchorage - Greater Anchorage Area Borough
School District Construction Advisory Committee to
assist and advise the Board of Education on the
design and specifications of school facilities and
the appropriate department of city operations on
municipal facilities.
         If, at the time this resolution is ap-
proved and adopted, there exists such a Construction Advisory Committee serving the City of Anchorage, the Assembly will authorize the School Board
to request the City to constitute that Committee,
including all of its then appointed members, as a
joint City-Borough Committee to serve both entities.
         (b) Advice and recommendations of the Advisory
Committee in the matter of school facilities will
be made directly to the Board of Education which
will take such advice and recommendations into
consideration in formulating final recommendations
to the Borough Assembly for approval and adoption.

SECTION 5. School Facility Construction or Furnishing Contracts

(a) In the matter of acquisition of school facilities the Board of Education is charged with responsibility of advertising for bids or proposals, evaluating the said bids or proposals and making recommendation to the Borough Assembly for final action. The Board shall further, following Assembly approval, be charged with the management of contracts so awarded.

(1) Upon award of a contract for construction or furnishing a school facility the Board of Education shall manage the contract, coordinating activities of the Architect Engineer and the contractor in carrying out all conditions of the contract documents.

(2) The Board of Education shall select and recommend to the Borough Assembly for approval and employment such professional employees as it may deem necessary in the supervision and inspection of all school facility construction while in progress.

(3) All orders of change to the contract shall be first reviewed and approved by the Board of Education before being submitted to the Borough Assembly for final action.

In order that construction on any school facility may proceed with a minimum of delay, the Assembly hereby authorizes the Board to approve any contract change, the amount of which does not exceed $3,000.00, subject, however, to ratification by the Assembly.

(4) If school facilities being acquired are of a leased nature the Board of Education shall be responsible for recommending Assembly approval of the lease contract provisions.

SECTION 6. School Facility Equipment

(a) The Board of Education is charged with the responsibility for planning the proper equipment and furnishings for all school facilities including existing or remodeled as well as new facilities.

(b) It shall be the responsibility of the Board to prepare school facility equipment lists, inviting bids or quotations for supplying and recommending final bid award by the Borough Assembly.

(c) Equipment for school facilities shall be delivered to the care of the School District and it shall be the responsibility of the District to require compliance with bid conditions.

SECTION 7. School Facility Casualty, Liability Insurance

(a) The Board of Education shall be responsible for maintaining an adequate casualty and liability insurance program in connection with school facilities for which it serves as agent of the Borough.

(b) Casualty and liability insurance plans proposed by the Board of Education shall be submitted to the Borough Assembly for approval.

SECTION 8. Fund Requirements by General Obligation Bonds

(a) The Borough Board of Education is hereby charged with the responsibility of preparing for Borough Assembly approval recommendations for general obligation bond authorization elections for acquiring school facilities.

Following Assembly approval to hold a general obligation bond authorization election, the Board is further charged with the responsibility of preparing for public dissemination supporting information on the bond needs for school facilities.

(1) The Board shall, in presenting for Assembly consideration its general obligation bond recommendations, include data on needed school facilities, current bond indebtedness, projected costs of debt retirement based upon estimated property valuations and other pertinent information.

(b) The Board is hereby charged with recommending for Assembly approval the schedules of bond sales for school facilities.

(c) The Board is hereby charged with the responsibility of preparing basic resolutions, bond sale prospecti and all other required supporting documents necessary to the sale of general obligation bonds for school facilities.

(1) The Board is authorized to seek the services of a financial consultant individual or firm to act as fiscal agent of the Borough in the sale of general obligation bonds for school facilities, recommending the selected individual or firm for final employment by Borough Assembly.

SELECTED BIBLIOGRAPHY

SELECTED BIBLIOGRAPHY

Books

Fiscal Problems of State and Local Governments.
University Park, Pa.: Pennsylvania State University Press, 1959. P. 92. Quoted in
Alaska, Alaska State Legislature, Legislative
Council, and Office of the Governor, Local Affairs Agency. Final Report on Borough Government. Juneau, January, 1961. P. 71.

Gruening, Ernest. The State of Alaska. New York:
Random House, 1954.

Keith, John P. City and County Rule in Texas.
Austin, Texas: Institute of Public Affairs,
University of Texas, 1951.

Lindman, Erick. A Foundation for Alaska's Public
Schools. Los Angeles, Calif.: Ford Foundation, September, 1961.

Rogers, George W. The Future of Alaska: Economic
Consequences of Statehood. Baltimore, Md.:
Johns Hopkins Press, 1962.

Publications and Reports of the Local Affairs Agency

Alaska, Department of Education, and Office of the
Governor, Local Affairs Agency. Borough
Manual. Vol. II: Schools. Juneau, 1963.

Alaska, Office of the Governor, Local Affairs
Agency. Alaska Local Government. Juneau,
May, 1961 - August, 1966.

_____. Alaska School Districts: Property Assess-
ments and Full Value Determination. Juneau,
1963.

_____. Borough Incorporation Manual. 1st ed.:
Juneau, May, 1961. 2d ed. revised: Juneau,
May, 1962.

_____. Borough Manual. Vol. III: Planning, Zon-
ing, and Public Services. Juneau, 1963.

_____. Borough Manual. Vol. IV: Assessment and
Tax Collection. Juneau, 1964.

_____. Incorporation of the Captain Cook Borough:
Report to the Local Boundary Commission on a
Proposal to Incorporate an Organized Borough
in the Anchorage Area. Juneau, May, 1963.

_____. Incorporation of the Chilkat Borough: Re-
port to the Local Boundary Commission on a
Proposal to Incorporate an Organized Borough
in the Haines-Fort Chilkoot Area. Juneau,
March, 1964.

_____. Incorporation of the Gateway Borough: Re-
port to the Local Boundary Commission on a
Proposal to Incorporate an Organized Borough
in the Ketchikan Area. Juneau, May, 1963.

_____. Incorporation of the Greater Sitka Borough:
Report to the Local Boundary Commission on a
Proposal to Incorporate an Organized Borough
in the Sitka Area. Juneau, July, 1963.

_____. Incorporation of the North Star Borough:
Report to the Local Boundary Commission on a
Proposal to Incorporate an Organized Borough
in the Fairbanks Area. Juneau, June, 1963.

_____. Major Differences Between First, Second,
Third and Fourth Class Cities in Alaska.
Juneau, n.d.

_____. Municipal Fiscal and Accounting Manual.
Juneau, October, 1966.

_____. Property Appraisal Manual for Alaska
Assessors. Juneau, 1963.

_____. The Proposed Homer-Ninilchik Borough: Re-
port to the Local Boundary Commission on a
Proposal to Incorporate an Organized Borough
in the Homer-Ninilchik-Anchor Point Area.
Juneau, April, 1963.

Reports of the Local
Boundary Commission

Alaska, Office of the Governor, Local Boundary Commission. First Report to the Second Session
of the First Alaska State Legislature. Juneau,
February 2, 1960.

_____. "Notice to the Secretary of State of the
Acceptance of a Petition for the Incorporation of the Captain Cook Borough." Proceedings for the Incorporation of an Organized
Borough. No. 4. Juneau, June, 1963.

_____. Recommendation for Changing the Boundaries
of the North Star Borough in the Fairbanks
Area. Juneau, January 29, 1964.

Publications and Reports of
the Legislative Council

Alaska, Alaska State Legislature, Legislative Council. Local Government in Alaska: Problems
and Alternatives. Publication No. 21-6.
Juneau, 1954.

_____. Minutes of the Alaska Constitutional Con-
vention. Minutes of the Daily Proceedings.
Juneau, March, 1965.

_____. Revenue and Taxation in Alaska. Part I:
A Handbook. Part II: Evaluation and Recommendations. Juneau, January, 1962.

_____. Taxes in Alaska--1963, A Handbook. Juneau,
December, 1963.

Other Reports and Documents

Alaska. Annual Report, 1961. Quoted in Alaska,
    Alaska State Legislature, Legislative Council.
    Revenue and Taxation in Alaska. Part II:
    Evaluation and Recommendations. Juneau, Janu-
    ary, 1962. P. 88.

Alaska, Alaska Constitutional Convention. Minutes
    of the Committee on Local Government. 1955-56.

_____. Committee on Local Government. "Commentary
    on Proposed Article on Local Government." De-
    cember 19, 1955. Quoted in Alaska, Supreme
    Court. Fairview Public Utility District No. 1
    v. Anchorage. Opinion No. 61 (File Nos. 69,
    71).

Alaska, Alaska State Legislature, Legislative Coun-
    cil, and Office of the Governor, Local Affairs
    Agency. Final Report on Borough Government.
    Juneau, January, 1961. (An early version of
    this report was published as: Preliminary Re-
    port on Borough Government. Juneau, December,
    1960.)

Alaska, Department of Administration. State Reve-
    nue Sources, Actual and Estimated, Fiscal
    Years 1959-60. Quoted in Alaska, Alaska
    State Legislature, Legislative Council. Reve-
    nue and Taxation in Alaska. Part II: Evalua-
    tion and Recommendations. Juneau, January,
    1962. P. 88.

Alaska, Department of Commerce, Alaska State Hous-
    ing Authority. Comprehensive Plan, Kodiak,
    Alaska. Anchorage, December, 1962.

Alaska, Department of Education. Schools Involved
    in Boroughs Contemplated in Chapter 52, SLA
    1963. Juneau, May, 1963.

Alaska Municipal League, Legislative Committee.
    Draft Bill. Juneau, October, 1966.

Alaska, Public Administration Service. Constitu-
    tional Studies. Prepared on behalf of the
    Alaska Statehood Committee. 3 vols. Chicago,
    November, 1955.

_____. Local Government Under the Alaska Constitu-
    tion. Chicago, January 9, 1959.

Anchorage Borough-City Study Committee. Minutes.
    Anchorage, 1966.

                Legislative Journals and Rules

Alaska, Alaska State Legislature. House Journal.
    Juneau, 1959-66.

_____. Senate Journal. Juneau, 1959-66.

_____. Uniform Rules. Juneau, March 11, 1963 -
    January 31, 1966.

Rader, John L. "An Explanation of a Bill for the
    Incorporation of First Class Organized Bor-
    oughs." Supplement to House Journal. Juneau,
    February 25, 1963.

_____. "A Sectional Analysis of Committee Substi-
    tute for House Bill No. 90." Supplement to
    House Journal. Juneau, March 14, 1963.

            Constitutions, Statutes, and
                    Regulations

Alaska. Alaska Administrative Code. Title 6,
    Division 2.

_____. Alaska Compiled Laws Annotated. Section 16. 1949.

_____. Alaska State Constitution.

_____. Alaska Statutes.

AS 07 (Boroughs)
AS 14 (Education)
AS 15 (Elections)
AS 18 (Health and Safety)
AS 22 (Judiciary)
AS 24 (Legislature)
AS 29 (Municipal Corporations)
AS 38 (Public Lands)
AS 40 (Public Records and Recorders)
AS 42 (Public Utilities and Carriers)
AS 43 (Revenue and Taxation)
AS 44 (State Government)

_____. Session Laws of Alaska. 1923, 1950-66.

Legislative Bills*

Alaska, Alaska State Legislature, 1963:

House Bill No. 62. An Act relating to the incorporation of second class organized boroughs for school purposes.

Senate Bill No. 17. An Act to change the date of termination of powers and functions of special service districts.

_____, 1964:

Committee Substitute for House Bill No. 345. An Act dissolving mandatorily-incorporated organized boroughs.

Committee Substitute for House Bill No. 390.

Committee Substitute for Senate Bill No. 298.

House Bill No. 345. An Act repealing the mandatory borough legislation of 1963.

*Includes only those bills that did not become law.

House Bill No. 387. An Act relating to initial assessment payments to certain boroughs.

House Bill No. 390. An Act relating to the transfer of state lands to organized boroughs.

House Bill No. 401. An Act relating to organized boroughs.

House Bill No. 408. An Act to permit referenda within organized boroughs to determine whether or not partisan elections should be permitted.

Senate Bill No. 298. An Act relating to borough elections.

Senate Bill No. 348. An Act relating to initial assessment payments to certain boroughs.

_____, 1965:

Senate Bill No. 101 (and Committee Substitutes). An Act to revise and codify the law relating to cities and boroughs.

_____, 1966:

House Bill No. 409. An Act authorizing a borough and first class and home rule cities within the borough to form a single unit of local government upon approval by public referendum.

Alaska Court Cases

Superior Court

City of Juneau v. Greater Juneau Borough. First Judicial District (Juneau). Civil Action No. 65-317. (Pending Suit.)

Walters and Mullen v. Cease, et al. Third Judicial
    District (Anchorage). No. 63-1411. November
    14, 1963.

Walters and Mullen v. Cease, et al. No. 63-1411
    and Gill and Norene v. Cease, et al. No.
    63-1763. (Cases Consolidated.) Third Judi-
    cial District (Anchorage). June 25, 1964.

                    Supreme Court

Fairview Public Utility District No. 1 v. City of
    Anchorage. 368 P. 2d. 540. 1962.

Walters and Mullen v. Cease, et al. 388 P. 2d.
    263. 1964.

Walters and Mullen v. Cease, et al. 394 P. 2d.
    670. 1964.

             Letters, Memoranda, Opinions,
                    and Speeches

Alaska, Department of Law, Office of the Attorney
    General. Letter [Unpublished Opinion] from
    Warren C. Colver, Attorney General, to T. E.
    Elliott, Executive Director, Alaska State
    Housing Authority. October 6, 1964.

_____. Opinion No. 25. 1963.

_____. Opinions Nos. 3 and 11. 1964.

_____. Opinions Nos. 1, 5, 6, 7, and 9. 1965.

_____. Opinion No. 5. 1966.

_____. Unpublished Opinion of the Attorney General
    to State Representative Harold Z. Hansen.
    March 15, 1961.

_____. Unpublished Opinion of the Attorney General
    to Roger W. Pegues, Director of the Local Af-
    fairs Agency. June 13, 1961.

_____. Unpublished Opinion of the Attorney General
to Roger W. Pegues, Director of the Local Affairs Agency. July 9, 1962.

_____. Unpublished Opinion of the Attorney General
to Dennis E. Cook, Acting Director of the Local
Affairs Agency. August 4, 1964.

_____. Unpublished Opinion of the Attorney General
to Dennis E. Cook, Acting Director of the Local
Affairs Agency. September 29, 1964.

_____. Unpublished Opinion of the Attorney General
to State Representative E. N. Orbeck. March
19, 1965.

Dalton, Mrs. James. Letter to Local Boundary Commission. Fairbanks, November 29, 1962. Quoted
in Alaska, Office of the Governor, Local Boundary Commission. Minutes, Island Homes Annexation Hearing. Fairbanks, November 29, 1962.

Eastaugh, F. O., Borough Attorney. Letter to
Claude Millsap, Chairman, Greater Juneau Borough. Juneau, April 17, 1964.

Egan, Governor William A. Keynote Address. Thir-
teenth Annual Convention of the Alaska Munici-
pal League. Seward, October 23-26, 1963.
Quoted in Alaska, Office of the Governor,
Local Affairs Agency, Alaska Local Government.
October, 1963. P. 5.

_____. Letter to Hon. Hugh J. Wade, Secretary of
State. Juneau, May 2, 1966.

Fischer, Victor. Speech before the Anchorage Chamber of Commerce. Anchorage, n.d.

Lafferty, Charles, Superintendent, Fairbanks Independent School District. Memorandum. Subject:
"House Bill No. 488." Fairbanks, March 30,
1962.

Pegues, Roger W., Director, Local Affairs Agency.
Letter to Ronald C. Cease, Assistant Professor
of Political Science, University of Alaska,
College, Alaska. Juneau, September 29, 1961.

_____, Seattle, Washington. Letter to Ronald C.
Cease, Portland, Oregon. November 15, 1966.

Wade, Hugh J., Acting Governor. Letter to President of the Senate, Alaska State Legislature.
Juneau, April 10, 1959.

                Newspapers: General References

Alaska Empire (Daily Alaska Empire to July, 1964)
(Juneau). September, 1962 - January, 1967.

Anchorage Daily News. September, 1962 - January,
1967.

Anchorage Times. September, 1962 - January, 1967.

Cheechako News (Kenai). September, 1962 - April,
1964.

The Daily Sentinel (Sitka). September, 1962 -
April, 1964.

Fairbanks Daily News-Miner. September, 1960 -
January, 1967.

The Frontiersman (Palmer). September, 1962 -
April, 1964.

Jessen's Weekly (Fairbanks). September, 1962 -
April, 1964.

Ketchikan Daily News. September, 1962 - January,
1967.

Kodiak Mirror. September, 1962 - April, 1964.

Newspapers: Specific Citations

"The ABC's of Boroughs," Anchorage Times, September
     14, 1963.

Archibald, Janet.   "District's Future Is Clouded
     Issue," Anchorage Times, December 7, 1963.

"Assembly Chops Borough Budget $50,000," Daily
     Alaska Empire (Juneau), June 4, 1964.

"Boro Repeal Strong in Anchorage," Ketchikan Daily
     News, July 31, 1963.

"Borough Act Still Stands," Anchorage Daily News,
     September 11, 1963.

"Borough Chairman, Mayor Exchange Verbal Brickbats,"
     Fairbanks Daily News-Miner, August 10, 1964.

"Borough Okays School Budget After McCutcheon Ques-
     tions," Anchorage Times, August 4, 1964.

"Borough Poll Dropped for Election Bid," Anchorage
     Times, October 5, 1963.

"Boroughs Seen as Key Issue in '64 Legislature,"
     Anchorage Times, September 21, 1963.

"Borough Vote Here Tuesday," Fairbanks Daily News-
     Miner, September 23, 1963.

"Borough? Yes, Chairman? No," Fairbanks Daily News-
     Miner, September 23, 1963.

"Bureaucratic Action," Ketchikan Daily News, June
     7, 1963.

"City Says Borough Sales Tax Need Not Shown;
     'Takeover' Delay Asked," Fairbanks Daily News-
     Miner, June 19, 1964.

"Commission Bound Legally to Hold Hearings--
     Phillips: Local Affairs Action Opposes Bor-
     ough Law," The Frontiersman (Palmer), July 3,
     1963.

"Compromise Reported on Sales Tax Issue," Fairbanks Daily News-Miner, July 6, 1964.

"Controversy Seen at Borough Meet," Anchorage Times, August 13, 1964.

"Councilmen Say 'Tit for Tat,'" Fairbanks Daily News-Miner, June 6, 1964.

"Council Votes Down Tax Cut," Fairbanks Daily News-Miner, July 21, 1964.

"Do We Want an 'Area Governor'?" Fairbanks Daily News-Miner, December 2, 1963.

"Fairbanks Schools Granted $1,210,771," Fairbanks Daily News-Miner, June 9, 1964.

"First Class Borough, Manager Best for Area," Anchorage Times, December 2, 1963.

"The Folly of a Special Session," Anchorage Daily News, September 20, 1963.

"Injunction Filed on Sales Tax," Fairbanks Daily News-Miner, July 22, 1964.

Isenson, Ed. "The City Beat," Anchorage Daily News, May 6, 1966.

"July 15, Set for Takeover of Schools," Fairbanks Daily News-Miner, June 12, 1964.

"Kendall Ouster Said Borough Act 'Diversion,'" Anchorage Times, October 18, 1963.

"Kilcher Says Poll Request Exaggerated," Anchorage Times, September 23, 1963.

"Kilcher Urges Special Session on Borough Act," Anchorage Daily News, September 14, 1963.

"Legal Baloney or Free Choice?" Fairbanks Daily News-Miner, March 18, 1964.

"Legislative Council Votes Against Poll," Anchorage
    Daily News, September 20, 1963.

"Legislators Comment on Session Call," Anchorage
    Daily News, September 16, 1963.

"Legislature Asked to Convene," Anchorage Times,
    September 14, 1963.

"McMahon Criticized by Borough Chairman," Fairbanks
    Daily News-Miner, June 25, 1964.

"Matanuska-Susitna is Borough Name," The Frontiers-
    man (Palmer), January 23, 1964.

"Meeting Set for Poll of Legislators," Anchorage
    Times, September 16, 1963.

"No Matanuska-Susitna Hearing, Cease Says: Director
    Reverses Tuesday Statement," The Frontiersman
    (Palmer), June 20, 1963.

"On the Inside," Fairbanks Daily News-Miner, Decem-
    ber 20, 1963.

"Power of Negative Thinking," Fairbanks Daily News-
    Miner, July 23, 1964.

"Power of Negative Thinking," Fairbanks Daily News-
    Miner, August 10, 1964.

"Reluctant Secretary Certifies Borough Petition,"
    Daily Alaska Empire (Juneau), September 10,
    1963.

"Sailors Under Fire for Sales Tax Stand," Fairbanks
    Daily News-Miner, June 3, 1964.

"Sales Tax Cut Delayed by Borough," Fairbanks Daily
    News-Miner, July 24, 1964.

"Sales Tax Injunction Plans Hit," Fairbanks Daily
    News-Miner, July 9, 1964.

"Sales Tax Meeting Doesn't Solve Dispute," Fairbanks
    Daily News-Miner, June 16, 1964.

"Skimpy Vote Starts Election: Official Sticks with
    5,500 Turnout Guess," Fairbanks Daily News-
    Miner, September 24, 1963.

"State Funds Coming to Help Out Schools," Fairbanks
    Daily News-Miner, July 9, 1964.

"Statesmanlike Solution," Fairbanks Daily News-
    Miner, August 23, 1963.

"Too Much!" Anchorage Daily News, September 10,
    1963.

"2,252 Say 'No' to Borough," Fairbanks Daily News-
    Miner, September 25, 1963.

"Uniform Sales Tax Only Fair Answer," Fairbanks
    Daily News-Miner, July 9, 1964.

"What About the Merger?" Anchorage Daily News,
    February 14, 1966.

"Why Should the Borough Delay?" Fairbanks Daily
    News-Miner, June 22, 1964.

"You Can't Hurry a Borough," Anchorage Times, Feb-
    ruary 28, 1963.

ABOUT THE CONTRIBUTORS

RONALD C. CEASE
is Associate Professor of Political Science,
Portland State College, Portland, Oregon. He is
a graduate of Reed College and has a Master of
Public Administration degree from The Maxwell
Graduate School, Syracuse University, and a Ph.D.
from The Claremont Graduate School. Dr. Cease
was director of the Alaska Local Affairs Agency
from 1962 to 1966 and prior to that was Assistant
Professor of Political Science at the University
of Alaska. He is the author of several articles
in professional political science journals. Dr.
Cease is a consultant for one of the task forces
of the U.S. Joint Commission on Correctional Manpower and Training; for the Portland (Oregon)
Metropolitan Study Commission; and for the City
of Vancouver, Washington.

JEROME R. SAROFF
is Vice President of Development Research Associates, Inc., a private consulting firm in Juneau,
Alaska. In 1967, Mr. Saroff was elected to and
became the deputy chairman of the Greater Juneau
Charter Commission, which is engaged in preparing
a charter for the complete unification of local
government in Juneau. He is a graduate of
Antioch College and has a Master of City Planning
degree from the Massachusetts Institute of Tech-
nology. Mr. Saroff was Director of Planning and
Research for the State of Alaska in the Office of
the Governor from 1965 to 1967, and before that
he was Planning Director for the City of Anchorage, Alaska. He was a member of the research
faculty at the University of Alaska as coordinator of the Barrow Community Development Study.
He has written a number of articles and papers.

JOHN L. RADER
   is an attorney and an executive of the First
   Federal Savings and Loan Association of Anchorage, Alaska. He was Alaska's first State Attorney General (1959-60) and a member of the
   State House of Representatives during the first,
   third, and fourth legislative sessions, serving
   as the Democratic minority leader during the
   third State legislature (1963-64). Mr. Rader
   was the Anchorage city attorney from 1954 to
   1955.

THEODORE E. FLEISCHER
   is a staff attorney engaged in legal research
   with Albertson's, Inc., Boise, Idaho. He was
   a legal assistant with the Alaska Attorney General's office from 1964 to 1965 and Assistant
   State Attorney General from 1965 to 1966. He
   is the author of a number of leading opinions
   on Alaska local government.

ROBERT J. DUPERE
   is president of Dupere and Associates, Inc.,
   financial consultants to a number of cities and
   boroughs in Alaska. He was special assistant
   to the Commissioner of Administration for the
   State of Alaska from 1961 to 1964. Prior to
   that he was Comptroller-Treasurer, City of
   Fairbanks, Alaska, from 1958 to 1960.

BILLY G. BERRIER
   is attorney for the Greater Juneau Borough.
   He was an attorney with the Washington Title
   Insurance Company, Seattle and Everett, Washington, from 1954 to 1964.

DONALD M. DAFOE
   is Provost, University of Alaska, at Anchorage.
   He received his Ed.D. degree from Stanford University. He was formerly superintendent of the
   Anchorage borough school system (1961-66); head
   consultant, Title X, NDEA, U.S. Office of Education (1959-61); Commissioner of Education for
   the Territory of Alaska (1953-59); and superintendent for the Rupert, Idaho, schools and

the Minidoke County Unit, Rupert, Idaho (1944-
51). He is a past president of the Idaho Education Association (1949); an honorary vice
president of the NEA; and a member of the Alaska
Commission of the Education Commission of the
States. He has published numerous articles for
local and State educational journals.

CLAUDE MILLSAP, JR.
is director of the Alcoholic Beverage Control
Board, State of Alaska. He formerly was borough
chairman of the Greater Juneau Borough. He was
president and general manager of the Juneau
Credit Association from 1960 to 1963 and was a
principal in the firm of Cal-Dustrial Engineers,
Inc. from 1958 to 1962. He is a former member
of the State Central Committee of the Republican
Party of Alaska.

JOSEPH R. HENRI
is attorney for the City of Juneau. He is a
former district judge of the fourth judicial
district at Fairbanks and has served on the
staff of U.S. Senator Ernest Gruening of Alaska.
He is chairman of the Alaska Bar's legislative
committee and of the legislative committee of
the Alaska Municipal League.

RICHARD W. FISCHER
is president of Richard W. Fischer and Associates, real estate appraisers, and is a borough
assemblyman on the Greater Anchorage Area Borough Assembly. In 1965 he was president of the
Greater Anchorage Area Borough Assembly.

KARL WALTER
is attorney for the City of Anchorage. He is a
former member of the board of governors, Alaska
Bar Association (1962-63) and a past president
of the Alaska Bar Association (1965-66). He was
a member of the Alaska Public Service Commission
(1960-64) and was state chairman of the National
Institute of Municipal Law Officers (1966).